Beasts at Bedtime

BEASTS *at* BEDTIME

Revealing the Environmental Wisdom in Children's Literature

Liam Heneghan

THE UNIVERSITY OF CHICAGO PRESS

CHICAGO AND LONDON

The University of Chicago Press, Chicago 60637
The University of Chicago Press, Ltd., London
Published 2018
Printed in the United States of America

27 26 25 24 23 22 21 20 19 18   1 2 3 4 5

ISBN-13: 978-0-226-43138-3 (cloth)
ISBN-13: 978-0-226-43141-3 (e-book)
DOI: https://doi.org/10.7208/chicago/9780226431413.001.0001

Library of Congress Cataloging-in-Publication Data

Names: Heneghan, Liam, author.
Title: Beasts at bedtime: revealing the environmental wisdom in
    children's literature / Liam Heneghan.
Description: Chicago; London: The University of Chicago Press, 2018. |
    Includes bibliographical references and index.
Identifiers: LCCN 2017051961 | ISBN 9780226431383 (cloth: alk. paper) |
    ISBN 9780226431413 (e-book)
Subjects: LCSH: Children's literature—History and criticism. | Ecology in
    literature. | Environmentalism in literature.
Classification: LCC PN1009.5.E25 H46 2018 | DDC 809/.89282—dc23
LC record available at https://lccn.loc.gov/2017051961

♾ This paper meets the requirements of ANSI/NISO Z39.48-1992 (Permanence
of Paper).

I dedicate this book to my parents,
Mary and Paddy Heneghan,
who fledged their six chicks in a nest lined with books,

AND

to *Vassia,*
my *Once Upon a Time* and my *Happily Ever After,*
who has starred in every chapter of my adult life,

AND

to our boys, *Fiacha and Oisín,*
who always allowed me to add a poem or two to
their nightly stories about beasts

Contents

Introduction 1

Section One: On Reading

THE EXISTENTIAL PRINCESS: A FAIRY TALE 15

1 Beasts at Bedtime: Reading about Nature with Children 17
2 Doctor Dolittle and the Question of Reading 26

Section Two: Pastoral Stories

TOPOPHILIA 35

3 The Pastoral Promise: And They All Lived Happily Ever After 39
4 The Ecology of Pooh 49
5 Peter Rabbit's Brutal Paradise 59
6 In the Garden of Earthly Delights 71
7 Beyond the Pool of Darkness: The Pastoral Roots of
   Irish Stories 83

Section Three: Wilderness Stories

LOST IN THE POPO AGIE WILDERNESS 95

8 On the Mallard 98
9 Where the Wild Things Always Were 104

10 Wild and Grimm Fairy Tales: Wilderness on the Margins 119

11 "Gollumgate": Tolkien and Ireland 133

12 "I Am in Fact a Hobbit": Tolkien as Environmentalist 139

13 The Tin Woodman's Path of Carnage through the Land of Oz 152

14 Hunger and Thirst in Suzanne Collins's *Hunger Games* 156

Section Four: Children on Wild Islands

OLD TOM'S ISLAND 163

15 The Why and the What of Islands 165

16 Archmage Ged, Merlin, and Harry Potter and the Training of Wizards and Witches 178

17 Is L. T. Meade the *Real* Author of Enid Blyton's Famous Five? 191

18 *Robinson Crusoe*: Now Here's a Cannibalism Tale for Every Child 195

19 On Isles Benevolent; on Isles Malevolent 213

Section Five: Urban Stories

THE URBAN WILD 225

20 The Urban to Rural Gradient of Children's Stories: The Happy Prince 228

21 Antipathy to Urban Life in Nursery Rhymes 231

22 Urban Decay: R. Crumb in the Nursery 235

23 The Escape Artist: *Calvin and Hobbes* and the Suburban Idyll 239

24 Babar: Elephant and Urban Adapter 244

Section Six: Learning to Care

AND THE WORLD HUMMED BACK 255

25 Caring for the Rose: Environmental Literacy and Antoine de
Saint-Exupéry's *The Little Prince* 256
26 What Then Should We Do? The Lorax in the Twenty-First
Century 272

Section Seven: Good Night, Sleep Tight

IN THE TOT LOT 277

27 Bookend Conversations 281

Acknowledgments 291   Notes 295   Index 319

Introduction

The Care and Feeding of a Bird

Newly arrived in the United States and setting foot on the red soils of Georgia for the very first time, Fiacha, our eldest and then a three-year-old, perched himself on top of a fire ant mound. It's a rare child who makes that mistake a second time since fire ants sting ferociously.[1] We had moved into a small ranch house a few miles from the campus of the University of Georgia in Athens, where I was to work for four years. The house was aesthetically unremarkable. There were parched lawns to the front and rear, both of which hosted innumerable fire ant mounds. In the front yard, right outside the door, grew two desiccated shrubs. What that neighborhood lacked in conventional wildlife it made up for with feral dogs. They howled all night and packed together in the morning, leisurely roaming the neighborhood hunting for those who, like me, were foolish enough to go walking in the early hours. It was in this unpromising location that Fiacha—an Irish name that means "raven," and whose second name is Daedalus, the father of Icarus—became a bird.

The care and feeding of a bird who is morphologically and physiologically human, though psychologically somewhat avian, is not an entirely trivial undertaking. While he was in motion, there was little inconvenience to us—he simply flapped his featherless wings as he migrated from place to place. He was something of a restless bird: now in the living room, now the kitchen, and now perched in his bedroom. Whenever and wherever he perched, the primaries on his wings would tremble, occasionally he would ruffle the length of his wings, and, at times, he would fold them and tuck them close to his little body. We learned to live with the concerned glances of strangers. Feeding time could be a little strenuous, although we could entice him with shredded morsels that he would grab by his "beak" and toss back into his mouth. Sometimes he would disappear from the house, and after those initial panicked occasions where we searched high and low for him, we knew he could be found sequestered in one of those forlorn-looking shrubs in the front yard. He would cling to a lower branch, peering out at the world through the patchy foliage. At least he was safely out of the reach of the packs of dogs and the fire ants.

In those early years, we read a lot about birds, looked at a lot of birds, and drew a lot of birds; and by sketching birds on folded pieces of paper and then cutting them out, we made innumerable models of birds. It led to a later interest of his in dinosaurs, then aircraft, then military history, after which there was another thousand twists and turns in his interests. That bird now studies philosophy, but he remains an avid birder. He admitted to me recently that he occasionally writes with a quill. To this day if you look at him long enough, you may still spot his flight feathers flutter ever so slightly, even on windless afternoons.

This book is written for the parents, teachers, librarians, and guardians of children who may think they are birds. It's possible, of course, and not at all uncommon, that your child might assume themselves to be a cat or a dog; this book is for these families also. It's also for the family of a child I've learned of recently who alternates between a crocodile, a rhino, and a snake. When she was quite young, a friend imagined herself to be a gorilla. A child of another friend thinks he is deep-sea shrimp that scares predators who get too close by squirting out a glowing substance. He alternates this with being a porcupine. You should give this child a wide berth. Other friends reported variously that their child is a tiger, a monkey, and, more exotically, an octopus or a river otter. I've even know of one child who is a lion but prefers these days to be called "Gecko." The poet Jan Bottiglieri took her identification with beasts to the next level: she told me she most often imagined herself to be her parents' deceased boxer dog, Major, no doubt to her parents' consternation and sorrow, for Major, apparently, had been a much-loved animal. Later, at age seven, Jan drafted a pamphlet on "How to Be Different Animals," which, she explained to me, drew upon her "vast field experience." Some children do not identify with being any animal other than the higher primates they already are. The stories that I write about here will be instructive to guardians of these children also, for it's a rare child who is not already inclined toward nature.[2]

Central to the task of caring for your little creature is to create the most nurturing environment for them. This, quite obviously, is not as simple as attending to their peculiar physical needs. It requires a careful tending to their spirits. This latter task can be assisted by the stories you tell and read to them. To help with the task, this book is intended to illustrate the thematic richness of children's stories. There is a surprising depth of environmental information in many of the titles that children find immensely appealing. The environmental components can oftentimes go unnoticed. In the chapters that follow, I will thus excavate the hidden environmental wisdom of these books.

Beasts at Bedtime is designed to reveal just how ecologically sophisticated such stories can be, with a view to helping you become a better steward of your child's environmental and, by extension, ethical education.

☾ ★

A few months before our family moved to Georgia, now more than two decades ago, I attended the Sixth International Congress of Ecology in Manchester. The program was entitled "Progress to Meet the Challenge of Environmental Change." Researchers came in from around the globe to address how ecology, as a strictly scientific discipline, should respond to the increasingly compelling evidence that humans were experiencing an unprecedented global environmental crisis of our own creation. Should our discipline become more directly engaged in environmental advocacy—a step that some scientists were reluctant to take, fearing that advocacy interferes with the objectivity of our science. Can the public trust the research of a scholar who is already socially engaged on an issue? One especially forceful case in favor of advocacy and public scholarship was made at this conference by Dr. Ravi Chellam, an Indian conservation biologist who was, and remains to this day, involved in the protection of the rare Asiatic lion.[3] Not only was the very charismatic Chellam—he has always been a rather leonine presence—engaged with assessing populations, surveying habitat, and undertaking all the routine demographic work that, by necessity, is conducted on species of conservation concern; he was also involved in planning lion reintroduction efforts into Indian preserves. Chellam was an advocate for outreach efforts with the public, since people were justifiably anxious about living in proximity to this impressive predator. Chellam had analyzed the data on human-lion conflicts near the Gir Forest in Gujarat state in western India and reported an average of around fifteen attacks by lions resulting in a couple of death-by-lion attacks annually between 1978 and 1991.[4] Chellam's conclusion was that a resolution to such conflicts might entail reducing the lion population by relocating or culling some animals. I found Chellam's talk edifying, and I recall it decades later. Here was a model of rigorous science and public engagement that I might emulate.

In addition, I recall Chellam's work, in part, because it was relevant to my own little outreach project on the home front—namely, the instruction of our youngster. Scientists are people too! Not only do we have a responsibility for communicating information to peers and to a larger public, our work, surely, can inform our behavior in the domestic sphere. It so happened that Fiacha's favorite poem at the time was William Blake's "The Tyger" (1794).[5] It's a poem about another, very different, Asiatic large cat that inhabited the "forests of the night." Our child had learned this poem by heart almost as soon as he could talk—a tribute to the value of endless repetition of verse to children. The sensational information I brought home about animals and people in India (and elsewhere) was a valuable supplement when we read and chatted about Blake's poem. Might not children who love such poems—and I learned much later that lions and tigers have a prominent place in children's literature in India—be more supportive of conservation efforts later on in their lives? A child in Ireland or India reading about big cats might be inspired to care for such creatures when they grow up.[6]

At the time I attended this meeting, I was due to defend my PhD dissertation on the issue of acid rain back in Dublin the following month.[7] This meeting, more than any other, confirmed to me that by doing basic science with a view to encouraging advocacy, I was on a useful path, and certainly one that suited me. And though atmospheric pollution is, admittedly, not as "sexy" as large cat conservation, I was determined not to be a scientist merely engaged with matters of theory while ignoring questions of how we might repair our relations with each other and with the natural world. This book is, in large measure, a response to a promise to myself to keep ruminating on the connections between environmental science and everyday life.

In retrospect, however, another aspect of this trip to Manchester has had quietly enduring implications for me, although it was many years before I understood them. This had nothing to do with a complex presentation of the ecological data or declarations concerning our current environmental predicament. I visited a Manchester children's bookstore, where I discovered a recently published book by the South African children's writer Paul Geraghty. The book was called *The Great Green Forest* (1994), and it was to become Fiacha's favorite.[8] At his request, I read it aloud over and over again. I read it so often, in fact, that all these years later, I can still recall every word of it. It begins, "High up in the great green forest, the sun began to rise. Way down in the deep dark shadows, a tree mouse was curling up to sleep. . . ." However, to her growing agitation, the tree mouse has her sleep interrupted by the calls of a rich variety of creatures with whom she shares her forest home. Ultimately, the noises of the *Great Green Forest* are quelled by the overwhelming sound of an approaching bulldozer ripping through the forest. The tree mouse confronts the bulldozer and yells, "Stop that noise!" The driver abandons the wheel and leaves the Great Green Forest, never to return.

Conversations about the book with Fiacha were simple to begin with, of course. He was, after all, a three-year-old! But his interest in the story lasted quite a few years. Where on Earth was the Great Green Forest? What exactly is a tree mouse, and why was the tree mouse sleeping while the other beasts remained awake? Why do different animals make unique sounds? Why did the animals go silent when the bulldozer approached? What could we do to help the tree mouse protect her home? And why, oh why, would anyone want to cut down the forest in the first place?

The knowledge contained in the book, despite the seeming sparseness of the storytelling, is actually quite complex. In discussing this favorite book with my son, and in responding to his questions, we brushed up against some important components of ecological knowledge, including the distribution of the world biomes and the natural history of tropical animals. We chatted about an especially significant environmental problem and sketched out the rudiments of conservation biology. We discussed our individual capacity to solve these problems—something psychologists call "locus of control"—that is, a belief that any of us have power over events in our lives.[9] Naturally, this conversation occurred without a technical vocabulary. Our bedtime chats, after all, were just about a tree mouse trying to snooze in the rain forest. Nevertheless, these bookish conversations invariably opened out to interesting terrain.

At the time I started to contemplate writing this book, Fiacha had just left home, and our younger son, Oisín, was preparing to graduate from high school. It's a bleak thing, by the by, to secure your door at night knowing that you are not locking your child in, but locking them out. Upon reflection, my wife and I have been more fortunate as parents than some, and I feel confident that they are ready to take on adult joys and responsibilities. These young men have their flaws, I suppose—it's not a father's task to keep comprehensive books on such things—but they are undeniably robust citizens and fellows of good humor and expansive empathy. Both are lovers of animals, and both have an appetite for the great outdoors. And yet both are readers and are reflective to the degree that youth can be. Having bought many of the books they loved in childhood—the classics as well as the less salutary titles (I'm on the fence, for example, on the Captain Underpants series!)—I had wondered if there was a connection between their reflective lives as readers, their appreciation of the outdoors, and their concern for our environmental future. As I sorted through their library, in an effort to relocate their books from their deserted bedrooms to the basement, I'd noticed that *many* of these books had an environmental flavor to them. Of course, some—like Geraghty's *The Great Green Forest*—are deliberately and provocatively environmental. But mostly our kids read what other kids read: Beatrix Potter's *The Tale of Peter Rabbit*, A. A. Milne's *Winnie-the-Pooh*, Laura Ingalls Wilder's *Little House on the Prairie*, Frances Hodgson Burnett's *The Secret Garden*, J. R. R. Tolkien's *The Hobbit*, J. K. Rowling's *Harry Potter*, and so on. Many of these latter stories are undeniably terrific, although the environmental themes are baked in the pie, so to speak. *Beasts at Bedtime*, then, is a response to my subsequent rereading of a large number of these books, investigating the hunch that collectively they offer a fairly complete guide to environmental literacy. This suspicion is largely confirmed. The book was subsequently written to provide parents, guardians, educators (both formal and informal), and scholars interested in children's literature a resource for recognizing environmental themes and a language for excavating the green content in favorite books of their own.

I have spent a long period of my life thinking about environmental issues. But for many years at the end of the day—in fact, quite literally at the end of each day—I spent part of my evenings as just another parent reading to a child who, like that tree mouse, was getting ready for sleep. Cozy times such as these may, I now realize, represent the greatest opportunity we have to share our excitement about the joys of the natural world and to cultivate wisdom on how we can all protect it. What I have learned, over the years, is that the parent assuredly doesn't need a training in the sciences, nor do they need to choose explicitly environmentally themed books, in order to pass on a love for the natural world to their kids.

Reading *Beasts at Bedtime*

I am a zoologist—an animal biologist—by training, a degree almost as rare these days as an education in alchemy. I specialized in ecology, investigating how acid rain influences the community of invertebrate animals living in soil. More recently, my work has been on conservation of biodiversity. Though I have graduate training in contemporary philosophy and, therefore, am a humanist of sorts, I am not, however, a specialist in children's literature. Nor am I a literary critic. This book is thus written by an environmental biologist inclining toward stories, and not by a literary scholar interested in environmental scholarship. I mention my training since I'd like it to be clear to the reader that although I know there is an enormous, and interesting, technical literature on children's literature, I am not presenting an extensive review of this work.[10] I am a parent writing for others with an interest in the cultivation of environmental sensibilities in kids. The book is entitled *Beasts at Bedtime*, recognizing that many of the great stories for children feature animals; however, in the pages that follow, I discuss plants and other living things, and more generally themes that are considered environmental.

I realize that the definition of "environment" I am employing throughout the book, and the themes I associate with this term, might perplex some readers. I emphatically don't intend to restrict the term "environment" to issues of concern to those natural sciences related to our green surroundings. Nor, of course, do I exclude them, for in some cases this is exactly what I will be discussing: food webs, energy flow, material cycles, soil processes, and so forth. However, since the term "environment" derives etymologically from "environs"—that which surrounds—the difficulty is that "environment" can seem to mean just about anything. At a pinch, one might, additionally, refer to one's inner environment (things below the level of the skin, say), in which case "environment" becomes so expansive that one might just as well be done with it and call it the "universe."[11] Nothing, in this view of things, is excluded from environmental thought. And though expansiveness may be satisfying in some ways, in order for "environment" to be a useful and implementable term (in this book and in an academic discipline), a certain amount of definition (a border, so to speak) must be given to it. My placement of this border is undoubtedly thematically broader than that which many of my colleagues might tolerate, but, nonetheless, it stops short of including everything in the universe. I mean it to encompass the green stuff of the world and that which eats the green; the decaying brown stuff of the world and that which eats the brown. I mean it also to accommodate reflections on human cognitive entanglements with the natural things of the world and our attunement to those things. I mean it to include our grappling with concepts of the wild and wilderness, and ruminating on encounters with vast landscapes that are both vertiginously terrifying and yet enticing. I mean it to extend to that sense we might have of tranquility in a garden. I mean it to include cogitation on the sources of our material well-being as well as on that which contributes to our sense of spiritual well-being (if by spiritual we don't think the super-mundane). I mean it as an inspection of what we eat, what we shit, what we leave behind, and what we waste. I mean it to include an analysis of the impact of this waste, and how waste and environmental damage impact all of us, but especially the planet's most vulnerable people. I mean it to include the way technology has and always will mediate our exchanges with the natural world. I mean it to include our inclination toward trees, our attachment to animals, as well as an introspection about our negligence of trees and animals and other living beings. I mean it to include our empathy for, and our ongoing disengagement from, the wild world. I mean our sense of dwelling and our sense of displacement, and an interrogation about that which makes us feel at home in the world, as well as thoughts about that which is uncanny, weird, and that evokes a creeping suspicion of not being at home in the world. And, inasmuch as love between humans entails the material, the inspirational, the ethical, and the hopeful, I mean "environment" to extend to thoughts concerning our love for one another. For humans, in all their mystifying achievement and their mystifying failure, are environmental beings.

Concretely, this means that an environmental theme in this book will include all that falls under the inspection of environmental science and ecology, environmental social science, environmental psychology, environmental philosophy, ecocriticism, environmental policy, and environmental justice. Indeed, any discipline that one can stick an *eco-* or another environmental prefix to is fair game.

In writing this book, I tried out a number of organizational schemes at different points in time. My first draft attempted to provide a short course on topics in the discipline of environmental studies with meticulous notes on where to find each concept illustrated in children's books. This scheme had the virtue of being systematic, but it also had some notable drawbacks. The text was as dull as ditchwater. It was also overly didactic. I hope, emphatically, that you learn something as you read these chapters, and I suspect the book will empower you to lend an environmental perspective to stories that you read with your child. That being said, I would regret it if this book was used to turn story time into an occasion for a laborious tutorial on ecology. It doesn't provide a magical formula for turning out young ecological savants.

Recognizing that there is no ideal way of organizing a book like this, the framework I finally adopted arrays children's books along a gradient of human involvement in the landscapes in which the story is set. These habitats range from wilderness to densely urban habitats (stories in urban habitats are less common). Several stories and works of children's literature are set in the middle landscape between the wild and the humanized, in pastoral landscapes. There are also a great number of stories set on islands: some tame, some wild, and all distinctive. Of course, many stories are not confined to one landscape and flit from one to the next: for example, the great Harry Potter is occasionally in London, occasionally in the scary wilds of the Forbidden Forest, and more often than not in the sometimes peaceable setting of Hogwarts School of Witchcraft and Wizardry in the Highlands of Scotland or in its somewhat pastoral grounds. The story also has its island moments: when, in *Harry Potter and the Philosopher's Stone* (1997), Vernon Dursley desperately tries to prevent the flow of letters inviting Harry to enroll in Hogwarts, he takes the family to a rocky island, where they endure a ferocious storm and a visit from Hagrid, the school's groundskeeper and gamekeeper and "Keeper of Keys and Grounds!"[12] Rather than discussing the books I've chosen in their entirety, I simply draw upon representative sections from several stories that illustrate the themes of islands, wilderness, pastoral, and the urban. By organizing a set of detailed readings of stories across a complete gradient of story landscapes, I have tried to capture a very broad set of environmental topics. The passages dealing with each book—especially the longer readings—should be regarded as "case studies" of sorts. That is, after completing this book, the reader should be able to see environmental aspects in any children's book—I defy you to find any book that has none—and perhaps do so with insights that go beyond what I have discussed here.

I have written this book so that the sections can be read in any order—you can parachute in to your favorite story—that being said, there's no real advantage to *not* reading it from cover to cover. Even if you are already environmentally literate, I hope that there will be insights in the pages ahead that will entertain you and provide you with some fresh perspectives on your favorite books. I hope, as well, that in reading this volume, you'll be tempted to dust off a best-loved story or perhaps read a book you have never encountered before.

Finally, a word or two on how I selected stories for inclusion in this volume. In selecting books to discuss, I have relied heavily on lists of award-winning books. In the United States, there's the John Newbery Medal and the Caldecott Medal; in Britain, the Guardian Children's Fiction Prize; as well as international awards like the Hans Christian Andersen Award and so on. I found a list of one hundred books selected by the National Education Association in 1999 to be very helpful and supplemented this with many other such "best of" lists.[13] With the help of my students, I conducted some informal surveys of my own. Though I have relied on such lists—books on which are often considered to be classics—I have also used my own judgment and have included several books and stories that, as an insatiable lifetime reader, I deem to be excellent. Not all of these are as well-known as some old favorites. You may also discover that several books you assumed would be included in the pages that follow are not here. Sometimes their exclusion is deliberate—I just don't have a taste for them—but sometimes I may not know them. Writing a book is an impressive reminder of our limitations and our finitude.

In writing this book, I have developed a renewed affection for some of the older tales—for example, I've relearned an immense number of nursery rhymes—and I've come to a new appreciation for some emerging classics. Contemporary titles like Suzanne Collins's

Hunger Games trilogy (2008–10) and J. K. Rowling's Harry Potter series (1997–2007) are far more compelling as environmental tales than I suspected before I started writing this book. Now, when I see other adults reading such titles on my daily commute, I salute them, knowing that an affinity with such stories is a powerful preparation for the environmental challenges of the future.

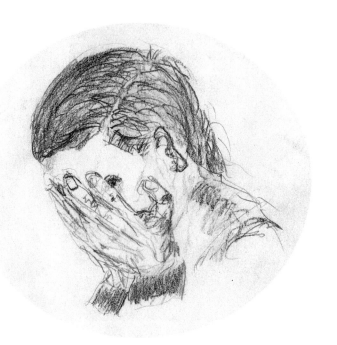

Section One

On Reading

THE EXISTENTIAL PRINCESS: A FAIRY TALE

Once upon a time, there was a princess who lived on a small blue-green world that orbited a medium-sized but feisty sun. Now this particular princess came from a long line of primates that had evolved slowly on the equatorial band of her world. She was fang-less and claw-less and relatively hairless, and alas several very formidable cats had discovered that her kind was remarkably tasty.

But the princess possessed a remarkable gift: she could imagine the future. After consulting with her scientists—who also shared this gift, for this was their unique possession—she learned that one day she must die, just as the scientists, too, must surely die. Moreover, she learned that everything that lives must perish. She learned, too, that the feisty sun that shone so gaily in sky would steadily increase in luminosity and one day would engulf the small blue-green planet.

The princess placed her forehead—behind which was stored the peculiarly ample brain that characterized her people—in her hands and she wept. After a while her weeping turned to a quiet sobbing, and the sobbing became a mild shuddering, and eventually the shuddering came to an end. The princess looked up at last and saw a child pass by where she sat. And knowing that this child, too, would die, she spoke unto the child saying: "Once upon a time . . ."

Once upon a time, there was a ferocious cat . . .

Once upon a time, there were three bears . . .

Once upon a time, there was a woodcutter with a beautiful daughter . . .

Once upon a time, there was an ogre who loved flowers . . .

Once upon a time, there was a princess . . .

Once upon a time . . .

1

Beasts at Bedtime

There are times when Skyping with my father that, for a moment or so, I confuse his image on the screen with mine. We are both gray-haired now and bearded, and though his facial wrinkles are more deltaic than mine, the resemblance between us is close enough to fool me briefly. After all, in my first memories of him, he was fully eight times my age. Now that gap has shrunk, and he is less than twice as old as me. But for the saving graces of some sort of Zeno's paradox of aging, I might catch up with him soon.[1]

Those first memories of my father are of him reading to me. Or rather, they are of him reading to all of us, in turn, seven pages each. In the earliest memories, there were three of us, later six. We would be in my sisters' room, each tucked in, me at the tail end of my sister Anne's bed. Clare, the eldest, was first, then Anne, and then me, each of us indifferent to the stories read to the others. Clare pulled on our father's earlobe, sucked her thumb, and listened. By my turn he was often sleepy, though if he nodded off, he was prodded back to his duties. I can still recall some of those early stories. There was Ben Ross Berenberg's *The Churkendoose* (1946), an unfortunate creature, ambiguously part chicken, turkey, duck, and goose.[2] There was Noel Barr's *Ned the Lonely Donkey* (1952), the farmyard beast who does his best to make friends.[3] There were also plenty of books of rhymes, books on animals in prehistory, and bird books. We also read the heroic Irish stories of Fionn mac Cumhaill, his warrior Fenians, and his poet-soldier son, Oisín, whose mother, Sadhbh, under an enchantment, took the form of a deer. I loved the old stories of Cú Chulainn, the boy who kills a hound and takes its place as a guard dog.[4]

Some years later, my teacher Mr. O'Leary would read J. R. R. Tolkien's *The Hobbit* (1937) in school as a reward for good behavior. I was enchanted by the story, so my father bought me a copy, and it became the first volume to give me that distinctive pride that comes from possessing a special book.[5] From my reading of *The Hobbit*, I date my love of woodlands, a love that has shaped much of my life. Two decades later, I read to my eldest child from that same special copy.

Those bedtime stories, read in the crevices of the day's end, were meant to prepare us for a night of that twitching repose that passes for childhood sleep. But looking back on them now, the nightly stories also irrigated our imaginations, preparing us for the day that followed. They steadied us for the small tribulations of school and primed us for expeditions to the outdoors of garden and neighborhood and, during the weekends at least, our visits to the beaches of Dublin.

Though we began with lonely donkeys and confused wildfowl, some years later my father and I scrutinized nature guides together, learning the names of actual creatures and their habits. My father was always deeply interested in nature. As an amateur malacologist, or student of mollusks, he used to bring us to the beaches of the eastern Irish seaboard on Saturday mornings to search for shells. We would pile into his old Morris Oxford and spend the morning scouring the Dublin sands, looking for surf-heaved treasure, our guidebooks at the ready. Of course, mornings after storms were best, meaning that these tended to be wintry expeditions. We patrolled deserted strands under gray skies, just beyond the reach of the apocalyptic fingerlike chimneys of Poolbeg power station, which dominated Dublin Bay. I don't recall that we were especially scientific in our collections, even though, in addition to guidebooks, my father had weighty monographs on the topic about the house, monographs whose wonderful illustrations we would pore over with him. To this day, I know the Latin binomials of most mollusks of the Irish coastline.

My father kept a saltwater aquarium, which I am told is quite difficult to maintain. The hermit crabs, my favorites, mostly kept to themselves—for such are the ways of crabs—though they would come out to devour morsels of ham. Once a year, the family bath was repurposed as a tank for raising tadpoles. The first truly scientific text I read, in fact, was on the life cycle of the frog. As their frog legs emerged, we would provide lollipop sticks as floating islands, and they would crawl out of the shallow water upon them, recapitulating the first moments of terrestrial life. They, too, had a taste for ham. I once saw a frog emerge from our back garden and look at me as if trying to place a memory, before leaping into the street beneath an oncoming car and making a soft, though audible "pop."

We kept pets and studied books on their maintenance. We had budgies (parakeets), rabbits, and a tortoise named Bert. Bobby the budgie had the somewhat understandable, though wholly unforgivable, habit of clinging fiercely to his perch on one's finger while taking a shit. His little pink feet would burn with the evacuatory strain. I don't recall this problem mentioned in Enid Blyton's Adventure Series, books that I had devoured years earlier, where Jack's parrot Kiki was more a helpful conversationalist than a muttering mess-maker.

Bert the tortoise was a special favorite of my mother's. He would scamper, to the best of his ability, to meet her, his nails clicking on the pavement like a nervous lover tapping on a windowpane. Bert liked to have his throat scratched: he would extend his head upon the improbable stalk of his neck toward her, and my mother would oblige. He went missing one late autumn. We assumed, based on our reading of a book on tortoise care, that he had hibernated in the garden. When we found him much later, our hearts were broken, as it was clear he had upturned himself and died on his back, beyond the help of the family that cared for him. Bobby's passing was also a torment. He was slaughtered, in his birdcage, by a cat who managed to open the clasp of its door. I did have one defense against these dismal existential events. By the time of the flattened frog and Bert's and Bobby's sad demises, I'd been mainlining dozens of nature books that filled my head with many details about the sterner aspects of ecological life. I learned to expect to find death in nature.

When people ask me what experiences made me want to be an environmental scientist, I usually think first of adventures with pets, shell collecting along Dublin's strands, maintaining the aquarium with my father, and much later the college summers I spent collecting insects in Ireland's national parks. But it seems clear to me now that time spent indoors, reading and being read to, had an equally powerful effect on me. Reading introduced me to nature—the sort of ordinary but wholly involving nature I encountered right outside my door.

I've been thinking about the environmentally salutary implications of children's books a lot lately, and not only for their value in minting the next generation of naturalists. Richard Louv's *Last Child in the Woods* (2005) has launched a movement encouraging this more sedentary generation of children to get outdoors, but I wonder if there might also be an environmental benefit to be gained by fortifying those intimate indoor moments when parents read to their children.[6] Are there special books that parents should choose for the Great Indoors? Are there special ways to read them?

Having now spent considerable time examining the content of contemporary children's bookshelves—visiting the local library, compiling and analyzing lists of children's classics, chatting with friends and neighbors who have small children—I have come to the conclusion that reading about nature might be simply unavoidable, since it is hard to find kids' books that are not about our feathered and furry friends or their prehistoric ancestors.

Of course, in an important sense, every book ever written is about nature. Even a writer as arcane and minimalist as Samuel Beckett knew he was reflecting on the environment. In Beckett's novel *The*

Unnamable (1953), the eponymous narrator is alone, despite his promise that "I shall not be alone, in the beginning." He goes on: "I am of
course alone. Alone. Things have to be soon said. And how can one
be sure, in the darkness?"[7]

Beckett's story could not be more spare, more replete with loneliness, hopelessness, emptiness, and despair. But despite the stripped-
down nature of the story, *The Unnamable* is essentially a meditation
on nature: the nature of the human body and its physical and social
needs, and the natural world as conjured up by mere utterance. "In
the world of nature, the world of man," the narrator asks, "where is
nature, where is man, where are you, what are you seeking?" To those
readers who find this work uninterpretable, John Calder, Beckett's
publisher, asks them to consider "how well they understand not only
their own lives, but what they see when they look out at the world;
how they interpret what they see, little of which could be understood
anyway."[8] *The Unnamable* is thus not only about nature but is itself
like an object of nature, simultaneously presenting itself and receding from human apprehension. If this is the case, then the canon
of nature writing could be broadened. In the end, it might be more
difficult to decide which great novels aren't environmental classics.

I recently examined the lists of the top novels of the previous century, including an especially influential one published by the Modern
Library, to contrast the prevalence of nature as a theme in adult literature and in books for children.[9] And indeed, given time and ingenuity, one can make the case for most novels on the adult list being
a little tinged by green. Even, for instance, the obscure farce *Zuleika
Dobson* (1911), by Max Beerbohm, a witty tale set in Oxford of a mass
undergraduate suicide for the sake of love, has occasional environmental touches.[10] For example, two black owls ominously perch on
the battlements of the Duke of Dorset's hereditary home, Tanker-
ton Hall, portending his death. Frankly though, an attempt to find
the environmental significance becomes strenuous, and the connection is, I suppose, quite tenuous. In the end, one must concede that

there are not many novels on the Modern Library's list that qualify explicitly as environmentally themed. One that certainly makes the cut, however, is Jack London's *The Call of the Wild* (1903): the hero is a dog named Buck, who initially lives comfortably in California, but who is sold as an Alaskan sled dog and adaptively sheds his domesticated traits.[11] Though London had not necessarily intended it to be for young readers, *The Call of the Wild* remains popular with teenagers and might be considered a cross-over adult/young adult classic. George Orwell's *Animal Farm* (1945) qualifies too, though presumably we readers know that his primary purpose is to tutor us on fascism, not induct us into the ways of the barnyard.[12]

Yet there are no great strains of interpretation needed to find nature in children's literature. I performed the same analysis of comparable lists of the best children's literature, relying heavily on lists provided by the National Education Association. I reviewed the titles in every age category and scored them for their environmental relevance. Being the father of two children, I knew many of them already, but I also reviewed those titles that were new to me. I found that a full 100 percent of books recommended for preschoolers are environmentally themed. And not in the way that Beckett's *The Unnamable* or Max Beerbohm's *Zuleika Dobson* are environmental. No, these titles include *The Very Hungry Caterpillar* (1969) by Eric Carle, which is quite simply about a very hungry caterpillar.[13] *Brown Bear, Brown Bear, What Do You See?* (1967), written by Bill Martin Jr. and illustrated by Carle, is about what the said bear and other animals see.[14] *The Rainbow Fish* (1992) by Marcus Pfister is about the development of social behavior in a very colorful fish.[15] And *The Runaway Bunny* (1942), written by Margaret Wise Brown and illustrated by Clement Hurd, is about a rabbit tempted to bolt from home and his mother, who is determined to follow him.[16] Nature is everywhere in the preschooler canon.

The proportion seems to slip steadily as children get older. Sixty percent of the 36 books recommended for four- to eight-year-olds feature animals or are in other ways concerned with nature. For the nine-to-twelve age group, it's just over 50 percent. However, it's fair to say that all of the (admittedly much smaller selection of) books for young adults could be described as promoting environmental sensibilities in its readers. These include the aforementioned ecologically rich *The Hobbit*; *Summer of the Monkeys* (1976) by Wilson Rawls, in which a young boy attempts to return chimps to a traveling circus; and *The Cay* (1969) by Theodore Taylor, a survival tale set in the Caribbean Sea.[17]

When I look back at it now, my father's choice of reading material for us was not simply an expression of his own inclinations. Sticking to the classics, it would have been impossible for him to avoid reading to us about nature.

Although children's books are emphatically nature-themed, the animals in them are often anthropomorphized. Only rarely do popular books written for the youngest children provide accurate natural history information. The caterpillar, brown bear, fish, and bunny in children's books do not behave in species-appropriate ways. One doubts, for instance, that in ordinary circumstances a colorful fish would be overly concerned with the hurt feelings of friends, nor would that fish, I suppose, engage an octopus as a life coach. It would seem that animals give voice to an adult world that wants to inculcate children with commendable virtues. Therefore, might animals play a starring role in children's books independent of children's particular interest in animals? After all, how better to socialize the young human animal than with tales of other well-behaved animals? In this model, as the child gets older and becomes more successfully acculturated, there is less of a need to invoke our animal pals, which explains why we see nature fading out of children's literature as they grow older.

There is now, however, compelling evidence that children's interest in animals might reflect innate desires of their own, rather than some adult indoctrination scheme. The ecopsychologist Olin Eugene Myers Jr. from Western Washington University has written that, for children, "the animal emerges . . . as a truly subjective other whose immediate presence is compelling."[18] Vanessa LoBue and her colleagues at Rutgers University and the University of Virginia published a research paper in 2013 showing that children under four responded preferentially to live animals—fish, hamsters, snakes, and spiders—than to "interesting" toys.[19] The children gestured more frequently to the animals, talked more to them, and asked more questions about them, and parents encouraged this interest.

Whether or not children's identification with animals is artificially manufactured by parents, has some innate basis, or—as seems most likely—is a combination of both nature and nurture, the inclusion of animals in tales written for the purposes of instruction is an old habit. Animals perform their roles as moral educators in contemporary children's books much in the way that they did in Aesop's time. One of the first children's books, John Newbery's *A Little Pretty Pocket-Book* (1744), provides several fables featuring animals.[20] By the turn of the twentieth century, anthropomorphic animals had become very popular. *The Tale of Peter Rabbit* (1902) by Beatrix Potter features animals wearing clothing, and *The Wind in the Willows* (1908) by Kenneth Grahame continued the trend, although Potter balked at Toad combing his hair, complaining that it was a "mistake to fly in the face of nature."[21] And in today's world of Pixar and Disney, the pattern of anthropomorphizing animals for purposes of moral instruction continues unabated.

There is strong evidence that having animals in a child's life is important for that child's moral development. A connection with live animals can increase a child's empathy and has been the basis for a number of important children's programs, and even used as part of therapies for troubled children.[22] But, so far, there has been much less attention given to the significance of fictional creatures in a child's life. At the very least, it seems highly likely that reading stories to children about nature provides an opportunity to foster an environmental ethic.

Even if all parents read stories to their children and discuss them patiently, not every parent is environmentally literate. As the US National Environmental Education Foundation stated in their report *Environmental Literacy in America* (2005): "Most Americans believe they know more about the environment than they actually do."[23] They reported that about 80 percent of Americans rely upon incorrect or outdated myths about the environment. Often, parents might not know enough to answer the questions that arise from even the simplest of children's books.

Since most of the books we read to our children are environmentally themed, it is clear that without improvement in environmental literacy, parents are squandering one of the greatest opportunities they have to cultivate in their children a love for the natural world that we all depend upon.

☾⋆

All parents have their own reasons for reading to their children, but surely most suppose that it will make them smarter people, better communicators, and more ethically inclined. Many will hope, no doubt, that their children will care for both the people and the creatures of the world that surround them. But to achieve these objectives, parents might need to do some reading themselves, so that their children can learn something more than good manners from the enchanted beasts of bedtime.

2

Doctor Dolittle and the Question of Reading

Learning from the Great Indoors

Practical writing on the environment has traditionally aimed at coaxing us from the soft comforts of our homes and off to experience the grandeur of the Great Outdoors. The champions of the American wilderness tradition—John Muir, Henry David Thoreau, and their intellectual descendants—have encouraged us to get out into wild places and in so doing to cultivate our own rugged natures.[1] Thoreau sets a rather high bar for gallivanting out-of-doors. In his essay "Walking" (1861), he wrote:

> I think that I cannot preserve my health and spirits unless I spend *four hours a day at least*—and it is commonly more than that—sauntering through the woods and over the hills and fields absolutely free from all worldly engagements. (emphasis mine)[2]

A recent manifestation of the inclination in environmentalism toward the out-of-doors can be seen in the national Leave No Child Inside movement.[3] A central motivation for this program—inspired by journalist Richard Louv's 2005 best-seller *Last Child in the Woods: Saving Our Children from Nature-Deficit Disorder*—is a supposed correlation between attention-deficit disorder and obesity, and the other prevalent malaises of our times, and a greatly reduced contact by kids these days with nature.[4] Encouraging youths to get out-of-doors—even less than four hours a day will do—is done with a view to improving their physical and psychological health.[5] Most parents who read this will suspect that their kids spend less time outside than they did themselves in their youth.[6] Reversing the trend of kids spending more time on the couch and hitched to their screens is seen as vital to their health and the health of the natural world.[7] It is assumed that a love of nature is key to preserving the wildest places and creatures. We protect most, the argument goes, what best we understand.[8]

Though the task of my book is not to undermine the important insights that are now emerging from the Leave No Child Inside movement, nonetheless, we should pause to remember this obvious truth: the great naturalists, even after their most arduous trips, returned home. In fact, much of what we learn about the wildest of places was written by men and women who, by necessity, do their reading and writing inside and typically behind a desk. Thoreau's journals alone contain two million words: even writing at a thousand words a day (which is twice my daily average) translates into a lot of desk time (almost six years of writing: no days off). Another exemplary naturalist, Darwin (who was no slouch when it came to exploring the Great Outdoors—his *Voyage of the Beagle* reports on his almost five years away from England exploring the globe) settled down in later life to a quieter life of reading, reflection, and ingenious observation of what was close at hand.[9] Reflection on the outdoors is often intensified and enriched indoors.

I don't suppose there is any environmental educator advocating for kids to walk for four hours each day in the woods. Nor would any expect a child to avoid indoor pleasures in their entirety. What should be encouraged is a more favorable ratio of life indoors and out-of-doors than our culture currently fosters. Thoreau and Darwin may not, of course, be the most apt role models for today's youth since they were, in essence, vocational naturalists (most of us assume,

I suppose, that our children will not be). Yet the role of reading, reflection, and action in the lives of those exemplary fellows who helped frame our contemporary understanding of the natural world is worth taking note of. The goal in all our lives is surely to get this balance right. It is a balance that will change at different life stages. One might hope, for example, that children spend more time outside than they often do. Yet one might also hope that when they are inside, the quality of this experience can be enriched by more time with stories and with their own creative preoccupations. The task is to transform the quality of the Great Indoors. By all means, "leave no child inside," but with this addendum: "leave no child inside without a book." Environmental education begins at the hearth.

Mirroring the tensions between balancing inside and outside time is a less well-known antagonism in somewhat rarefied debates over environmental literacy; for now, let us define environmental literacy simply as having knowledge about nature versus formal literacy—reading, writing, and arithmetic. This tension can be boiled down to the question: Does a bookish child neglect the cultivation of those skills needed to "read the book of nature"?[10]

Doctor Dolittle and the Question of Environmental Literacy: Does a Naturalist Need to Read and Write?

In the unlikely event that you are about to read Hugh Lofting's classic *The Story of Doctor Dolittle* (1920) to your child, I encourage you to stop reading before Chapter IX, "The Monkey's Council." Of course, if you can stomach references to "The Land of the White Men," then by all means forge ahead. But you should certainly proceed with enormous caution before embarking on Chapter XI, "The Black Prince," in which we first meet Prince Bumpo, an African prince from the kingdom of Jolliginki. The prince is a recurrent character in the Dolittle books—he becomes the Doctor's friend and traveling companion.

When we meet him first, Prince Bumpo is addicted to fairy tales and wants to become a white prince so as not to perturb Sleeping Beauty, who would, he fears, upon waking, be offended by his blackness. To this enterprise, the Doctor lends his reluctant assistance, though his solution—a face wash comprised of an admixture of medicines—was only temporarily successful.[11] Up to that point in the book, the Dolittle stories can be profitably read to and by youthful readers, as can some of those of the Newbery Award–winning *The Voyages of Doctor Dolittle* (1922). This latter book is, besides, especially interesting on the question of how much formal literacy is needed to complement environmental literacy, or indeed in questioning if these two forms of literacy have contradictory tendencies.[12]

Although Dolittle is a medical man by training and a veterinarian by necessity, the Doctor is a naturalist by avocation. This becomes strenuously part of his self-description in *The Voyages of Doctor Dolittle*, the main adventure of which consists of Dolittle's bid to rescue that other great naturalist, the "Red Indian" Long Arrow, son of Golden Arrow. Long Arrow had last been seen on Spidermonkey Island, a floating island, typically found close to Brazil. He must be found!

Proclaiming oneself a naturalist may sound as anachronistic these days as being an apothecary or, say, a typewriter manufacturer, since the term and the accompanying field of natural history has somewhat fallen out of favor. So what, exactly, is a naturalist? The *Bloomsbury Good Word Guide* helpfully distinguishes "naturalist" from the phonically similar "naturist."[13] Don't confuse the two: the latter person dispenses with clothing, whereas, in my experience at least, the former has much need of pockets. A good naturalist carries specimens, notebooks, magnifying glasses, small vials of alcohol, killing jars, and other tools of the trade about their person. The *Oxford English Dictionary* more emphatically defines a naturalist as a person who has a special interest in, or makes a special study of, plants or animals, although in the classic age of natural history—the centuries after the onset of the Enlightenment up until the early twentieth century—the term also included geology, meteorology, and so on.[14] Natural history can thus be described as the systematic inspection and description of the phenomena of nature. Naturalists typically observe nature rather than performing elaborate field or laboratory experiments—which characterizes the contemporary discipline of ecology as a science. Though it is now a pejorative to dismiss a scientist as a mere "bug hunter," I suspect that Darwin would have been pleased enough with the label. One of the more famous drawings of Darwin from his college days has him riding the back of a ground beetle with the caption, "Go it, Charlie."[15]

Those of us who advocate for a more eclectic definition of environmental literacy might be wary of the writing of some scientists who encourage a narrow ecological training of youthful natural historians.[16] Frank Golley's otherwise excellent *A Primer for Environmental Literacy* (1998) can serve to represent this narrower inspection of environmental literacy.[17] This book presents the inculcation of environmental literacy as entailing technical principles of scientific ecology. In fairness though—and I might point out here that Frank was a cherished mentor of mine at the University of Georgia—Golley acknowledges that "environmental literacy connotes more than knowing the names of the organisms and understanding geomorphology." Recognizing that "experience is the trigger for environmental literacy," it is necessary, Golley writes, "to go beyond books and libraries and experience nature directly." Such reflections will remind us that even the most methodologically minded of young naturalists need to put down the books at times.[18] But can we dispense with formal literacy altogether—putting down the books altogether, or perhaps never even taking them up at all? Or to press the question even deeper: Does formal literacy get in the way of environmental literacy? It's one of the more extraordinary facets of *The Voyages of Doctor Dolittle* that our good Doctor reflects upon this very perplexing question.

☾ ⋆

The narrator of *The Voyages of Doctor Dolittle* is young Tommy Stubbins, who is an illiterate boy when he first meets the Doctor. He promptly declares his wish to become a naturalist. Since Dolittle's exploits were undertaken in the early to mid-nineteenth century—a golden age for natural history—this was a reasonably aspiration. Would Stubbins need to learn to read and write to achieve his aim? In assessing the need for formal literacy, Dolittle calls to mind some of the great natural historians. Of Darwin, for example, Dolittle says, "This young fellow . . . reads and writes very well," and Cuvier, the doctor admits, "used to be a tutor." However, one of the greatest naturalists of them all, Dolittle claims, is Long Arrow, who "doesn't even need to know how to write his own name nor to read the A B C." Would young Stubbins go the path of a Long Arrow or a Darwin (or, indeed, a Dolittle)?

What does Dolittle think contributes to Long Arrow's effectiveness as a naturalist in the absence of formal literacy? First, he is nomadic, never staying in the same place for very long: he's "a sort of Indian tramp." Second, he lives with the animals and with the various tribes of Indians, usually in the mountains of Peru. Third, he has specialized knowledge: Long Arrow is especially good on bees and beetles. It turns out, if you'll forgive me for spoiling the plot, Long Arrow is trapped in a cave on Spidermonkey Island. He ingeniously ties a leaf parchment with explanatory pictograms of his location on the leg of the very rare Jabrizi beetle, and this leads to his rescue by our doctor. Finally, perhaps it is Long Arrow's *lack* of book learning, his facility for dealing with the immediacy of nature, that makes him more effective than lesser naturalists, like Darwin and Cuvier. For it is the ability to observe things closely that is most determinative of excellence in natural history. In an exchange between Tommy Stubbins and Polynesia, the Doctor's parrot—an inarguably offensive parrot—we learn further secrets to becoming a naturalist. Polynesia asks Tommy, "Are you a good noticer?—Do you notice things well?" She then provides several instructive examples of noticing, such as this one, "Supposing you saw two cock-starlings on an apple tree, and you only took one good look at them—would you be able to tell one from the other if you saw them the next day?" If you care to be a naturalist of Long Arrow's caliber, you must commit yourself to such feats of observation.

These days there is, presumably, little doubt that formal literacy is a jolly good thing—though it is certainly a costly enterprise. Though most kids learn to talk without much coaxing, reading and writing requires some ingenious inculcation. Somewhat surprisingly, however, there remains some debate in environmental circles about the environmental costs of formal literacy. A champion of the viewpoint that literacy is a mixed blessing is David Abram—an exceptionally good writer—who in his book *The Spell of the Sensuous* (1997) argues that the alphabet, and the distraction of the written word in general, cultivated a turning away from the immediate natural world.[19] Writing things down, which augments memory, at the same time induces a forgetfulness of the world.

David Abram was not the first, of course, to question the implications of writing—famous critics of writing includes Socrates—and while it is not a widespread opinion, it nonetheless comes up in environmental circles and is worth reflecting upon.[20] It is tempting to assume that there is a lot of folk knowledge about nature embedded in oral cultures, knowledge that has been left aside in these more literate times.[21] In the end Dolittle, at least, determined that formal literacy must indeed be valuable, for we know that ultimately Stubbins learned his ABC's. It is Tommy Stubbins, as I have mentioned, who is the supposed scribe of *The Voyages*. Stubbins is Dolittle's student and Dolittle is, after all, the greatest naturalist of them all and is a literate man besides.

What makes Dolittle a better naturalist than Long Arrow, since the unalphabeted Indian surpassed even Darwin and Cuvier? By Doctor Dolittle's own admission, he surpasses Long Arrow because his methods are more up-to-date, and, thus, it is not his literacy per se.

We learn a lot about the great naturalist's methods, some of which are quite counter-intuitive, as the Dolittle stories progress. First, Dolittle seems to have a knack for getting things wrong, and yet his outcomes are generally fine. For example, he is not much of a sailor, and his voyages typically get deflected by shipwreck. No shame in that; indeed, the great naturalist and co-discoverer of natural selection Alfred Russel Wallace was shipwrecked more than once, though, of course, Wallace was not a skipper of his own vessel.[22] But Dolittle is adept at learning from his mistakes. This is the hallmark of a good scientist.

Key to Doctor Dolittle's methods is the curious novelty—which remarkably we have yet to discuss—that he can talk to the animals. So crucial is this to the Dolittle universe that in some of the movie renderings of Doctor Dolittle, this is the only plot element from Lofting's stories that is retained. How is this unprecedented feat achieved? Not, it turns out, by means of a superpower, not by a freak accident, and not related to his capacity for reading and writing. Doctor Dolittle learns the language of animals by dint of sustained effort. How he accomplishes this is a matter for another day.

Richard Louv—whose work, as we have seen, inspired recent environmental education programs that encourage kids to go outside and be in nature—does not, of course, suggest being outdoors should be encouraged at the expense of reading or any other aspect of formal literacy. "Reading," Louv writes in *The Last Child in the Woods*, "stimulates the ecology of the imagination." The work of environmental educators will be to balance the salutary effects of being outside, whilst encouraging the best use of time indoors. The transformation of the experience of the Great Indoors by encouraging a balanced life of reading, reflection, and experience is the next great challenge.

Alan
CJH
2015

Section Two

Pastoral Stories

TOPOPHILIA

For my twenty-first birthday, my youngest brother, Paul, gave me a collected volume of John Betjeman's poetry. Betjeman remains one of the most popular of the English poets and, though I no longer read him regularly, if every so often in the late summer I describe an especially sun-kissed friend as being "furnish'd and burnish'd by Aldershot sun," it is Betjeman's "A Subaltern's Love Song" that I am quoting.

There is undeniably a lovely specificity to Betjeman's observations about people, and his writing has a rootedness in the distinctive English countryside. In describing Betjeman's world and work, the poet W. H. Auden coined the term "topophilia." The word has its etymologically roots in the Greek *topos* meaning "place" and *philia* meaning "love." Betjeman had a peculiarly acute visual imagination that Auden felt he himself had not. In his self-assessment Auden deemed himself to be too much of a "thinking type." Even for those who are not as cerebral as Auden imagines himself to be, reading Betjeman poems draws attention to something that we may not have even noticed missing in ourselves until we see it expressed in one of those poems. However, a Betjeman poem does not, I think, merely alert us to our deficiencies—for that would be sad—but rather coaches us to notice how the specifics of the places in which the events of our lives take place may intensify all of our experiences.

Topophilia is, to my ear at least, a pretty word, but that alone should not justify its use. If it means no more than a literal "love of place," might it not be better for us just using that term? Thus, if the word had evolved no further than Auden's initial use of it in reference to Betjeman's work, then it would be reasonable to drop it. However, topophilia has been adopted and put to good use by philosophers, geographers, and environmental psychologists in recent decades, and though its meaning has not, in fact, migrated tremendously far beyond Auden's definition, nonetheless, it is now associated with and enriched by some fascinating new research arenas.

Environmental psychologists have tried, for example, to discover what specifically determines the human subjective experience of the physical environment. What are the elements of landscape that trigger our preferences? Is there a genetic component to our sense of place? It is clear from such research that our subjective responses to landscapes are complex, but they are undeniably whole body responses: the sight, smell, and sound of a landscape may influence us. Furthermore, memories associated with these perceptions are crucial in determining whether our present evaluation of a place is positive or negative. Close your eyes: recall, say, what it felt like to have that warm breeze blow across the sand as you played on your favorite beach as a child. The plashing of the waves, the tinkling notes in the distance of other children's merriment, the compliant whisper of the sand as you slice it with your spade. And oh, such a lovely sound the tree outside the bedroom window made as the wind swept through the night leaves as you curled up in your bed during your childhood years! Listen to how Betjeman captures the feeling of Christmastime:

> The holly in the windy hedge
> And round the Manor House the yew
> Will soon be stripped to deck the ledge,
> The altar, font and arch and pew,

So that the villagers can say
'The church looks nice' on Christmas Day.[1]

What's that you are feeling? It may be topophilia.

I grew up in a relatively large city, Dublin, though my topophilic
inclinations are toward the pastoral regions beyond the limits of the
city. The village where we lived was called Templeogue; it was right at
the trailing edge of Dublin in the 1950s when a suburb grew around
the old village. To the north, and toward the city, was Terenure Village and beyond this Rathgar, where in 1882 James Joyce was born.
Farther north still was Rathmines and then, five miles or so from
our home, was Dublin city center. For most of my youth, however, I
obeyed a gravitational pull to the south. In those days, if you chose
your route carefully, you could walk through farmland from beyond
our garden wall all the way to base of Montpelier Hill in the foothills
of the Dublin mountains, where stands the remains of a large hunting lodge built in 1725 (on top of a Neolithic tomb), and subsequently
used by the infamous and allegedly satanic Hellfire Club for nefarious
purposes.[2] The devil, apparently, had interrupted a card game at the
lodge, and the building went up in flames. Today the hill is owned
by the Irish state and is flanked by forestry plantations, dedicated to
less sinister pastimes like orienteering, jogging, and nature walks.
Both of these poles, north to the city and south toward the mountains, influenced me and my later professional direction.

As a child, I split my free time between the back garden (favorite activity: collecting wasps in jam jars—first step, eat jam), the
farm fields—often admittedly to engage there in pitched battles with
neighboring kids—and, finally, the foothills leading up to the Hellfire
Club, to which I cycled and walked. Though this was not the wildest
of terrain, nonetheless, it was wild enough to be both educational
and perilous. Once, for example, when cycling at considerable speed
down the mountain from the Hellfire Club, my cycling companion

was knocked off his bicycle by an especially ill-tempered goat. If a goat charges you on the hillside, it may quite possibly be the devil. Pan, the goat god and lord of the pastoral, is, however, the more likely candidate.

It's the pastoral middle ground—that ecological sweet spot—that comforts me most.

3

The Pastoral Promise

AND THEY ALL LIVED HAPPILY EVER AFTER

Versions of the Children's Pastoral

At the secret core of many stories lies the promise of a happy ending: *And they all lived happily ever after*. I call this the pastoral promise—it's a promise of a perfect world set beyond the action that gripped us as we read the story. It's an idea rooted in ancient thought and one that provides a powerful goad for environmental action. It implies that there is a harmony, a oneness, and a peaceful end game beyond the complications of the moment. Once the words "and they all lived happily ever after" appear, they indicate that those tensions that have maintained the story, the ones that propelled us along, have been dissipated. The world is restored to harmony. After this the curtain descends, and we are to learn nothing more of our heroes. The prince and the princess have wed, the wolf has died, the evil witch has perished, the children have been restored to their parents, and all is well with the world, in perpetuity. Never-ending happiness— impossible in our everyday lives, though we may crave it—exists as a private world beyond the limits of the page.

In one of my favorite stories, "The Parable of the Prodigal Son," frequently adapted from Luke's Gospel as a children's story, a younger son takes his inheritance and leaves his father's home. He squanders his share of the estate on wild living. But the land to which he traveled suffers famine. The son hires himself out to watch over swine. As he considers eating the pigs' food, he realizes that his father's servants are more fortunate than he is. He sets off for home. His father sees him from afar and runs to embrace him. The son begs for forgiveness, declaring his unworthiness to be his father's son. But the father calls to his servants to bring the errant son his best robe; a ring is placed on his finger and sandals on his feet. A fattened calf is prepared for a feast. Joyfully, the father says: "This son of mine was dead and is alive again; he was lost and is found." Now, of course, the story does not end here. The elder son, who had all the while remained at his father's side, complains about the celebration for his brother, for he, who had slaved away on the home front, has never received so much as a goat to feast on with his friends. But the father reassures him that all he has is his sons. Of the prodigal son, the father says to his grumbling son, repeating the words he had uttered to the servants: "But we had to celebrate and be glad, because this brother of yours was dead and is alive again; he was lost and is found." And they all lived happily ever after. Or, at least, this is what we must assume, for we hear no more of this story. Though it is hard to imagine that the prodigal son—who is, no doubt, transformed by his experiences— will ever be satisfied back home.

To err with the prospect of redemption: this, in part, is the pastoral dream. Forgiveness is a general comfort, but it's especially reassuring for a child and is, unsurprisingly, a prevalent motif in children's stories. Even as grievously as the prodigal son has sinned, he is to be welcomed home. The little rapscallion of Margaret Wise Brown's *The Runaway Bunny* (1942) is the young child's equivalent of the prodigal son, though presumably the former is fluffier and less culpable.[1] After all, there is no mention of the bunny squandering a fortune.

Sometimes the pastoral function of a story is to remind us that there can be a return, and all, then, will be well with the world. Bilbo Baggins, for example, begins and ends his adventures in the pastoral haven of the Shire. We first meet our hobbit "in the quiet of the world, when there was less noise, and more green, and the hobbits were still prosperous. . . ." Something adventurous gets awoken in this initially rather self-satisfied hobbit, and so he ventures forth with wizard and dwarfs. But it is not the Bilbo of old who later returns to the Shire. He has been hardened by the road, by adventures, by an encounter with a dragon, and by battle. Bilbo is changed and yet the Shire endures. Tolkien writes: "As all things come to an end, even this story, a day came at last when they were in sight of the country where Bilbo had been born and bred, where the shapes of the land and the trees were as well known to him as his hands and toes." And if we didn't know that *The Hobbit; or, There and Back Again* (1937) was a beginning and not an end, we might imagine Bilbo—queerer, to be sure, than he was before he left, safely ensconced in Bag-End—smoking his pipe, tending to his flowers, noodling with his memoirs, and "being quite a little fellow in a wide world."[2] Later at the Council of Elrond, in *The Fellowship of the Ring* (1954), Bilbo confesses that he had hoped to finish his memoirs with the phrase: "and he lived happily ever afterwards to the end of his days."[3]

At its most elemental, the pastoral refers to people associated with the tending of livestock, especially shepherds. This much is implied in the etymology of "pastoral," which derives from the classical Latin word *pastoralis*, relating to the tending of livestock. The father in the story of the prodigal son is thus a literal pastoralist—he cares for his flocks. In the case of the errant son, he resorts, in troubled times, to the less seemly aspect of pastoralism: the tending of swine. In the earliest Greek pastoral poems, such as those by the Greek poet Theocritus (c. 310–250 BC), the lives, the loves, and the laments of shepherds in remote mountainous region of Greece were recorded and idealized.[4] So influential did the literary form that sprang up from such ancient literature become that one can say that parents, when they snuggle up to read a bedtime story with their child, still echo sentiments first provoked by life in the remote valleys of the ancient world.

The environmental setting of the original pastoral poems was a rural one, and generally in classical pastoral literature, life is pre-

sented in an idealized or romantic form. Such poems are referred to as
"idylls" or "bucolic" poems. From this we get an association between
the terms "idyllic" and "bucolic" and notions of a life of ease and harmony. Especially influential versions of pastoral poems include those
of the Roman poet Virgil (70–19 BC). These are called the *Eclogues* or
Bucolics.[5] Some of the poems are set in Arcadia in the Greek Pelopon-
nese. Arcadia was the home of the god Pan, who retains a strange
appeal even in contemporary literature for both adults and children.
For example, in the effervescent tale *The Wind in the Willows* (1908) by
Kenneth Grahame, our heroes, a mole and a river rat, have an encounter with Pan.[6] In the chapter titled "The Piper at the Gates of Dawn,"
Mole and Rat search for the missing son of the Otter and discover him
on a small island in the river under the care of Pan. It is such an odd
encounter that critics have often expressed themselves nonplussed
by it. It's as if it's a feral chapter from another book. But perhaps this
should always be the case when one meets a god of the old world:
it should seem like a departure from the mainstream of any plot.

If the conventional pastoral has been eclipsed in poetry, it endures
in other aspects of culture.[7] The appeal of the pastoral remains conspicuous in both children's stories and in environmental thought.
Visions of peaceful and harmonious times in rustic settings have
been foundational to utopian visions; a life of simplicity, outside in
nature, under clement skies, and quitting "the rat race" is the stuff
of green dreams.

☾ ⋆
⋆

Taken together, the essence of the pastoral tradition, according to
the poet and critic William Empson, is twofold. In Empson's classic,
if somewhat cryptic, overview of the genre, *Some Versions of Pastoral*
(1935), he states that in the pastoral, the complex is expressed simply, and, moreover, simple people express strong feelings.[8] The parable of the prodigal son conforms to Empson's pastoral tropes: it is a
simple story in which supposedly simple people express strong emo-

tions. A son leaves and returns home, but the feelings expressed—the comforting lure of home, a sense of belonging, and the fidelity of a father's love—are far from simple. These themes are also universal. Once again *Wind in the Willows*, that classic children's pastoral tale, depicts this theme beautifully. As Rat and Mole are traversing a field, Mole passes near his own burrow, which he had abandoned when we first encountered him at the start of the novel. He senses he is close. Grahame describes the moment when it hits Mole:

> He stopped dead in his tracks, his nose searching hither and thither in its efforts to recapture the fine filament, the telegraphic current, that had so strongly moved him. A moment, and he had caught it again; and with it this time came recollection in fullest flood. Home!

Mole is overcome by emotion by this discovery (and by Rat's initial inability to discern its importance to his friend). Mole blurts out: "'I know it's a—shabby, dingy little place,' he sobbed forth at last, brokenly: 'not like—your cosy quarters—or Toad's beautiful hall—or Badger's great house—but it was my own little home—and I was fond of it—and I went away and forgot all about it—and then I smelt it suddenly—on the road. . . .'"

Mole and Rat spend the night in Mole's old home. And though that place still exercises its charms on Mole, he nonetheless realizes that it is not yet time for him to return there. After all, he does not want "to abandon the new life and its splendid spaces, to turn his back on sun and air and all they offered him and creep home and stay there." So Mole leaves home once again.

The pastoral embraces the dream of a homecoming—back to the environment from which we came—to be sure, and also those of comfort, security, and belonging; but, additionally, the pastoral is concerned with health and vigor, with a carefree life in peaceful places, with un-perplexing friendships, with serenely beautiful things, and with harmony in all its dimensions. Harmony and composure ground pastoral stories. As often as not, the pastoral dream is a reverie enjoyed in a leafy place, typically an environment beyond the tribulations of urban concerns. Gardens abound as settings for children's stories, as do gardens in that more figurative sense: those fertile pastures where natural and human action felicitously combine.

Pastoral stories are a distinct category of children's literature, even if the term is not in wide use among youthful readers or their parents. Critics of children's literature—by which I mean, those writers, often academics, who analyze stories for children—typically diagnose the pastoral style of literature by the presence of anthropomorphized animals in benevolent rural settings. Beatrix Potter's *Peter Rabbit* stories or A. A. Milne's *Winnie-the-Pooh* serve as exemplary stories of the genre. William Empson remarked that

> children feel at home with animals conceived as human; the animal can be made affectionate without its making serious emotional demands on them, does not want to educate them, is at least unconventional in the sense that it does not impose its conventions, and does not make a secret of the processes of nature.

In the child's pastoral story, harmony prevails for the most part, despite the occurrence of those mild tensions that move the plot along. There is an important exception to the pastoral's emphasis on harmony that we will discuss presently—death is woven into its fabric in an important way. But, generally, adult concerns do not intrude, especially in stories for the very young. The characters do not, for example, typically have financial concerns. Winnie-the-Pooh never mentions his mortgage or car payments. There is no mention of a Mrs. Winnie-the-Pooh. Nor are infidelities, botched friendships (though Winnie is a master at navigating his relationships), and so forth suitable topics for the children's pastoral, at least not those written for those of the most tender years. *Winnie-the-Pooh* is not without its emotional nuances, though: Eeyore's gloominess is only the most conspicuous of its psychological depths.

The danger with the pastoral is that as a literary form, it is so polymorphic, so embracing of good things, of sweet environments, of the pleasing middle ground, that it can almost seem to embrace everything. But something that is everything can seem to be nothing at all. The trick, then, is how to figure out how to operationalize the idea in concrete and recognizable ways.

Fortunately, from our discussion above, we already have clues that will allow us to operationalize the pastoral. The pastoral flags an occupation: shepherds and those who tend to flocking animals and other peaceful creatures; a place: primarily rural or gently humanized landscapes, at times gardens and oases of green; a mood: nostalgic, a sense of belonging, of being at home; a tone: harmony and balance; a spirituality: that oceanic feeling of connection with nature, an inclination toward the great god Pan; a technological orientation: modest and appropriate; a hypothesis about the Good Life: well-being derives from proximity to nature. The pastoral thus offers these human consolations: redemption and recovery.

For a definition to work, it must limit at the same time as it includes. If all children's stories were pastoral stories of a sort, we could dispense with the term "pastoral" and just call them stories. So what stories are emphatically non-pastoral?[9] The pastoral generally excludes the urban, the industrial, the rootless, and the aggressive. Importantly, however, the pastoral does not exclude death. The mention of death in the pastoral requires a brief explication here; we will return to it again below. Death has long been an inclusion in pastoral art, both literary and visual. For example, Nicolas Poussin's (1594–1665) renowned painting *Et in Arcadia Ego*, also known as *The Arcadian Shepherds*, illustrates this darker mood that can nibble at the edges of pastoral tranquility. In the painting, Arcadian shepherds inspect the inscription on a tomb. "Et in Arcadia ego" is translated as "Even in Arcadia, there am I"; the "I" being death. The painting, and several others that mimic the theme, derive their inspiration from Virgil's *Eclogue V*, where shepherds mourn the death of Daphnis, commemorating him with the following inscription: "Daphnis was I amid the woods, known from here even to the stars. Fair was my flock, but fairer I, their shepherd."

Pastoral-inspired stories for children and young adults can thus simultaneously be concerned with the difficulty, indeed at times the impossibility, of achieving harmony and balance. In Chinua Achebe's fable concerning the limits of animal community harmony, *How the Leopard Got His Claws* (1972), we learn that at one time "all the animals in the forest lived as friends."[10] Few of them had sharp teeth or claws. They had no need since the animals got along. The dog was the exception, and he violently usurped the leopard, who was king. Rejected by his people, the leopard had teeth and claws forged by the blacksmith. From the thunder he was given a new voice, and he regained his standing. But thereafter, considering the other animals "miserable worms" and "shameless cowards," he ruled the forest with terror. The dog slunk off and become the slave of people.

Death, too, intrudes into children's pastoral stories. For example, in Katherine Paterson's controversial novel *The Bridge to Terabithia* (1977), two friends escape their lonely lives by creating an idyllic leafy kingdom.[11] However, death intrudes into this pastoral world—indeed, it is, ultimately, as one of the characters is crossing into Terabithia, the children's shared pastoral oasis, that she loses her life. Perhaps the most moving death scene in children's pastoral literature comes at the end of E. B. White's *Charlotte's Web* (1952). White describes the spider's death:

> The Fair Grounds were soon deserted. The sheds and buildings were empty and forlorn. The infield was littered with bottles and

trash. Nobody, of the hundreds of people that had visited the Fair, knew that a grey spider had played the most important part of all. No one was with her when she died.[12]

My advice to you, reader, is not to be caught out by reading this sad passage in a public place.

A story can be pastoral, holding out the possibility of peace and harmony, only to have those possibilities shattered—we may want peace, we may want carefree days in a verdant place, but this will not be our lot. It is, perhaps, because some of us may hope for a world in which death is expunged—or at the very least want our children's realizations of it deferred—that makes Paterson's award-winning novel so controversial. Death is sad, but Virgil would have understood this story quite well.

€ ★
★

Books end; even in their physicality, books are intimations of mortality. Dust to dust jacket, and then the story is over.

Stories of all sorts, bucolic and otherwise, may conclude with a promise, offered in the form of the comforting thought that our heroes' drama is over. Gray skies will not return. Pastoral stories often make this promise most vigorously: they end very happily as often as not. Not all, however, always end with the literal words "and they all lived happily ever after."[13] Some of the Grimm fairy tales end with close variants. For example, "The Little Donkey"—a tale about a prince in the form of a donkey who marries a princess and is revealed in the end as a noble-looking youth—concludes on a blemish-free note of happiness and good fortune: "After the death of his own father, he received yet another kingdom and lived in happiness and wealth." Similarly, "The Little Lamb and the Little Fish" ends with the word "happy." A more prevalent ending to fairy tales—and one that, depending on your perspective, could also be regarded as happy, I suppose—are alacritous accounts of the demise of the villain. Noth-

ing says "perpetuity" quite like the death of an enemy. In "The Wolf
and the Seven Kids," the wolf falls into a well, and "when the seven
kids saw this, they came running and dancing joyfully around the
well." In "The Three Little Men in the Forest," a wicked stepmother
and her daughter are dispatched horrifyingly: "They were cast into
the forest to be devoured by wild animals." "The Twelve Brothers"
also has a gruesome finale. This time it's a mother-in-law who dies:
"They stuck her into a barrel full of boiling oil and poisonous snakes,
and she died a gruesome death." "Little Brother and Little Sister,"
another frightful stepmother tale, combines the demise of the evil
stepmother with a mention of perpetual happiness for our protagonists. It ends thusly: "The evil stepmother was burned at the stake ...
and brother and sister were once again together and lived happily
until the end of their days." "The Old Woman in the Forest" ends with
the witch's demise and a poor servant girl's marriage to a prince: "And
the couple got married and lived a happy life."

The conclusion of a young child's pastoral story is often bittersweet. *Winnie-the-Pooh* concludes plaintively: "But wherever they go,
and whatever happens to them on the way, in that enchanted place
on the top of the Forest, a little boy and his Bear will always be playing." And Beatrix Potter's *Peter Rabbit* stories, every last one of them,
conclude with a return to the security of the hearth.

Whether a story ends with *happy every after*s, with the death of an
enemy, or with relaxation by a toasty fire, the implication is always
the same: Life is complex, and stories are complex, but happiness in
the form of the obliteration of problems, the removal of threat, and
a stay against calamity might just be possible. Let us hope for sim-
pler times ahead. If the stars align and the environment is just right,
felicity, prosperity, health, and harmony in sun-dappled valleys are
ours for the taking. This is the essence of the environmental pastoral. The page ends. But not ours, not yet.

4

The Ecology of Pooh

When Winnie-the-Pooh got stuck in the doorway of Rabbit's home after feasting on large amounts of honey, he was assisted by a great and very strange chain of being. In E. H. Shepard's illustration, Christopher Robin can be seen tugging on the wedged bear, followed by four rabbits, a stoat, a mouse, Piglet, three more mice, and a hedgehog. Yet another mouse scampers to join the effort. A beetle is landing behind the mouse, and aloft are two more beetles, a dragonfly, and, finally, a butterfly. In Disney's animated film, made five decades later—and a hemisphere away—the chain is foreshortened and adapted to a New World audience. Pooh remains stuck, of course, and Christopher Robin still leads the effort, but lined up behind him are Kanga, Eeyore, Roo, and a gopher! In the cartoon, Gopher makes it clear, and Pooh reiterates it, that he "is not in the book." A translocation to a new place can be unnerving: though some things remain the same, alterations are inevitable.

I recently sat with pencil sharpened and notebook at the ready, like an anthropologist in exotic terrain, to watch Disney's *The Many Adventures of Winnie the Pooh* (1977), a feature-length collection of the earlier animated shorts. What happened, I wondered, when England's most famous fictional bear migrated across the Atlantic and settled into an American landscape? Like Pooh, I had grown up on an island west of the European mainland (in my case, Ireland) and in my ripe maturity had emigrated to the United States. Like Pooh, I had spent much of my time out-of-doors. Over the back wall of our family home in south county Dublin were mile after mile of farm fields, interspersed with shrubby hedgerows. Not quite as bucolic as

Pooh's Hundred Acre Wood, perhaps, but there, until the summer dusk drove us home, was where we largely spent our childhood vacations. Like the transplanted Pooh, the terrain in which I now dwell in the New World is hospitable enough in many ways, and yet it is also uncanny. It is not quite home. The suspicion I am investigating here is that, from an environmental perspective, there is more to this bear of "very little brain" than meets the eye.

When Pooh arrived in the United States, he de-hyphenated his name—perhaps a result of some tweaking at Ellis Island. Christopher Robin admirably retained his English accent, and Owl's accent was plummy, though at times I think he hammed it up for his US audience. But Pooh's, Piglet's, Rabbit's, Tigger's, Kanga's, and Roo's accents became appropriately American. The process of assimilation had begun. As often happens in cases of faunal introductions, the aliens must interact with new critters. Gopher—a small burrowing rodent endemic to North America, enterprising and mercantile—worked out a quote for removing the wedged Pooh from Rabbit's door. Gopher figured his hourly rate, at overtime with 10 percent added, and assessed how much explosives might be needed for the job. No, we are not in England anymore!

Despite all this, much in the film survives largely unchanged from the books. Scenes often start or end with reproductions of Shepard's drawings taken from the original books, and the stories are rather faithfully retold. I would have preferred that Disney ended *The Many Adventures* with A. A. Milne's sentence: "But wherever they go, and whatever happens to them on the way, in that enchanted place on the top of the Forest, a little boy and his Bear will always be playing." In Disney's version, a Bear alone awaits a boy's return. Now, that's depressing.

Unlike most exiles, Pooh seems to have made a rather easy transition to the New World, and in fact he and his friends seem to have traveled from England with their entire ecological entourage. In other words, home traveled with them. The trees, the grasses, the features in the landscape, are all the same. Sandpits, bridges, even their furniture came, too. Unlike Pooh, who emigrated with Disney's help, most immigrants do not have the luxury of traveling with their physical landscape (although there's a long history of immigrants reshaping the land in the image of home). Most of us find ourselves distant and dislocated from all that reminds us of home. And this is true even for those who do not migrate, for adulthood is its own form of exile, in time if not in space.

One spring afternoon in the early years of this century, I took a stroll through the East Woods at the Morton Arboretum near Lisle, Illinois. The trees were still leafless and the light was very fierce, so much so that I shielded my eyes with my hand, as if I were saluting my companion, Christopher Dunn, who at that time was the Arboretum's director of research. We were admiring the ecological restoration work that had been accomplished in the woodland over the years that I had been visiting. Dominated by oaks and sugar maples, the East Woods is about 1,100 acres, a sixth of the size of Ashdown Forest in Sussex, England, where the Pooh stories are set. In fact, the part in which we rambled was about the same dimensions as that part of the forest around Owl's house known to Pooh and his friends as the Hundred Acre Wood.

Here and there between the trees, we could see clumps of green where European buckthorn, an invasive shrub, was leafing out, taking advantage of the early spring light before other vegetation had emerged from its winter quiescence. On my early visits, the East Woods had been heavily invaded by this aggressive exotic Old World shrub, which, though infrequently found in its native range, has become one of the major impediments to conservation efforts in midwestern woodlands. Through active management, the buckthorn population in the East Woods had now been markedly diminished.

Both Christopher and I are Old World transplants (Christopher is a Scot), but unlike buckthorn, which has been in the region since the mid-1800s, we are very recent arrivals: he as a teenager and I when a little over thirty. During our walk, we stopped at a point where we could look over the terrain and admire the fidelity with which the restoration work has returned it to the structure of a pre-settlement midwestern woodland. Here we turned to each other, and—simultaneously it seems—both had the same thought: "There is something not quite right about this." In a nostalgic moment, both of us recalled the woodlands of Ireland and Scotland, especially the wilder places that Christopher and I both preferred: darker, more tightly packed woods on craggier terrain than is usually the case in this flatter part of the world. We were, for a moment at least, contrasting the East Woods not with its healthy ancestral state, freed from the injurious impacts of the past century, but with the woodlands of our personal memories, against which any woodland might seem like a collection of so many living sticks.

The fact is we are living in times of great transplantation. About 1.5 percent of the US population moves between the major regions every year: about 5 or 6 percent move across county lines. Internationally, the numbers of people crossing borders is staggering. For instance, if all those who migrated internationally in 2010 (about 216 million people) converged on an uninhabited region (say Antarctica), it would make that country the fifth most populous country on Earth. Accompanying the flow of goods, services, and people is a great biological interchange where species that were formerly restricted to one biogeographical zone are transported, either deliberately or unintentionally, to areas outside their native range. Christopher and I, standing in our Hundred Acre Woods, personified these frenzied exchanges. Old World islanders in the US Midwest, we were discussing a European botanical rarity that was now thriving in Chicago woodland.

Since a person's attunement toward nature is most often determined by youthful encounters with place, that which is most delightful to us in nature as adults is that which we remember from our youth. Thus, the landscapes of our adulthood, whether we have moved 300 miles or 3,000, tend to remain somewhat unfamiliar to us and, as a consequence, difficult to understand, much less to love. This is one of the neglected consequences of the great transplantation: I call it the "uncanny landscape hypothesis." Does this make it difficult for us to care for the landscapes in which we find ourselves, whether pristine, managed, or restored? Perhaps more positively, do we need new tools—tools of initiation, imagination, and empathy—to fit into a landscape that is new to us?

That we can read Milne's *Winnie-the-Pooh* (1926) and view Disney's later adaptations through an ecological lens at all is a testament to the fidelity with which both Milne and Shepard, his illustrator, reproduced the landscapes of Ashdown Forest in Sussex in which the original stories were set.[1] The Pooh stories captured a cultural landscape at a time when its human and natural elements were felicitously combined, as well as the special intimate relationship between a child and that landscape. It is very clear that the boy (based on Christopher Milne, the author's son) loved his bear and loved the landscape in which they had their escapades.

The connection between children and nature has taken on considerable urgency in recent years. Evidence is accumulating that access to outdoor experiences is vital for children's physical and mental health. The absence of such opportunities manifests itself in "nature-deficit disorder," a term coined by the American writer Richard Louv in *Last Child in the Woods* (2005).[2] Viewed from this perspective, Winnie-the-Pooh and the biographical elements that the book imports from Christopher Milne's life are an informative case study of the connections between a child and a landscape. Inside the house, Pooh is just a stuffed animal being dragged along by a cartoon boy; outside, all comes to life.

In his autobiography *The Enchanted Places* (1974), Christopher Milne recalled his real adventures in the Sussex countryside surrounding Cotchford Farm, which his family bought in 1925 when Christopher was four.[3] They spent their weekends and holidays there, and—in the company of his father or, more often, his nanny—Christopher made progressively deeper forays from garden to farmland and into the woodland and forest beyond, always on foot and, as he got older, on his own. Over time, his walks got longer and his intimacy with the landscape grew. He remembers, many years later, what it was like to be a child lost in nature:

> I would go down to the river and find a quiet place, secluded, hidden . . . and sit there for hours, watching the water as it gently twisted and eddied past me. Then perhaps I would see something: an eel wiggling its way upstream; a grass snake with just its black head showing above the surface, moving gently from side to side; damsel flies, their wings making a dry whispering sound as they came to investigate me; the plop of a water vole, and if you looked quickly you might see it running underwater along the river bed; a shy moorhen, a noisy mallard, a flashing kingfisher, whistling urgently.

As Christopher's ambit broadened, he encountered the locations that his father would later write into his books: Poohsticks Bridge was on the way into Posingford Wood near Cotchford. Farther along the road is Ashdown Forest, the forest of the books. From Gills Lap (Galleons Lap), one could walk down into a valley and up again toward some distant trees. This is the Hundred Acre Wood (in reality, a Five Hundred Acre Wood). Unlike the more open landscape of Posingford, this wood is darker and in it grew ancient beech trees. You might recall from the books that Piglet lived in one of those beech trees. The Hundred Acre Wood was also home to Owl. Some of these trees were felled during the Second World War, to Christopher Milne's regret, because, as he wrote, "among them was a tree I was particularly fond of."

Memories of the natural splendors surrounding his childhood

home sustained Christopher Milne through his military service in the Second World War. However, he destroyed all of his early efforts to write about that enchanted place. It would be thirty years before he could do so, and if that late account celebrates his early connection with nature, it also provides a cautionary tale. Christopher Milne famously resented the Christopher Robin of his father's tales and the tensions this caused with his father. The perennial child "Christopher Robin" outshone the adult "Christopher Milne." In later years, when Christopher Milne was asked if it saddened him not to have his toys with him anymore (they now live in a glass case at the New York Public Library), he responded: "Not really . . . I like to have around me the things I like today, not the things I once liked many years ago." In ending *The House at Pooh Corner* (1929) as he did, A. A. Milne anticipated the problem by leaving the little boy and his bear at play in their enchanted place. Christopher Robin, the boy, remained perennially on the hill, even after Christopher Milne, the man, had long vacated the spot.

Childhood might be the time when connection with place is fiercest. As we grow up, the adult and the quotidian envelop us. Often we set aside more than just our childish things: we vacate our childhood world. It was perhaps inevitable, given the nature of the story he had to tell, that Christopher Milne's autobiography returned to the world of Pooh and the childhood world of Christopher Robin. There is no sense in *The Enchanted Places* of Christopher Milne's adult connection with nature or place. In one passage in his book, he recalled in great detail where different flowers were found near Cotchford: the ash plantations for orchids; cowslips at the top of a field; the large wood for bluebells. He and Nanny would pick basketsful of flowers. After mentioning this, he wrote what seems to me the most bittersweet line of his memoir: "And it was here . . . I would find that splendour in the grass, that glory in the flower, that today I find no more." No, there is no going home again, nor can the man become the boy.

€ ⋆

There exists a rich literary record on the human connection with place, but serious scholarly investigation of the psychology of this relationship and how it might change during a lifetime has only begun in the last few decades.[4] The full panoply of associated psychological attributes is only now being excavated—under the banners of E. O. Wilson's biophilia hypothesis, Yi-Fu Tuan's notion of topophilia (and Gaston Bachelard's phenomenological account of topophilia that predates this), Jay Appleton's symbolic analysis of landscapes, Louv's nature-deficit disorder, and a variety of ecopsychological investigations.[5] Many of these trace their roots to the pioneering work of environmentalist and counterculture historian Theodore Roszak.[6]

All of these theoretical accounts ask whether we have a genetic predisposition to certain landscapes, how our cultural identity with place is formed, and so on. However, according to environmental philosopher Glenn Albrecht, professor of sustainability at Murdoch University in Western Australia, we do not yet have an adequate vocabulary to address our "psychoterratic" states—or how the state of the Earth relates to our states of mind. To balance the negative psychological state of "nostalgia," a couple of years ago Albrecht proposed "endemophilia" (the sense of being truly at home within one's place and culture—or "homewellness"). To balance the term "topophilia," a love of place, Albrecht opposes "solastalgia"—the desolate feeling associated with the chronic decline of a homescape.[7] "Solastalgia" names the emotions we have at the loss of species and habitats through climate change and other environmental changes. We should all expect a lot more of it.

We could say, then, that the tales of Pooh and his friends are a celebration of "endemophilia": a deep at-homeness in place and time. On the other hand, Christopher Milne's memoir has elements of solastalgia, as in the pain he associates with the loss of those beech trees.

Indeed, he warned the readers of *The Enchanted Places* that though they could try to follow his map of the Cotchford terrain, they might not be able to do so, as the landscape could have changed. Solastalgia could be the ruling mood of our age.

But there is another sadness recorded in Christopher Milne's story, a sadness that most of us experience, I expect: the loss of connection with place, especially a natural one, that happens as we grow older. I propose, in the spirit of Albrecht, to call this "toponesia" (from the Greek *topos*, place, and *amnesia*, loss of memory). Even if the world stood still, we would still spin away from it, dragged into the orbit of our private economies and that series of mischiefs that we call our adult life. These psychological factors associated with the Winnie-the-Pooh stories—their nostalgia, solastalgia, and toponesia—combine to make the stories a surprisingly powerful meditation on place, as much as a source of simple pleasure.

The Winnie-the-Pooh stories express the powerful and intimate connections that we form as children, not only with our toys, which we imbue with life, but also with place, which serves as both cradle and companion. A larger inspection of the books (and the real life of their central character) manifests both the delights and the discomfiting aspects of our relationship with place. Connections with nature that many of us nourish in memory are hard to retain in adulthood. An inspection of Christopher Milne's story brings to mind that we grow up and we change, as do landscapes, as do our relationships. We leave our childhood places behind us, sometimes literally, by thousands of miles, traversing several biomes before alighting like storm-tossed petrels in deeply unfamiliar territory.

Discovering how to develop an affiliation for new places might be the major environmental task of our age. Even those who do not move at all will find themselves in places that feel new, as habitat damage and climate change take effect. And if we do leave, we need to learn to love the places in which we find ourselves.

What tools are available to us? A. A. Milne's method was the vicarious: as Christopher Milne wrote in his memoir, "My father, who had derived such happiness from his childhood, found in me the companion with whom he could return there." We can see the world through our children's eyes. Recently, I saw a father leaning over his child, who was enraptured by a bird hopping on a city sidewalk. Mimicking his child's enthusiasm, he whispered in his best David Attenborough voice, "I think it's a sparrow." We think we need to inculcate in our children a love of the wild, but I suspect we misunderstand the direction in which instruction must flow.

But there are other ways, I think, in which we could gain as adults a love for those places, uncanny though they might be, in which we find ourselves newly arrived, or in which old certainties are disrupted. My model in this regard is Tim Robinson, an English writer who in the 1970s showed up on the west coast of Ireland. Over the subsequent decades, by dint of his mapmaking, his writing (about Aran and Connemara), and his scrupulous attention to people and place, Robinson has become almost synonymous with the west of Ireland.[8] His basic methodology is walking and listening: just as Christopher Milne and his imaginary companions before him were wont to do. If we are to regain intimacy with this place, this Earth, we might have to take up again those ancient and revolutionary tools, walking and listening, listening and walking.

5

Peter Rabbit's Brutal Paradise

When Beatrix Potter died in December 1943, at age seventy-seven, she left nearly all her property to the British National Trust, along with her prized cattle and sheep. The land that she left to the state became the core of the Lake District National Park in northwest England. It should not surprise us that Potter, whose many children's books include the especially beloved Peter Rabbit series, was a notable conservationist. Her books reflect the observations of a keen naturalist combined with a storyteller's instincts. Had she lived in other times, Potter might have devoted her energies to science. That she wrote animal stories and in her later years devoted her energy to traditional farming practices and to land conservation assures her a place as one of Britain's great environmentalists.[1]

Despite my adult appreciation of Potter's books and her conservation legacy, as a youth I felt much less appreciative of her work. In large part this chapter reflects my rediscovery of the power of her work. Ten-year-old me would be horrified.

For my *eleventh* birthday, my father brought me and a small group of my friends to see Bruce Lee's kung fu classic *Enter the Dragon*. It seemed a little incautious of him, in retrospect, to expose impressionable youth to such horrifying violence. The outing was, I suspect, in compensation for a birthday disaster the previous year. That year we had been deposited at the Classic Cinema in Harold's Cross, a small distance from our home, to see *The Tales of Beatrix Potter*, a filmed ballet. My father bought the tickets and the popcorn, and promptly drove away. In fairness, none of us, neither boys nor parents (I hope), knew that the movie starred the members of the Royal Ballet, pirou-etting about in animal costumes. Squirrel Nutkin, Mr. Jeremy Fisher, Jemima Puddle-Duck, Peter Rabbit, and the whole menagerie of Pot-ter's anthropomorphized animals were featured. I can't tell you much about the film, since within a frame or two, the lads got fidgety, and restlessness quickly turned to revolt. We left the cinema.

Now, in those moments as we were determining to leave, I felt fairly confident that I knew the direction home, but once we were outside, blinking in the bright sun of an early June afternoon, I real-ized that I did not, in fact, know where we were. None of the lads, all of whom were from the same neighborhood, had the faintest idea either. We set off, a small gang of latter-day Dublin Hansels, look-ing for faint clues that would lead back home. Mild trauma that it was, I now have no recollection of how we safely returned. Perhaps we stumbled upon the neighborhood park and knew our way after that. I also have a trace of memory that my father located us and drove us home; perhaps we telephoned him. Upon our return, my mother expressed her surprise at our early homecoming. Then she remarked, "But I thought you loved Peter Rabbit." My pals regarded me with grave suspicion.

The following year, all boys, my dad included, remained glued to our seats as Bruce Lee dispensed highly choreographed justice to the evil Han and his henchmen. Not a single *chassé* or *pas de deux* in the film. We applauded when the villain was impaled upon his own spear.

My primary youthful memory of Beatrix Potter is this episode—though, apparently before the movie expedition, I liked the stories well enough. Of all the books I've reread over the past year while writ-ing this book, few have made a greater renewed impression on me. Not only is Potter a teller of tight stories and a peerless illustrator of animal life, she had, besides, a naturalist's practiced eye, a con-servationist's regard for the beauty of landscapes, and a scientist's non-sentimentality in confrontation with the facts of life. Potter's stories illuminate so many facets of the children's pastoral story that we will examine them in some detail, before taking up the individual components of the pastoral in subsequent sections.

Beatrix Potter was born at No. 2 Bolton Gardens, Kensington, in London in 1866 into a prosperous middle-class family. Potter was educated at home by a series of governesses. Her brother, Bertram, was six years her senior. Bertram, later an artist, was her companion during the holidays, but otherwise he was away at school. Her biographers remark that her upbringing was somewhat dull and sheltered. Undoubtedly, life at No. 2 was a highly regulated affair. A cutlet and rice pudding were sent in to the nursery at one o'clock every afternoon. At six, dinner was served in the dining room. The family ate in silence. To judge from the journal that Potter wrote in code from ages fourteen until thirty, she, nonetheless, kept herself rather well occupied; she was alone, but not especially lonely. The journal reports on innumerable walks in Kensington Garden and visits to adjacent museums and art galleries in the company of her governess. In addition to her keeping notes on the art she viewed, the young Potter remarked extensively on her menagerie of pet animals. On Thursday, July 19, 1883, for example, Judy, her pet lizard, laid an egg. Beneath the egg's transparent shell, Beatrix observed that it was "wriggling with large eyes, tail curled twice, veins and bladder or fluid like a chicken." However, she had more eccentric pets than mere lizards. On December 8, 1883, she recorded the death of her family of pet snails, exclaiming that they had met with "an awful tragedy." Right after this obituary, Potter reported the death of architect Richard Doyle. "How time does go," she wrote, "and once past it can never be regained."[2] Snails and famous architects secured the young Potter's empathy in almost equal measure.

In the summertime, the family vacationed in southern Scotland's and northern England's Lake District. Years later when reflecting on those summers, she wrote, "I remember every stone, every tree, the scent of the heather, the music sweetest mortal ears can hear, the murmuring of the wind through the fir trees. Even when the thunder growled in the distance, and the wind swept up the valley in fitful gusts, oh, it was always beautiful, home sweet home, I knew nothing of trouble then."[3]

Eventually, Sawrey in the Furness area of Cumbria, near Lake Windermere, became her home. England's most important bucolic poet, William Wordsworth, is associated with the Lake District. Potter mentions him only in passing in her journal and repeated a local claim that Dorothy Wordsworth, William's sister, was the better poet.

Potter was a product of these two worlds, the urban and the rural. From her London pastime of gallery visiting, she drew much inspiration for her draftsmanship, and from her rural vacations, she developed an abiding love for the countryside and nature. In the countryside, she and her older brother captured and kept small animals, like rabbits and hedgehogs, to add to their collection. These, too, became early models for her sketches. A lifetime of attention to such small animals as these accounts for the accuracy of those renderings that decorated the later stories. Potter's mature genius was to bring these two worlds, urban and rural, together using her marvelous skills as illustrator, and her perceptive and empathic ability to capture rural detail.

The origins of *The Tale of Peter Rabbit* are from a series of illustrated letters that Potter wrote to the children of Annie Carter, who had been the last of her governesses, and only a few years senior to Beatrix. The tale, in all its basic narrative and pictorial elements, was in the letter. Such was their popularity among that first audience that Potter self-published the tale. Subsequently, Frederick Warne and Company republished the book and went on to publish twenty-three of her stories between 1902 and 1930.

The Tale of Peter Rabbit was Potter's first success and remains her most beloved story. Peter features in four of Potter's stories: the eponymous *The Tale of Peter Rabbit* (1902), followed by *The Tale of Benjamin*

Bunny (1904), *The Tale of the Flopsy Bunnies* (1909), and concluding with *The Tale of Mr. Tod* (1912). The appeal of these stories comes, in part, from Potter's disinclination to talk down to children. She often uses a fine vocabulary word or two. Lettuces being "soporific" for rabbits is merely the most famous of her grand words. But for all of that, Potter's sentences are crisp and her paragraphs are short. The stories unfold, as do all of Potter's, in a series of short paragraphs with adjacent illustrations. More than any other writer, the effect Potter created emerges from the skillful positioning of picture and text on the page. The illustrations amplify the stories in important ways. When we first meet Peter in *The Tale of Peter Rabbit*, he is naked. Or, at least, coatless. He occupies the center of the first illustration, staring over his shoulder at us readers. It is hard to gauge his mood. Neutral, indifferent, I'd say. The text reads, "Once upon a time there were four little rabbits, and their names were Flopsy, Mopsy, Cotton-tail, and Peter." Already we can tell that Peter is an exceptional rabbit: no rabbity name for him. In the next illustration, Peter is robed in his blue jacket with brass buttons. This is an attire that, when clothed at least, he retained throughout his life. His sisters in red coats crowd around Mrs. Rabbit, but Peter stands aloof. Once again he eyes us; his expression is remote.

Let us briskly recall the plots of each story before remarking on them in some detail. The first story begins and ends in the Rabbit family home. They live under the root of a "very big fir tree." Mrs. Rabbit is about to set off from home and through the woodland to the baker's. We should note here, in passing, that Potter rarely neglects the material needs of her characters—they are well-provisioned animals. She instructs the youngsters that in her absence they may go into the fields or down the lane, but are cautioned against visiting Mr. McGregor's garden. After all, Peter's father had met with "an accident" there and ended up in a pie. This historical trauma is illustrated: Mrs. McGregor sets down the ample rabbit pie on the table, a McGregor child peeps over his shoulder, the family dog looks on,

and Mr. McGregor's burly hands are just within the frame, his knife
and fork at the ready. *Et in Arcadia Ego.*

Mrs. Rabbit leaves. Peter heads straight for McGregor's garden.
Peter's predilection for risky living has, it would seem, been inherited from his father. In the garden, he gorges on a variety of vegetables. He runs into McGregor, who gives chase, rake in hand. As he
flees, Peter loses his shoes and then his jacket. The chase continues
into the toolshed. Peter escapes the shed, and McGregor abandons
the chase and returns to gardening. A doleful Peter wanders around
the garden, meets a mouse, avoids a cat, and makes his way out of the
garden and back to the woods. He returns home, goes to bed, and is
fed a medicinal dose of "camomile tea" by Mrs. Rabbit. It is then that
we learn that this is the second time in two weeks Peter has lost his
jacket and shoes. The inclination for recklessness is strong within
him, it seems. Mr. McGregor hangs Peter's clothes on a scarecrow.
Blackbirds look up at it fretfully.

Benjamin Bunny, Peter's cousin, is quite the personality. In the
tale that bears his name, he urges the still-naked Peter back into
the McGregor garden. Their mission is to retrieve Peter's jacket and
shoes. Peter, it seems, has learned his lesson and doesn't want to
return, but is persuaded to join Benjamin for one last heist, as it were.
High adventure ensues. They find themselves, eventually, trapped
under a basket by a cat. Benjamin's father comes to their rescue. The
rabbit boys return home as heroes, with Peter's clothes rescued and
a small crop of onions secured.

The Tale of the Flopsy Bunnies concludes the long-running cam-
paign between the bunnies and Mr. McGregor. Peter's appearance in
this story is brief. Benjamin, now grown up, is married to his cousin
Flopsy, Peter's sister. They have a large family, as rabbits are wont to
do, and are occasionally short of food. Peter, a gardener himself now,
provides, when he can, cabbages for his fecund relatives. When Peter
cannot provide, Benjamin and his offspring, collectively called the
Flopsy Bunnies after their mother, raid McGregor's rubbish heap—

destitute bunnies as they are—foraging for scraps. On the occasion of the story, they find and eat spoiled lettuce. Lettuce being "soporific," at least for rabbits, the rabbits fall asleep. As they slumber, McGregor comes upon them, and they are captured. Benjamin escapes. Rather macabrely, Mr. McGregor counts them off, "One, two, three, four, five, six leetle rabbits!" and places the sleeping Flopsy bunnies in a sack. No doubt, Mr. McGregor is remembering what a tasty pie their late grandfather made. Benjamin Bunny remains at large. With the help of a mouse, Mrs. Tittlemouse, an old friend of Peter's whom we met in the first tale, the rabbits are freed from the sack. In their place, Benjamin leaves McGregor with a sack of moldering vegetables. Upon being presented with these, Mrs. McGregor expresses her displeasure by throwing the vegetables at her husband.

Peter makes his final cameo appearance in *The Tale of Mr. Tod*. This is a darker and more menacing tale. There is, as far as I know, no movie version of this tale, but it is cinematic and terrifying. It features two villains, Tommy Brock, a badger, and Mr. Tod, a fox, and the tale centers, as did *The Tale of the Flopsy Bunnies*, on a compelling search-and-rescue mission. Young bunnies are kidnapped by the badger, who sets the bunnies aside for later consumption. Peter and Benjamin go off in hot pursuit. The bunnies are eventually rescued, just in the nick of time, from the oven in which Tommy Brock intends to cook them!

The plots of the rabbit stories seem simple enough—being pastoral tales—but there is more complexity to them than first meets the eye. Potter's body of work is so rich, in fact, that there is almost a cottage industry of literary criticism on her writing. For example, novelist Graham Greene discussed Potter's work with the same degree of seriousness that he devoted to more high-brow novelists such as Henry James, with whom he directly compared her. Pointing out that the great characters of fiction often come in pairs—Don Quixote and Sancho Panza, for instance—Green described Peter Rabbit and Benjamin Bunny as "two epic personalities." Benjamin has a "coolness and practicality" that serves as foil to "the nerves and clumsiness of his cousin."[4] Between 1907 and 1909, Greene detected a change in Potter's style. Mr. Tod suggested to him that a darker mood prevailed and that it had "changed the character of her genius." It hints, he continued, that Potter endured in the intervening years an emotional ordeal of some sort. Perhaps Greene crossed a line with the grandness of his criticism. An unimpressed Potter responded to Greene's 1933 essay. She denied any emotional disturbance in those years, saying that she was merely suffering the aftereffects of the flu. She added, however, that she did not ascribe to "the Freudian school" of criticism.

So let us proceed with an analysis of Potter's work with caution. In reality, an environmental reading of Potter does not require taking any huge liberties with her stories. An inspection of Potter's life reveals that she was from a young age a serious observer of nature, and as she got older, she became an accomplished naturalist and a committed conservationist.

The tales of Beatrix Potter illustrate key aspects of the children's pastoral: they feature the antics of anthropomorphized animals in rural locations. Although the plots are simple, fittingly so, considering their audience, thematically the stories reflect in sophisticated ways upon notions of home and belonging, upon the practicalities of life in the countryside, with order and, just as importantly, with the restoring of order after stressful episodes. All of these are suitable literary subjects, of course, but are also emphatically environmental.

Potter's tales are classified in critical circles as "animal tales." This is a somewhat inglorious term for a wide variety of stories that share the commonality of featuring animals. In some ways it's no more satisfactory than referencing all other fiction as "human tales." Animal tales are often characterized by the presence of anthropomorphized animals. Animals in these stories have human characteristics: they talk, walk, dress, emote, relate, or possess some combination of these qualities. The humanization of the character can amount to virtually taking over of the animal. The Arthur series by Marc Brown, for example, features a fully kid-like aardvark. That being said, in the first of these stories, *Arthur's Nose* (1976), Arthur is teased about the length of his nose and contemplates surgery.[5] His nose is all aardvark; his situation is fully human. Anthropomorphism can be expressed to a milder degree. The rabbits of *Watership Down* (1972) by Richard Adams, for example, are quite rabbit-like, though they are rather warrior-like, and some of them have clairvoyant aptitudes, a contentious claim for rabbits and humans alike.[6] The animals in Virginia Hamilton's superb collection of American black folktales, *The People Could Fly* (1985), are a hybrid of human and animal characteristics.[7]

What sets Potter's animal tales apart from others in the genre is the attractive blending one finds in them of realism and the suspension of disbelief. Potter's rabbits undoubtedly possess a range of human-like qualities. A mother cautions her young ones, makes veiled references to the death and consumption of her late husband, and then goes shopping for currant buns at the baker's. A delinquent bunny deliberates his escape from a garden and frets over the loss of his clothing. A series of rescues are planned. And yet, for all of this, Potter's bunnies are faithfully rendered in the illustrations and in many aspects of the text. In many, not all, of the illustrations, Peter and family are merely attractive rabbits in a dangerous world. Their physical form and the outward expression of their behavior are all pure rabbit. Peter stares at us from the opening illustrations, attentive while also being alert to any lurking danger. This cautiousness lurking behind bravado will be recognizable to any rabbit fancier. Peter's locomotion is also faithful to his kind. At times he sprints, and then, for instance, after the first round of the chase with McGregor, he slows to an unperturbed "lippety-lippety." Potter's ability to present these creatures to us as both heroes in an adventure tale and also in their rather uncanny rabbitness derives from a lifetime of observation of animals. It may not surprise anyone that both Peter and Benjamin were based upon real rabbits. Neither led such dramatic lives as their fictional counterparts; nonetheless, their lives were not event-less. Of the real Benjamin—Benjamin Bouncer to give him his full name—Potter wrote, "He is a real coward, but believes in bluster, could stare our old dog out of his countenance, chase a cat that had turned tail." He was also quite a silly fellow. He once fell into an aquarium and "sat in the water which he could not get out of, pretending to eat a piece of string." Peter was, similarly, a well-loved rabbit. When he died at age nine, she wrote: "An affectionate companion and a quiet friend."[8]

In addition to her faithful observation of pet animals, there was quite a serious aspect to Potter's interest in science. She was a truly accomplished naturalist and a scientific observer of the natural world surrounding her. Her investigations into the germination of fungi and the biology of lichens produced genuinely important results. On April 1, 1898, Potter's paper "On the Germination of the Spores of Agaricineae" by Miss Helen B. Potter was presented at the Linnean Society. Miss Potter was not there to hear it since women were excluded from the society. Years later the Linnean Society wrote her a letter of apology, but it was too late. The world may have lost a talented mycologist; on the bright side, we gained a storyteller of genius.[9]

There are three habitats in which Potter's rabbit tales unfold. These include the immediate environs of the very big fir tree where Peter and his family make their home. On one side of home lay the wood, on the other the McGregor's garden—both with their lurking dangers. We learn more about the wider wooded lands beyond the margins in *The Tale of Mr. Tod*. That world is replete with dangers, including animals who would happily make a supper of our heroes. But for the most part, it is the drama of the garden that occupies us most in the quintet of rabbit stories. Mr. McGregor presides there as lord of his domain, doling out justice to herbivores. A lot of McGregor's time is spent weeding his vegetable patches and sowing his cabbages. We rarely see Mr. McGregor without an implement in his hand. Later, when Peter turns gardener himself, perhaps he was more sympathetic to his old foe. It's likely that Peter may have had a rabbit problem of his own!

Gardens are curious affairs. We speak of growing vegetables, but, in fact, vegetables grow themselves. Indeed, it is the vegetables that grow us. Gardens are, to write philosophically, a strange amalgam of control and spontaneity. A wild garden, maintained for aesthetic reasons, requires limited control. Spontaneity is tolerated there. A productive food garden, in contrast, requires a surfeit of control. The task of the vegetable grower is to foster the conditions under which the edibles will grow. And this, as often as not, requires the killing of herbivorous creatures. McGregor is the controller-in-chief of his garden. A story written from McGregor's perspective would be a tale of labor and frustration, with the rare comforts of a nice meat pie.

McGregor's garden is no pastoral haven to be sure. It does, however, provide a short course on the workings of the ecological world. In that garden, a veritable ecological island, there exists a little community consisting of a profusion of edible plants, a guild of herbivorous animals—one rabbit and one mouse being emblems of a larger hungry collective—and one human in competitive struggle to be the garden's top consumer. The brute fact that we have to eat, and at times kill, is foundational to ecology. Food concerns are paramount in Potter's work. There is, as I mentioned, rarely a tale in which the characters do not get a square meal.

The garden is not harmonious, but there is a type of stability there. McGregor is there when Peter is youthful, and persists there, managing the affairs of the garden, when Peter is an adult; years of planting, weeding, maintaining a mulch pile, and occasionally feeding upon his competitors when he can catch them. Like most predators, he is occasionally successful and rabbit is served for supper, but, more often than not, he does not capture his prey and is merely content with running them off.

The most strikingly ecological aspects of Potter's writing are the non-sentimentality with which she writes of the natural interactions in the garden. Graham Greene put it best when he wrote that Potter "puts aside love and death with a gentle detachment." However, Potter's depiction of life in the garden is not the only one where earthly delights and contemplations of mortality are envisioned side-by-side, a topic to which we turn to next.

6

In the Garden
of Earthly Delights

More ink has been spilled interpreting Hieronymus Bosch's master-piece *The Garden of Earthly Delights* than the oil applied to the panels on which it is painted. The painting, which dates to the early 1500s, now hangs in the Prado, in Madrid. The left panel of this triptych depicts a youthful God, presumably Christ, presenting Eve to a dazed Adam. Around the First Couple cavorts an assortment of animals, some recognizable and some surreal. The panel to the right depicts Hell. A man is being eaten by a seated bird-headed creature. His head is in the beast's mouth; birds fly out of his posterior. Around the bird-headed figure are grimly fascinating scenes of torture and vicious cruelty. A rabbit, as innocent-looking as Beatrix Potter's Peter Rabbit, carries off an impaled and bloodied man. At the center of the canvas, a hollowed-out man is supported by a rotting tree trunk. Balanced on this head is a disk bearing a set of bagpipes. Yes, there will be bagpipes in Hell.

Sandwiched between Paradise and Hell is the scene that gives the painting its modern name: *The Garden of Earthly Delights*. This panel depicts hundreds of carnally engaged couples, enormous birds, flying fish, and an abundance of strange vegetation. A theme of excess dominates: excessive sex, pleasure, and fructification. In the center of this panel, which is therefore at the very center of the entire work, a blue orb emerges from the middle of a lake. Through a window in the globe, a man can be seen gently cupping his partner's genitals. A rotund bottom intrudes into the scene. Is this an earthy paradise depicted? Is it the world shown as shamelessly fecund as it could be? Or, does the image, which like other triptychs is read from left to right, serve to remind us that our time on Earth is just an ephemeral way station in our inexorable migration along the path to some sort of Hell? In the end, we're all perhaps destined, sooner rather than later, to be consumed by the bird demon, with birds flying out our asses.[1]

There are important lessons for us in Bosch's painting. First, although the central panel is the Garden of Earthly Delights proper, all panels in the triptych depict gardens of a sort and can be helpful in questioning what a garden is. Paradise and Earth share the same sky, and both have water and lush greenery. The landscape of Hell is less garden-like for sure, but is at the very least on the threshold of being a garden. It is vegetated, if we can designate the hollowed-out tree-man as a type of grotesque plant life; and it is, besides, an arena of both (macabre) spontaneity and (vicious) control (spontaneity and control being features, as we will see, of gardens). Though we might incline to think of gardens as pleasant places—and many are—gardens don't, in fact, have a built-in moral register. Gardens can be, on the one hand, the most nurturing of places or else, quite rarely, they can be hostile to human welfare. Although Bosch's Paradise is undeniably a garden, and Hell is a garden of a hideous sort, the earthly garden is neither perfect, nor is it horrifying. It's an amalgam of sorts. The garden we live in may be what we make of it: if your life is not sensual, pleasurable, or fruitful enough, you have just a moment or two to repair the situation, for one may not tarry in the Garden of Earthly Delights.

If gardens are not necessarily defined by their agreeability, since there are some terrifying gardens—what, after all, are graveyards if not gardens where we plant our dead, oftentimes in the hope of seeding the afterlife—what then defines a garden? How does a garden differ from any other component of the landscape? What are its properties? Let me pose this question in this way: If you were transported, say, in a dream, to the Garden of Eden, how would you know you were in that garden?[2] You may, in this improbable circumstance, bring to mind from your biblical (or Koranic) reading the micro-geography of that garden. Eden, we are told in Genesis, contains "every tree that is pleasant to the sight, and good for food," as well as "the tree of life" and "the tree of knowledge of good and evil." The river that flows from Eden has four branches: the Pishon, the Gihon, the Tigris, and the Euphrates. However, even if you are aware of these topographical markers, it might still be difficult to know that you are in Eden: there'll be no signage in Paradise.

Let's say that you, too, are told, as were Adam and Eve, to leave the garden.[3] How, exactly, would you know when you have left? Would you know it from a change in vegetation? Gardens, after all, often have clusters of ornamental plants and a generous ratio of fruiting trees compared to inedible ones. Perhaps you noticed a nice bed of carrots on your way out? Or maybe you had to clamber over a wall or hop over a gate: was the garden enclosed? Enclosure and the presence of cultivation are the heart of most definitions of gardens—for example, in the *Oxford English Dictionary*'s definition: "enclosed piece of ground devoted to the cultivation of flowers, fruit, or vegetables."[4] We thus leave a garden when we leave cultivation behind and leave the enclosure. There is also a sense of ownership in the matter of gardens—property rights might make our minimal list of garden properties. Thus the Garden of Eden, planted by God, was His to expel Adam and Eve from. In a lower key, is it not understandable that Farmer McGregor, owner of his own plots, fiercely protects his crop?

It may surprise you—it certainly surprised me—to learn that there has been considerable philosophical attention devoted to gardens.[5] From a philosophical perspective, Mara Miller in *The Garden as an Art* (1993) describes a garden as "any purposeful arrangement of natural objects with exposure to the sky or open air, in which the form is not fully accounted for by the purely practical considerations such as convenience."[6]

It might be said that philosophy's main historical contribution to reflection on the garden has been to encourage us to disregard them. For example, no less a figure than Georg Wilhelm Friedrich Hegel, the great German Enlightenment philosopher, valued gardens for the "cheerful surrounds" that they produce, and yet he thought them "worth nothing in themselves."[7] Other philosophical attention to gardens is devoted to clarifying why exactly gardens are a lesser form of art.[8] Such dismissals may derive from the fact that gardens are hard to pin down: are they purely natural objects, or are they, as some master gardeners have insisted, great works of art? Philosophers of art oftentimes dismiss gardens as having too much nature. Environmental thinkers, on the other hand, find in gardens too little of nature and rather too much art. If gardens are neither fully art nor fully natural, what sort of weird composite of the natural and artifice are they? It may be best, considering this tension, to evaluate gardens in terms of the balancing of spontaneity and control. In some cases, gardens have a surplus of control over spontaneity. In others, the relinquishing of control and the deliberate promotion of wildness can be precisely the gardener's aim.[9]

One recent expression of the disdain in which gardens are held in environmental circles is the dismissal, by some wilderness advocates, of many contemporary landscape management practices, including ecological restoration, as "mere gardening."[10] On the other hand, environmental writer Emma Marris points out in *Rambunctious Garden: Saving Nature in a Post-Wild World* (2011) that it may be better to accept that Earth is now more garden-like than wild and, contra several environmental thinkers, accept that this does not signify an end of nature, merely a more appropriate way of thinking about it.[11] Whichever side of this debate persuades you, it seems clear that one way or another, gardens are less-than-wild nature. Some environmentalists are untroubled by this; others are outraged.

Gardens cannot exist without the forces of nature, nor can they exist without intention and the sweat of human labor. Perhaps this is why so many great stories are set in gardens—a garden setting can provide the comforts of a controlled world but is also infused by forces beyond the ken of ordinary mortals.

Master Gardener of Fairy Tales: Hans Christian Andersen

The action of several of the stories collected by the Brothers Grimm center on gardens. Some others start in a garden but the action radiates from there to a wider, wilder world. In one of the most famous of such garden stories, a husband steals rampion—also called Rapunzel—from the walled garden of a fairy. The leaves of rampion were once eaten in salads. The unfortunate man fetches this plant for his pregnant wife, who refused to eat anything else. His wife's craving is not sated by the first stolen harvest, and so the husband, fearing for his wife's health, returns to the garden for more. The fairy catches the thief and, upon hearing that the wife cannot survive without rampion, permits the husband to take all he wants in return for his agreeing to turn over their unborn child, Rapunzel. The remainder of the action of the story is familiar enough: the girl's confinement in a tower by the fairy, the astonishing means of entering and egressing from the tower by climbing Rapunzel's long hair, the prince who learns of this secret, his visits and his being blinded by thorns, the final reuniting of the lovers, and the restoration of the prince's sight. But is there not something of a plant motif running through the entire story? Rapunzel is confined within the walls of the tower in a garden: rooted in one spot like the garden plant after which she was named; Rapunzel's hair descends tendril-like from her tower to the earth below; and our prince climbs the stalk-like tower to pollinate the loveliest flower that ever grew beneath the sun (in the saucier original version of the tale Rapunzel becomes pregnant).

The tradition of fairy tales set in, or radiating out from, a garden is perfected by the master gardener of such stories, Hans Christian Andersen.[12] These stories include a tale of justifiable revenge exacted on a murderer by an elf so small he can live in a rose bloom ("The Elf of the Rose"; 1839). In another, a single leaf from the garden of heaven falls to Earth and blooms in a forest. It is neglected by all but a little girl who recognized its beauty and value ("A Leaf from Heaven"; 1855). One story, "The Snail and the Rose-Tree" (1861), relates an existential conversation in a garden between a rose who cannot help but bloom, and to rejoice in blooming, and a snail who merely spat at the world—such is the haughty nature of snails. In another called "The Thistle's Experiences" (1869), a large thistle lived outside the garden, "by the palings at the road-side." The thistle longs to be among the other blooms. One of her flowers ends up being chosen by a Scottish maiden for her suitor, and the couple wed, and thus "this thistle-calyx came into the garden, and into the house, and into the drawing-room." What the thistle could not attain, her children did.

The loveliest, and most heartbreaking, of these Andersen garden stories is "The Daisy" (1838). On a fresh bank in a flower garden by a farmhouse in the countryside grew a daisy. This lowly daisy loved a lark, and the lark sung to the daisy. It flew down and kissed the flower and flew back into the blue sky. And how the tulips hated the daisy; how very sulky were the peonies. But the lark was captured and put in a cage, and the daisy was sad for it, but being a flower it could say nothing. The boys who captured the lark then placed the clump of turf in which the daisy grew into the lark's cage. Alas, the captors did not remember to leave water for the bird. The flower could not move to console the lark, but the fragrance of the daisy provided a small comfort to the bird. The bird then died and was buried with honors by the remorseful boys. The wilted flower that loved the bird, and who provided it with a tiny service as it died, was thrown out onto the dusty highway. For is it not the way of the world that the services of seemingly insignificant things go unremarked.

"The Garden of Paradise" (1838) is a more complex story still. It concerns a prince who searched in vain in his library for the precise location of the garden of paradise. When he locates it, he finds that the Island of Happiness is ruled over by a fairy queen. This garden is lush beyond all imagining. Lions and tigers gamboled there like playful cats. Antelope looked upon them without fear. The prince is invited to stay a hundred years (though the time, he is told, would seem no more than one hundred hours). The only condition is that he should not follow the fairy queen when, inevitably, she would beckon to him in the evening. The queen slept beneath the Tree of Knowledge. Were the prince to kiss her there, "the garden of paradise would sink into the earth. . . ." And so begins the first night of the century to which he has committed himself. The prince does not last one single night—not a single night! He follows the fairy queen to her bed beneath the tree and lies beside her. She weeps in her sleep, and the prince bends to kiss the tears from her eyelashes. And all then is lost.

Quite famously Hans Christian Andersen's (1805–1875) stories contain autobiographical elements.[13] It is unsurprising, therefore, that many of stories refer to plants, since he described himself as a "swamp plant" who was reaching for the light. A common motif in his fairy stories is the discovery of the value of neglected creatures; the neglected creature he had in mind was, at times, himself. "The Ugly Duckling" (1843), considered to be autobiographical and perhaps his more famous story, illustrates the pattern. The homely duckling is rejected in the farmyard, but then becomes a swan, a bird of undeniable beauty, and takes its place in the stately company of these birds. Such stories of transformation were personal for the author, whose own transformation was impressive but arguably never quite complete. Certainly not in his own eyes, anyway.

Andersen is quite justifiably known as Denmark's most successful writer. However, his origins were very humble. He was born in the small walled city of Odense, Denmark, to a poor cobbler, also called Hans, and Anne Marie Andersdatter, a washerwoman. His father died young, and a youthful Hans Christian left for Copenhagen to make his fortune in the theater. His initial attempts failed, but he eventually secured recognition for his first novel, *The Improvisatore* (1835).[14] The book that followed contained his first stories for children, a collection of four fairy tales. Though later he was to write dozens of plays, poetry, and novels, it is for the fairy stories, almost two hundred of them, that he is best remembered. Of these two hundred, barely fifteen are frequently read these days. That being said, so beloved is this handful of stories, that it is reasonable to suggest that they have shaped the tender sensibilities of most children in the Western world.

Our ugly duckling eventually got the international recognition he craved, and in large part he earned the fortune that accompanies such fame. He cultivated important friends abroad. Once, for instance, he visited Charles Dickens in London, although it appears that he outstayed his welcome, and Dickens cut off their correspondence, much to Andersen's distress. At home in Denmark, his reputation was secure and he hobnobbed with the Danish elite. For all of this, Andersen never felt like he fully belonged in the upper reaches of Danish society. He was undoubtedly welcome into the homes of royalty and the expanding Danish bourgeoisie, but he would never fully assimilate. Despite the success, Andersen would always be the son of a cobbler and a washerwoman.

Adding to his disappointment, Andersen did not regard himself as the great writer he had hoped to be. Finally, to top it off, Andersen was never to be romantically happy; over the course of his life, he endured unrequited loves for both women and men. When he died, a letter for a girl he had loved, unrequitedly, decades before was found in a pouch on his chest.

Is this not the alchemy of all great literature: that it turns the base metal of the personal quotidian, including all of life's little sadnesses, into the gold of brilliant stories? Hans Christian Andersen, no less than James Joyce or Leo Tolstoy, used his own frustrations, his own struggles, to fuel his genius and create art. Fairy tales were uniquely successful for him as a means of expressing his prettiest dreams as well as his consuming frustrations.

That harsh critics of Hans Christian Andersen exist may be as surprising to learn as hearing that there are those who loathe a fragrant summer afternoon. But there is, indeed, a lively debate about his legacy. The disagreements revolve around the question of his originality and the revolutionary nature of his tales. After all, Andersen comes after the Brothers Grimm and E. T. A. Hoffmann (a writer of horror stories, who inspired our Dane), and his fairy tales, like most other aspects of his writing, were deeply influenced by a large body of German Romantic writing. Andersen was not the first to write fairy tales. But Andersen stumbled upon the fairy-tale form after trying several other literary styles, and he wrote them in a way that appealed to broad audiences—both children and adults—who were both entertained and perplexed by them. That you get both pleasure and consternation from Andersen tales may contribute to their enduring appeal.

Andersen critics see in his work the *prospect*, if not the *delivery*, of a truly revolutionary program. These are tales written by a ferociously talented underdog railing against an ossified elite. This might have made Andersen the voice of the downtrodden. But revolution was not to be Andersen's task. Jack Zipes, perhaps the best-known scholar of fairy tales, takes a dim view of Andersen and how he squandered his revolutionary potential. In his essay "Critical Reflections about Hans Christian Andersen, the Failed Revolutionary," Zipes writes:

> Overall Andersen was an imitative, eclectic, and sentimental writer who, despite his narcissism, is fascinating more for the way he cut out his own tongue and kowtowed to an upper-class elite and

religious reading public than he is for his prodigious writings and for transforming the fairy tale.[15]

But perhaps revolution, like pleasure, does not emanate exclusively from the revolutionary or pleasurable object. Andersen may have seethed about his social circumstances, but ultimately he conformed to conventional expectations and curried the favor of his patrons. But for many readers, Andersen really does provoke a sort of revolutionary thought: that we can transcend our momentary circumstances. I may indeed be an ugly duckling, but the future has not been set in stone; and who knows what I shall become? Admittedly, this may be the mildest form of revolution, but a person who lives to revolt another day may be in a better position than one who is squeezed dry by the pressures of a particularly ferocious moment. That person can continue to dream big dreams. Andersen's fairy stories allow us to vicariously reflect upon, and maybe even overcome, our own little worries, express our own limitations, and address the fragility of our egos.

Andersen uses references to the gardens and flowers in his stories to illustrate two important points. First, that which is neglected, despised, and treated cruelly has often the greatest value. "The Ugly Duckling" elucidates the attractive thought that things cast aside have a marvelous beauty and are capable of unexpected things. Those things least remarked upon, in fact, are often the most remarkable: an undesirable plant growing in the forest comes from heaven's garden; a thistle languishing outside the garden sealed the love between a man and woman. Moreover, there is a fierce beauty in very ordinary things. In "The Gardener and the Manor" (1872), for example, a flower beloved by a princess was not a lotus from the East but was an artichoke from a kitchen garden. Rather than disdaining the artichoke, the princess remarked that the humble gardener "had really opened our eyes to see the beauty of a flower in a place where we should not have thought to look for it."

Lessons from Hans Christian Andersen have unexpected parallels in the environmental realm. Andersen's insights that things (and people) of value are to be found where one least expects them, and his provocation that we reassess the significance of ordinary things and events—these are also deeply ecological thoughts. They are, besides, powerful and timely thoughts. All the manifestations of the natural world are subtended by the activity of cryptic beings toiling away behind the scenes. Fungal networks, bacterial cells, and a vast army of enigmatic animalcules orchestrate the processes of decay upon which the living rely. Pollinators buzz from plant to plant like amorous servants tending to needs of the blossoms in the garden. Certain relatively drab plants, especially wild beans and peas, can fix nitrogen from the atmosphere and add that key nutrient to the soil to the benefit of the entire community of plants.[16] Ecology, in many ways, is a discipline that mirrors in the sciences what Hans Christian Andersen did in the form of fairy tales. Both elevate the drab, the neglected, the minuscule, and demonstrate their vitality.

Fairy tales, like other short tales, are like gardens. We scramble over the wall to land in a world unlike the one from which we just came. When such enclosures are tended by a master gardener of Hans Christian Andersen's caliber, we notice there among cultivated things the spontaneous exuberance of a feral world. Fairy tales can thus comfort and terrify: they rupture our equanimity.

Nature heals. That two-word sentence, combining as it does one of the English language's most complex words with one of its most soothing, unites an antique intuition and an emerging science, and draws upon a body of thought distilled by the Romantics that remains compelling to contemporary environmental thinkers. Nature heals, and yet nature in a garden seems to intensify its healing salve. Though there is much in Andersen's stories of the power of gardens to soothe, healing gardens are more prominently featured in other books. *The Secret Garden* (1911) by Frances Hodgson Burnett and Johanna Spyri's *Heidi* (1881) (if we can admit that alpine meadows serve as gardens).[17] The lesson concerning the power of nature to heal could not be more clearly expressed than it is in *Heidi*. Heidi is taken from her alpine meadows, where she'd been living with her grandfather, to live in the city of Frankfurt. She is to keep Clara, a sick child, company. Heidi endears herself to Clara's family, and though she is fond of her new friend Clara, she pines for the mountainside. She herself becomes sick. Clara's father is convinced she must return home. When she does, she is restored to good health. A year later Clara visits Heidi in the mountains and she, too, gets better.

Fully a century before the topic of the healing power of nature became a topic of empirical research, the power of gardens, and pastoral nature more generally, to improve human well-being was intuited by children's writers imagining gardens.[18]

7

Beyond the Pool of Darkness

THE PASTORAL ROOTS OF IRISH STORIES

The first environmental scheme that I committed to as a budding environmentalist in the early 1980s was a plan, of my own conception, to declare all of the West of Ireland a national park. Lands west of the river Shannon—which at 360.5 kilometers is Ireland's longest river and separates Ireland's most western counties from the other regions—would be off-limits to all further economic development. My understanding at the time was that the lands of the Irish West were primarily wild, where historically the human influence was negligible. In my initial conception of the scheme, I generously envisioned a phased depopulation of the region—no forced removal of people in this plan. After some time of incentivized migration, these western lands could be set aside in perpetuity for nature to hold sway, and for the enjoyment of those, like me I suppose, who cared for more austere living.

This plan was consistent with that long-standing sentiment in environmental thought that places highest value on greener and wilder landscapes. The wilder the better, in fact. It was not atypical in those days for environmental scientists to be trained, as I was, in a city and yet to pine for remote landscapes. For my part, I could not wait to get out of Dublin and to start living closer to "real nature."

My inclination toward untamed lands and rough living was thus inspired, in part, by my environmental training. I was also influenced by those Irish stories of my childhood. Such stories are set, more often than not, in Ireland's wilder landscapes. The first discovery of

Ireland, for example, is romantically described in "The Story of Tuan Mac Cairill," in James Stephens's *Irish Fairy Tales* (1920), as follows:

> As we drew on Ireland from the sea the country seemed like an unending forest. Far as the eye could reach, and in whatever direction, there were trees; and from these came the unceasing singing of birds. Over all the land the sun shone warm and beautiful, so that to our sea-weary eyes, our wind-tormented ears, it seemed as if we were driving on Paradise.[1]

In a now-tamed world, it was nice to imagine that Ireland had, at one time at least, been marvelously wild. And if Ireland retained any of its primordial elements, surely these were to be found in the West of Ireland, remote from the influence of Dublin and the effete counties of the eastern seaboard.

In the fictional accounts that I consumed as a child, Ireland remained wild, in many parts at least, long after its initial colonization. Fionn and the warriors of the Fianna, the subject of one of the great cycles of Irish stories, gallivanted about in Ireland's more unruly places. The Fianna were a type of fictional hunter-gatherers, but the broader society in which they lived was a pastoral one, dominated by the activities of high-kings, druids, and clannish farmers and their domesticated animals. In fact, one of the greatest northern Irish epics, *Táin Bó Cúailnge*, often translated as *The Cattle Raid of Cooley*, is, as the title suggests, a tale of cattle rustling. *The Táin* is that rarer form of literature: the pastoral war story.[2]

But even in the world of old Celtic stories, a world that was, compared to ours, a relatively savage place, a nostalgia already existed for *even more* antique times—an era when the land was less domesticated and the people were fiercer, and their appetite for life lustier. In the Celtic imagination, the wildest pole in their mythological life was the land of the fairies, or the Sidhe (pronounced "Shee," as in Banshee, a female fairy) to give them their proper name. In the story "Mongan's

Frenzy," also in Stephens's collection, Fionn's travels to the land of Faery is described in colorful detail. In this account Faery and Ireland are remarkably similar except, as Stephens writes, "All things that are bright are there brighter. There is more gold in the sun and more silver in the moon of that land." Stephens goes on to describe the forests of Faery:

> When they had gone a little distance they came to a grove of ancient trees. Mightily tall and well-grown these trees were, and the trunk of each could not have been spanned by ten broad men. As they went among these quiet giants into the dappled obscurity and silence, their thoughts became grave and all the motions of their minds elevated, as though they must equal in greatness and dignity those ancient and glorious trees. (267)

This passage captures one of the more appealing facets of wild country: its ability to call upon us to be more than we are. The trees of Faery beckon; trees can coax the best out of us.

In some accounts, the land of Faery is a shadow world, one that we can catch glimpses of, but passage to which can be arduous. This is consistent with an account of the origins of the Sidhe as angels that fell from heaven but, rather than sinking to the underworld—and thus becoming the demonic subjects of that most famous of fallen angels, Lucifer—their descent was broken by the surface of the Earth. They now dwell close by, but belong to a different order of existence.

In other accounts, fairies are descendants, albeit mythological ones, of Ireland's oldest people, the Tuatha Dé Danann. After their defeat by a subsequent wave of colonizers, these ancestors were relegated to less desirable parts of the landscape. They now live around the hills and mountains of the countryside. Their realm is thus continuous with ours: their Ireland is our Ireland. Occasionally, a mortal strays into a hosting of the Sidhe but is discouraged from making such a mistake again. As befits Ireland's originary people, the

Sidhe are consistently described as more attuned with nature. This is whimsically signified by "the wearing of green," best known as the clothing hue of that most famous of solitary fairies, the Leprechaun. Irish fairies differ in most respects from J. R. R. Tolkien's ethereal elves. The Sidhe are creatures with more gargantuan appetites than mere mortals. They are also amoral, or, at very least, conscienceless. In William Allingham's poem "The Fairies" (1850), which my parents would recite for me without seeming to care a whit for the inner tumult it provoked, the fairies' terrifying inclination to snatch children is recorded:

> They stole little Bridget
> For seven years long;
> When she came down again
> Her friends were all gone.
> They took her lightly back
> Between the night and morrow;
> They thought she was fast asleep,
> But she was dead with sorrow.
> They have kept her ever since
> Deep within the lake,
> On a bed of flag-leaves,
> Watching till she wake.[3]

The fairies could also impose harmful mischief on adults, without always being aware, perhaps, of our frailties. W. B. Yeats noted the following cautionary tale in his *Fairy and Folk Tales of the Irish Peasantry* (1888): "Near the village of Ballisodare [near Sligo] is a little woman who lived amongst them seven years. When she came home she had no toes—she had danced them off."[4] Word to the wise: If you meet an Irish fairy, wear your stoutest dancing brogues.

It's hard to exaggerate the hold that fairies have exercised upon the

Irish imagination. Though he wrote about them extensively, Yeats was somewhat agnostic on the question of whether they were real. In his still wonderful to read collection *The Celtic Twilight* (1893), he asked if a sensible person could believe in fairies. This is what he wrote in response: "Even when I was a boy I could never walk in a wood without feeling that at any moment I might find before me somebody or something I had long looked for without knowing what I looked for. And now I will at times explore every little nook of some poor coppice with almost anxious footsteps, so deep a hold has this imagination upon me."[5]

For my own part, I have never seen a fairy, though my paternal grandfather—"Grandy" we called him—in his unraveling years told me that on one of his rambles in Kerry as a young man, he bent down to tie his shoelaces and saw a little man sitting on a tussock beside his feet. They both moved along, each in their own direction, without exchanging remarks. Certainly I have visited places where I know the feeling that Yeats described, where a mood descends upon you, a sense that there is something there with you that is grander even than the trees, more secretive even than the birds noiseless in the leafy branches, and busier than the beetles tending to their cryptic labors in the mossy undergrowth. Reenadina Woods in county Kerry is one such place, where stands one of Europe's last great yew woodlands; Glenveagh Valley in county Donegal also, where as one descends the wild mountainside with the sun setting to your left, and the mountains dark to your right and behind you, and where here and there invisible streams chortle beneath the gorse: aye, there may be fairies there all right.

The West of Ireland is richest in fairy lore and fairy places. It is rare that tales describe fairies in Dublin city. When one shows up, for example, in "Jamie Freel and the Young Lady: A Donegal Tale," the fairies were passing through Dublin and up to no good. In the great story collections, the counties of the West of Ireland frequently appear. Counties Donegal, Galway, Sligo, Clare, Kerry, and Leitrim all produce great fairy lore and, not coincidentally, are famous recorders of fairy tales. Certainly, a full "natural" history of fairies would report sightings in most other parts of the country. I've heard, for example, of a few reports from the verdant hills of county Meath, close by county Dublin, from where my maternal grandmother hailed. But western Irish counties provide the most excellent fairy habitat.

The West of Ireland provides the natural backdrop for folkloric tales, and unsurprisingly it remains a consistent, though not of course exclusive, element in the fiction of that region. Liam O'Flaherty, from the Irish-speaking town of Gort na gCapall, on Inis Mór (the largest of the Aran Islands), off the coast of county Galway is an exemplary figure in this regard.[6] His first story, he reported, was written when he was still a schoolboy. It concerned a murder, where a man killed his wife—she had let his tea go cold—and he attempted to bury her body in his farm field between the narrow rows of potatoes. A pastoral horror story. The story, apparently, merited a thrashing by his schoolmaster. O'Flaherty's mature stories had more of wild nature in them, but were not any less dramatic. A few of these are still read by children; some were on the curriculum for the Irish equivalent of middle school when I was growing up.

The subjects of O'Flaherty's published stories, especially his earliest ones, are oftentimes the objects of nature—dramatic, unpeopled landscapes. Is it, I wonder, unique in the history of literature to have an ocean wave as the central character in a short story? There are two main characters in "The Wave" (1924), a giant cliff face and the ocean wave that swells in with the tide and that undermines the cliff. In this tale, whose stylized naturalism was borrowed from the French literary genius Guy de Maupassant, the cliff, silent and austere, had withstood "thousands of years of battle" with the sea. This particular wave though, whose "awful mass of water advanced simultaneously from end to end of its length without breaking a ripple on its ice-smooth breast," surged toward the cliff and hit precisely a small cavern on the cliff already excavated by countless generations of smaller waves. The cliff, which had formerly dwarfed the tide, now "looked small in front of that moving wall of blue and green and white water." The cliff was reduced to rubble. That's it, that's the story! In another, perhaps O'Flaherty's best known short story, "His First Flight" (1924), we join a young seagull on a ledge, goading himself into taking the plunge off the brink, and out over the "great expanse of sea stretched beneath." His parents and sibling have abandoned him to his fate. He either flies or dies. His family, including his fledged brothers and sisters, are on a broad plateau halfway down the opposing cliff. He calls out to his mother, "Ga, ga, ga" and she replied, "Gaw-ool-ah." No, he'll get no direct help from her. She does, however, fly toward the ledge, a piece of fish in her beak, and hovers nearby, "her legs hanging limp, her wings motionless." Maddened by hunger, our hero dives for the fish and, lo, he is flying; it's his first flight. In "The Cow's Death" (1924), O'Flaherty reports a less successful flight by a cow as it plunges off a cliff toward the sea in search of the discarded corpse of her stillborn calf.

Though O'Flaherty was adept at setting up conversations between inanimate objects or between atypical characters—seagulls, cows, sheep, thrushes, wrens, cows, and so on—most of his stories have more conventional characters: boys and girls, revolutionaries, tramps, and farmers, for example. In a story I'd especially recommend, "Three Lambs" (1926), Little Michael leaves his family's cottage early in the morning to witness the black sheep birth her lamb. With tender felicity, O'Flaherty describes the boy on that grand morning: he runs down the lane, and "his sleeves, brushing against the evergreen bushes, were wetted by the dew, and the tip of his cap was just visible above the hedge, bobbing up and down as he ran." He finds the sheep and empathizes with her birthing pain, and wonders why her fellow sheep don't keep her company. He assists in the birth. To his delight though, the sheep gives birth to another lamb. "Oh, you devil," he exclaims, repeating a curse he's learned from his tougher friend, Little Jimmy. And then one more lamb is born—this time a black lamb. Little Michael runs home to report the news, and as he ran "he barked like a dog in his delight." But Little Michael is no nature saint: in another story, "The Wren's Nest" (1926), Little Michael and Little Jimmy squabble over and destroy the nest as the "two wrens were . . . hovering about screaming in an agonized state. . . ."

Having been raised on such stories, and on the romance of Ireland's folklore traditions, it is unsurprising that my adolescent compass pointed West. The Irish West, where grow the forests, though now in tatters and scraps, where the mountaintops are mauve with the heather, where the choppy Atlantic waters batter the ragged coastline, the West of the Faery—this, surely, was the "real" Ireland. In my imagination, at least, little scraps of that real Ireland must surely persist. This wildness must be preserved.

One justification for my poorly conceived national park scheme, mentioned earlier, was that it merely amplified the ongoing historical decline of the Irish West. For a variety of demographic and economic reasons, a depopulation of the region had been ongoing since the Great Potato Famine of the 1840s. Thus, instead of a continued investment in economic development to reverse the demographic hemorrhaging of rural Ireland, I was merely urging a hefty investment in nature and in a certain rudimentary, low-impact, style of human habitation.

My plan, I see now, was predicated on a laughably false understanding of the factors shaping the landscapes of western Ireland. These landscapes are indubitably wild. The twentieth-century Austrian philosopher Ludwig Wittgenstein—who lived briefly in Connemara, county Galway, in the 1940s—describes those lands as being the "last pool of darkness" in Europe. Wittgenstein meant this, it would seem, in a positive sense, since he got a lot of his inscrutable brand of writing done there. In recognition of their wild character, a national park was indeed established in Connemara in 1980, close enough to where Wittgenstein briefly lived. The creation of this park occurred around the time of my ruminations about this western park concept, though I don't claim any credit for it! I worked in the national park, doing insects surveys for a while in the 1980s. The centerpiece of the park is the Twelve Bens, a series of quartzite peaks that are truly remote and rugged.

Pool of darkness though they may be, the lands of Connemara and the Irish West are not, in fact, wild areas, for the most part, where nature alone runs riot. Ireland, a relatively small island, has been inhabited for the past eight thousand years. Little true wilderness remains. The landscapes of the Irish West were, for the most part, shaped by the activities of both people and nature. For example, the Burren, a distinctive karst limestone plateau in county Clare (the county just south of county Galway), hosts over three-quarters of Ireland's plants. These lands have been grazed for millennia. Thus, the Burren is a series of biologically rich pastures, and not merely manifestations of nature in the raw. Furthermore, blanket bog, the distinctive vegetation of the mountainy regions of Ireland and Britain, originates, as often as not, as a blending of both human and natural forces. Felling of trees thousands of years ago set in train a series of processes that deflected the ecological development of these landscapes from forest to peatland. Both of these landscapes, the limestone pavements of the Burren and the blanket bog, are pastoral landscapes of a sort.

A scheme, such as the one I proposed, that removed the deep historical human involvement in the landscape runs a grievous risk of depleting a landscape of its unexpectedly high biodiversity. Recognition of the often-benign cultural influences on these iconic landscapes should not be understood, I think, as opening the way for a havoc of contemporary and possibly damaging use. The point is that certain human pressures, historically mildly imposed, produced landscapes that, over long periods of time, were good for humans and the rest of nature.[7] Is such long-term mutuality between humans and the rest of nature not the very essence of sustainable practices?

I describe this small fiasco in my early thinking to make a couple of points. It illustrates the tendency in environmental thought—my youthful inclinations being quite consistent with such traditions in ecological thought—to prioritize wilder places over urban ones. This anti-urban bias remains pronounced in environmental science, although with the recent emergence of urban ecology, this long-standing attitude is fading somewhat. Furthermore, it underscores an enduring environmental presupposition, that lands free of human influence, "wilderness areas," are more authentically "natural" than those that had undergone any form of human modification. There are compelling reasons, of course, for suspecting that wilderness presents great opportunities for the protection of nature, especially the bigger, more ferocious species, of which there are none left in Ireland, unless of course you include frisky domesticated ones.[8] However, such preconceptions in environmental thought can at times be misanthropic. If my scheme had ever left the privacy of my personal notebook, and thankfully it did not—until now at least—it might rightly have been regarded as a cold miscalculation regarding the real history of these valuable lands and the importance of the long-term relationships fostered by generations who inhabited these lands. It was insensitive as well to the peoples of this region.

This then was my rookie mistake: I had felt the lure of wild places and misconstrued it as emanating from unpeopled lands. What I discerned had, in fact, been the call of the pastoral, a call that echoes through Ireland's older tales, and a smattering of more contemporary ones also. This, too, I now realize: the idea of the pastoral has played an important, though regularly neglected, role in shaping environmental sensibilities. The pastoral has often been overshadowed by its boisterous younger cousin, the idea of wilderness. The seductiveness of the wilderness idea compared to the pastoral may, for example, help explain environmentalists' perplexing antipathy toward agriculture as an activity. To illustrate, ecologist and historian Jared Diamond published an influential essay in 1987 entitled "The Worst Mistake in the History of the Human Race."[9] That mistake: the invention of agriculture, going back ten thousand years or so. And though Diamond's point, like other critiques of the agricultural revolution, is that it unleashed a population explosion, nonetheless attitudes to agriculture in environmental thought remain contentious.

My superficial understanding of the cultural history of the Irish West was symptomatic then of a neglect by environmental thinkers of the significance of cultural landscapes in general, and the pastoral in particular. The pastoral idea is not, of course, simply synonymous with agriculture—not all farm fields are bucolic. Nonetheless, a theme in both environmentalism and in literature, for both children and adults, posits an appealing middle space between urban decay and remote wilderness where peace and well-being prevail. This must be perennially rediscovered in environmental thinking. Once its qualities are recognized, or re-recognized, it is clear that it is the pastoral, as much as wilderness, that has both influenced our environmental longings and shaped our literature. After all, who among us does not dream of harmony in a temperate land of "milk and honey"?

Section Three

Wilderness Stories

LOST IN THE POPO AGIE WILDERNESS

Almost a decade ago I made a small blunder along the trail through the Popo Agie Wilderness that almost cost me my life. That Wyoming wilderness area encompasses over 100,000 acres of granite peaks, narrow canyons, glorious alpine valleys, and icy lakes and streams. Twenty of its peaks exceed 12,000 feet, including the Wind River Peak, which rises to 13,255 feet, and though it is frequently visited by climbers, for the most part we walked alone through the vast landscape.

I hiked in there for a few days with a veteran of those trails. His son-in-law was the third of our little party. It was late summer and there was already a slight bite in the air suggesting the oncoming of autumn.

Even now, these several years later, at times I glance at a map of the region reminding myself of where I lost the trail and struck out toward oblivion. It was late on the first evening of our hike, and we were hoping to make good progress into the back country before we made camp. Although I was a seasoned camper, having slept under canvas close by Irish national parks for part of each summer during my college years, I had never been in such formidable wilderness, nor had I ever been on so arduous a hike. But I was poorly prepared for the trip, having, in retrospect, a false confidence in my own charmed life and an assumption, that I now regard as almost fatally flawed, about the fundamentally benign nature of the world. No map, no compass, no food in my pack, no survival gear, no clue.

We had incautiously spread out along a mile or so of trail. I was to the rear, having deliberately slowed my progress so as to enjoy solitude. My wilderness reverie had been punctured a little by a small party who were packing out of the area. We nodded our *hellos* and on I walked, slightly vexed that our group was not, in fact, alone. They were the only people we saw that day. It was fortuitous that they were there it turned out.

The day wore on, the sun was low, and the sparkling gray of the granite was replaced by the slate gray of the early evening sky. On and on I trudged. Enough light remaining to illuminate a descent into the pretty valley where we were to camp, but not enough for me to clearly discern my companions, who, for all I knew, were now setting up their tents. Perhaps dinner would await me!

The sound of evening in the Popo Agie Wilderness is a rare delight. Crystal-clear alpine streams gurgle, birds fidget in the scrub, and the wind mutters through the grasses. As I walked along, I became aware of a muttering in quite a different key. Eventually, I turned and, scanning the horizon, I saw the hikers I had passed on the trail waving down the valley at me. They were, in fact, yelling at me, though the wind muted them. I waved back begrudgingly, not at all impressed to have the evening so disturbed. I turned back to the trail, but the yelling continued. The Popo Agie Wilderness gets an occasional grizzly bear, but it seemed unlikely that this was what they wished to warn me of. Perhaps I had missed some wonderful sight—the geology of the region is quite spectacular—I looked around that spot. Moments went by and though I could not make out what they were saying, nor could I discern the meaning of their gesticulations, all of a sudden, it dawned on me that I was going in the wrong direction and was heading *away* from rather than toward my companions. Thus, thanking those hikers with an acknowledging wave, I retraced my steps and eventually rejoined my friends.

Now, I realize that this may seem like the smallest of matters. After all, had I really been in all that much danger? I had been on the wrong trail for no more than thirty minutes, and a little light remained in the sky. Though in winter the temperatures in the Popo Agie, even in the valleys, can plunge to minus forty below, in late summer the nights were merely cool. Indeed, my misstep seemed so inconsequential that when I caught up with my party, I decided not mention it. Perhaps, though, it was shame.

In quiet moments ever since, I have speculated about the journey's end if those hikers had not intervened and had I simply marched on. When would I have realized I was not catching up? Was that trail leading to some temperate valley where I could have bedded down for the night, albeit hungrily, or down inhospitable scree and into a freezing lake? And having discovered myself alone and map-less, would I have subsequently hiked back successfully to Landers, the nearest town, or gotten lost in the 1,400-square-mile Wind River wilderness complex of which Popo Agie is just a tiny part.

What I learned—though not on that day, it's true, but rather in slightly panicked later reenactments as I looked at those maps—is that what the wilderness means is that to be unprepared is to flirt with perishing.

8

On the Mallard

I am sitting at a desk in Cedar Bark cabin, a log structure that used to float on Rainy Lake in northern Minnesota. I'm told this cabin once served as a brothel for loggers working in the watershed. The cabin is now anchored on Mallard Island, home for fifty years to Ernest "Ober" Oberholtzer (1884–1977), the wilderness advocate. The cabin houses more contemplative activities these days than in its rambunctious past. Some of the writers and painters and teachers and contemplatives—guests of the Oberholtzer Foundation who visit this island retreat for a week or so to chip away at their projects—are roomed in this cabin. The amenities on Mallard Island remain relatively primitive, though it now has the luxury of fairly sophisticated composting toilets. One of these toilets—the preferred one by many visitors—has a fan that circulates air below the bowl's surface to assist no doubt the processes of excremental decay, though it creates the rather amiable impression that you are shitting into a stiff breeze. Electricity now comes to the island by means of an underground cable. So each evening my cabin mate Thomas can play musical recordings on the deck. He accompanies these blues tracks, fabulously, on his harmonica. Every so often he sets down the instrument and looks contemplatively out across the lake and softly sings: his voice is a beautiful tremolo but is quiet, as if he's in a soft conversation with the past and with the waters that surround the island. The island is sad only to the extent that life is sad; the island is happy to the extent that this, too, is the way of the world.

The island is a mere acre and a half in extent and is dotted with a variety of buildings in addition to the one in which I am housed.

Many of these were commissioned by Ober and typically constructed by Emil Johnston, of whom it is said was a genius woodworker when he was sober.[1] He must have been sober more often than not, for there are many small, eccentric, and charming buildings here: the Japanese House, the Bird House, the Front House, the Winter House, the Old Man River House, the Wannigan (Kitchen Boat), and so on. It's like stumbling into a small village in the sort of dream where commonplace symmetry and order have been replaced by a perfectly intuitive alternative geometry. The vegetation of the island is relatively open, and, mirroring the buildings, it is an eclectic mix of strange companions: lilac bushes, cherry, raspberries, blackberries, blueberries, small ash trees, birch, cedar, aspen, oaks, some larger pines, and so on. Deer swim out to the island, and a mink plays under the deck outside the screened porch where I write. Nearby, the loons converse on the lake in the evenings and get raucous in their own distinctively elegant way as night falls on the island.

The outcrop of granite that forms the substrate of the island is the product of some of nature's more ancient business, the molten tumult that solidified into rock having settled down millions of years ago. But the ecology of the island is richer than it might otherwise be, for without the barges of soil and manure that Ober brought over to the island, a piece of rock of such a small size jutting but a few feet above the surface of the lake would host but a very modest ecological troop. Thus—and this is what I have been gearing up to say—atop this antique geological outcrop, the island has been shaped primarily by the intentions and inclinations of people.

This island's life is then a cultural affair, and was so, of course, even in Ober's day. Long before Ober's time, the island had been held sacred by the Ojibwe people. Of life on Mallard, Joe Paddock, Ober's biographer, has written: "There is in western civilization a nature-culture division that has become our sad heritage. Within himself and through the lifestyle he developed in the Mallard, Ober did much to solve, dissolve, and transcend that division."[2] But the

watershed of Rainy Lake has tipped, I imagine, even more to the cultural end of the spectrum than it had before. Water from the lake
had been directly drinkable in Ober's time; today it must be purified
by reverse osmosis! Though the open waters are clear and inviting,
so weedy are the lake channels between adjacent islands that swimming around the Mallard is in places like breast-stroking your way
through the crowns of a submerged forest. One night, the sounds of
selected recordings of classical lights—Vivaldi, Beethoven, Mozart,
and such company—streamed across the lake, played loudly upon
an adjacent island. Since Ober was a keen musician and a patron
of music, the sound of the classics played late into the night might
not have seemed strange while he lived here. Yet this recent music
seemed both haunting and irritating to me in equal measure. Such
audacity: to perturb the solitude of those who had, no doubt (though
perhaps in a smaller way), been disturbing yours! I am mindful here
that my tin whistle, which I play with spirit though not with musical
precision, has a pronounced tendency to travel on the air and doubtlessly reverberates around adjacent islands. Even more distracting
than classical music at vesper time are the motorboats, the Jet Skis,
and all the other mechanical toys that rip across the waters of the
lake and that erode, at times, the sense of companionable solitude
that we've cultivated on the island.

Mallard Island—home to the late Ernest Oberholtzer, the champion
of wilderness—is thus not itself a wilderness, and is even less so now
than it was in Ober's time on the island. But it was never intended
to be. Nonetheless, it is a fine place to contemplate and write about
wilderness, which is why I have come here. It is precisely because its
island life is calibrated to straddle the nature-culture divide that it
can serve in this way. One can, of course, contemplate wilderness in
places where nature alone holds sway, for reflection is, of course, an
ancient and presumably defining practice of humans. But to write

about wilderness requires the intrusion of culture. To hold a pencil, to scratch a note on paper, even if one were to do so surrounded by the vociferous wild, is to participate in a relatively new cultural practice. New at least if I can be granted the claim that any practice restricted to the past few millennia is a new addition to human culture.

Another reason why Mallard Island lends itself to the contemplation of wilderness is because it evokes a very particular "feeling" and therefore an orientation toward the wild. Mallard Island is ironically a physical reminder that wilderness may not itself be a physical place. Roderick Nash, the celebrated historian of the concept of wilderness, puts it thusly in the famous opening to his book *Wilderness and the American Mind* (1967): " 'Wilderness' has a deceptive concreteness at first glance. The difficulty is that while the word is a noun it acts like an adjective."[3] If wildness is a feeling or at least the subjective adjectival quality of a place, then, happily, wilderness is inextinguishable. Wilderness can be any place. But—and this is the difficult question I think—if wilderness is any place, is it anything at all?

So I sit here on Mallard Island, staring out on the water, glancing down at my screen, surrounded by a dreamtime village and by Ober's books (which, by the way, include quite a few volumes by that other great island man, the Aran writer Liam O'Flaherty, mentioned in a previous chapter), and in the companionship of poets and artists and dreamers, and wonder what exactly can one make of the concept of wilderness?

☾ ⋆
⋆

On Mallard Island, it occurred to me that the time has come to re-rethink the idea of wilderness, and the best resources for accomplishing the task are to be found in stories written for children. My optimism is that in re-rethinking wilderness in this way, one can acknowledge but go beyond the shortfalls of traditional wilderness thinking. I base this assessment on a reading of a wide array of children's stories for all age groups and from different cultural traditions.

In fact, all of the books I've read in assembling this volume were pre-paratory for the task of reasserting the value of the idea of wilderness.

Our traditional thinking about wilderness—the "first thinking"—was formulated in part by means of a largely secular reflection on stories of biblical wilderness: in wilderness, one encounters both the divine and the malign. The idea of wilderness as sacred space was incorporated into the writings of the hard men (they were typi-cally men and often men of stern disposition) who recreationally explored and charted the backcountry of the United States in the late nineteenth century. Wilderness, more generally, has been con-ceived as the realm of savage nature, where people can visit but do not remain. Wilderness, its advocates claim, challenges and restores a mind fatigued by the quotidian affairs of a civilized life. American frontier wilderness founded the American identity, and though rug-ged times are now past for most people, wilderness reminds a nation of its distinctive grounding. Besides, an encounter with wilderness reminds us all across the globe of our un-severed, though oftentimes concealed, unity with the rest of nature.

In recent decades, the idea of wilderness has been appropriately criticized and rethought based upon a concern for those experiences and literatures typically overlooked in the traditional wilderness dis-course. The perspectives of indigenous peoples had been notably absent in early discussions of wilderness and were excluded in a manner that, in some circumstances, has undermined their very lives and livelihoods. Wilderness preserves—those "untrammeled" lands where nature alone holds sway—were often formerly simply "home" to indigenous people. Those open meadows, scattered timberlands, seas of prairie grasses, and austere mountain peaks that were set aside as sanctuary for nature had often been carefully managed by the original denizens of the land. It's as if I came upon your flower garden shortly after you had been forcibly escorted off the property and in your absence mistook it for the work of providence alone. Moreover, what if I wrote the prettiest poems about your garden, photographed it exquisitely, and restricted access to permit holders whose papers were stamped and in order? What if, when the whims of climate ordained it, I let that garden burn to the ground and then rhapsodized about the glory of the flames? What if I truculently refused to acknowledge that this was ever your garden? What if I then declared that the appropriation of your sublime garden was America's finest idea and promoted the idea around the globe. That, according to its critics, is the problem with wilderness: the idea was built by ablating and fictionalizing genocides. And if these pernicious truths were not enough, the idea of wilderness as a place for nature alone, far from cultivating a sense of unity with nature, by definition inscribes the separation of humans from the rest of nature. Indeed, wilderness since 1964 is the law of the land; wilderness legislatively banished nature into tidy, though admittedly slightly dangerous, corrals. The idea of wilderness is all in all a bit of a mess.

So why, in all of this, are children's stories important for reasserting the value of the idea of wilderness? It's because the idea of wilderness in children's stories is more ecumenical than is the one in traditional environmental literature. This is not the idea of wilderness as reflected in stories about Moses, Isaiah, John the Baptist, and Jesus, or in the writings of more contemporary figures like John Muir, Henry David Thoreau, and Aldo Leopold. A child's wilderness can be found in the little room under the stairs, or in the garden shed, along a quiet stretch of road outside the city limits, or in the vastness of the Canadian wildlands. Indeed, an encounter with wild things can start in the bedroom as it did for Max, the naughty child in Maurice Sendak's *Where the Wild Things Are* (1963).

9

Where the Wild Things Always Were

Maurice Sendak's *Where the Wild Things Are* (1963) is two months older than I am. Since it was not a book that was regularly read in Ireland in my youth, I did not come across it until I read it to my children. The story is a simple one: A naughty little boy, Max, in an animal suit—generally it's assumed to be a wolf suit, though other guesses abound—is sent to his room without dinner. As his childish wrath begins to cool, Max closes his eyes—reflectively and not sleepily— and his room is transformed into a forest, a tree here and there at first, and then a shrub or two; two palm trees spring up (large ones though not fruiting), grass carpets the floor, vines dangle from the ceiling, and then the walls are gone: where once there was a bedroom, there is now "the world all around." Already Max is cheered; he steps into this forest. He boards a boat, a private one also named *Max*, and the little boy sails away. At journey's end, he reaches "the place where the wild things are." He's appointed king—this is accomplished by means of the mildest hypnosis; the wild things and wild Max rumpus. And that rumpus is excellent. Six out of thirty-four pages of the book are devoted to rumpusing; or to express it differently, *Where the Wild Things Are* is almost 18 percent rumpus. Fatigued, and no doubt hungry, Max's thoughts then turn, not to home exactly, but to where "someone loved him best of all." In their grief at the loss of their king, the wild things tell him that he is indeed loved, though admittedly they also threaten him with consumption. Max then reverses his journey, standing stiffly and with eyes closed at the prow of his ship. Dinner awaits him upon his return. All in all, Sendak tells the story in relatively few words: 338 to be precise. To illustrate how spare this is, this paragraph is also 338 words.

Sendak needed no more words than 338 to tell this story, though I need a few more to reflect upon his important book. What Sendak did not say in words, he communicated with illustrations. A picture paints a thousand words; Sendak's twenty pictures speak volumes. It would be a futile exercise, and a dull one besides, to transliterate Sendak's illustrations, yet they should not go unremarked, for the illustrations are undeniably marvelous in their expressive power. We do not need to read more about Max's naughtiness, for the events leading up to his banishment to his room are clear: childish frenzy is illustrated on his face. He'd been banging nails into the wall, he'd strung his teddy up with an improvised rope, and he'd been chasing the dog down the stairs with a fork! Once he is dispatched to his room, he glares over his shoulder at the closed door. The plant on a window-side table seems to lean toward the open window, for this is the way with plants. The moon, which is depicted in nine pictures, is in a waning crescent. By now Max has turned from the door, his eyes are closed, the expression on his face is more contemplative, his foot is arched up off the floor. The forest emerges in the bedroom. But now we spectators are seeing not the world as imagined by Sendak, but complicatedly we are seeing the world as imagined by Max, as imagined by Sendak. Perhaps few artists have so effectively captured the moment of active reverie. Relaxed though engaged, off Max goes on his wilderness adventure.

Maurice Sendak (1928–2012) was admirably self-effacing regarding his prodigious talents. He wrote that "it is not that I draw particularly better or write particularly better than other people. . . ." However, the consensus of critical opinion lines up against him on this issue: *Where the Wild Things Are* won a Caldecott Medal from children's librarians in 1964 and has been consistently ranked as a children's favorite. Sendak's accomplishments specifically as a visual artist are now well recognized. Selma G. Lanes's *The Art of Maurice Sendak* (1980) provides a nice selection of his illustrations and art from throughout his career. Even if we were to take Sendak at his word about his relative merits as an artist, how does *he* account for the appeal, especially to children, of his work? Sendak's speculation on that matter is that "I remember things that other people don't recall: the sounds and feelings and images—the emotional quality—of particular moments in childhood. . . . My most unusual gift is that my child self seems still to be alive and well."[1]

That Sendak's power as a storyteller comes from a happy coalescing of his technical skills and an ability to connect with his inner child seems a plausible thesis, for is this not the case with many brilliant writers for children? Sendak's art emerged from specific memories of his childhood in an immigrant Jewish-Polish family in New York. His relatives—who during his early years visited the Sendak home each Sunday and mercilessly pinched his cheeks, and whose every blemish he noted and filed away for later use—were the models for the wild things. But Sendak's work is powerful for additional reasons. His vision seems both specific and universal. Max's rambunctious behavior recalls our own childhood; his exile in his bedroom recalls our own penalties and the small humiliations that we each endured, and so on. These themes seem universal not just because most of us live relatively canalized lives—Max's life is reminiscent of our own—but rather they seem universal because Sendak has captured what it's like, psychologically, to be *any* human child. We were all impetuous; we all tested the limits of our guardians' patience, grew frustrated, and retreated—when the situation demanded it—to the resources of the imagination. There is something of the psychologist in Sendak in this to be sure, but at the same time something, as others have noticed before me, of the anthropologist and mythologist about him. He doesn't, in other words, just bring us back into our childhood, but he dispatches us on a journey in that universally possessed little boat of the imagination—the one named for each and every one of us—deep into the forests of the psyche, that place where, since the dawn of humankind, the wild things are.

Max's imaginative journey to where the wild things are is an encounter with the *idea* of wilderness, and not wilderness as a physical place. This idea of the wild is part of Max's mental constitution: it's undeniably real since our imagination is real, however intangible it may seem. Yet in his reverie, Max imagines being transported *somewhere*, for this is the classic trope of wilderness thinking: wilderness is where we are not. For all their initially frightening aspects, the wild things dwell in a place that is not altogether intimidating. Max, himself a wolf, rapidly quells the wild things. His is a dream of mastery over the wild, and the consequence of his trip is self-mastery over his inner tumult. The angry kid gets a grip on himself. When Max returns to self-presence, aware once again of being in his bedroom, he is ready for civilization. His appetite for the wild assuaged— and no longer threatening to eat the dog with a fork, and no longer claiming that he will eat his mother—he ingests a less exotic meal, one prepared for him by his mother.

The use of the idea of wilderness in *Where the Wild Things Are* is quite a simple one: it provides Max with a psychological salve for what ails him. For all its simplicity, this idea of wilderness nonetheless has some important components: It underscores an element of distance from both ordinary things and from the human community—wilderness can be solitary. It posits the rambunctiousness of diverse wild things and provides a realization that one cannot dwell forever in the wild. In this notion of wilderness, there is a heightened reminder that after our fill of wilderness, one can, or perhaps even should, return, replenished, to the comforts of home.

It would be glib to make strenuous comparisons between the picture books of Maurice Sendak and the oldest pictorial art that we have: namely, the rock and cave art of the Pleistocene. For all of the universality and subtlety of his work, Sendak's audience is youths and those who, like you and me, are perhaps nostalgic for childhood. In contrast, we can't be sure who Pleistocene art was created by or for. Second, for all the concision of his text, Sendak wrote a story with which his artful panels are in garrulous dialogue. We can't be sure what stories go along with Pleistocene art. The storytellers are long dead; and the cave panels are not lined up in a suggestive narrative sequence. However, as we shall see, while we don't have a fully satisfying account of why ancient artists created these works, the paintings on the cave walls of the Pleistocene are not exactly mute. Even if we can't transliterate them, these are surely the original beasts at bedtime stories, for animals dominate these rock "canvases." Over a century of scholarship has now been invested in interpreting this artwork, identifying the images, establishing their chronology, understanding their production techniques, and speculating about the cultural context in which they were created. We are now in a better position to speculate about them than ever before.

The work of any individual writer, even one of Sendak's genius, is inarguably eclipsed in importance compared to the work of an entire epoch. Pleistocene art is the work of thousands of generations of artists starting about thirty-five thousand years ago; this art has an almost cosmopolitan geographical distribution. Yet despite the difference in audience, the divergence in their scope and meaning, and the remaining debates concerning their meaning, it would be unfortunate to ignore the illuminating parallels between children's picture stories and individual works of Pleistocene art. Their shared preoccupation with animals is only the most obvious comparison.

In Jean Clottes's glorious book *Cave Art* (2008), the French prehistorian and cave art specialist provides what he describes as an "imaginary museum" of prehistoric images.[2] In recent days, I have wandered through Clottes's "museum" jotting down notes, not as I do when reading a book, nor even as I might walking by conventional museum exhibits, but as I do when strolling through a living community. Here's a bear, there's a bison; a herd of aurochs (wild cattle) stampede. A mammoth with enormous tusks stands right there, and close by two rhinos clash. I witness a pride of lions chasing down bison. And every once in a while, I see a human being—that most rare of the Pleistocene creatures. But I look again: the human appears to be half bird and half man. I see a woman: she's naked and standing with a bison. Indeed, she may be part woman, part bison. Perhaps she is wearing a bison suit? Perhaps the man was wearing a bird mask? I wheel around and hear the thundering of hooves; horses speed by me.

My "field notes" from a virtual nature walk through the Chauvet Cave in France (with art from ca. 30,000 BC) revealed that I had encountered the following: 34 lions, 27 rhinos, 23 horses, 13 bison, 6 mammoths, 5 aurochs, 3 cave bears, 2 deer, and 1 spectacular owl, who glared at me with his head pivoted 180 degrees from his front. One hundred fourteen animals in all. It's by no means an exhaustive roster of the community; after all, Clottes could not exhibit the entire Chauvet collection in his book and therefore made a selection of the images to present. He highlighted the more impressive images and the rarer finds. Be that as it may, this community of animals is diverse. It is diverse in both of the ways that ecologists evaluate such things: the species number is fairly high (nine species) and the number of individuals are distributed across these species in a relatively even way: lions and rhinos are fairly common, and owls are rare. To compare this diversity, I calculated a metric that I often use for living communities. The Shannon diversity index, though it has its methodological shortfalls, is often employed by ecologists because it captures both the diversity and evenness of creatures in a biological community. The Shannon diversity of the Chauvet fauna based upon my "visit" was 1.77.[3] To put this in context, the diversity of the birds in one of my favorite Irish woodlands is a little over 2. That the diversity of animals depicted in the Chauvet Cave is not that much lower than in many natural communities alerts us to the sheer diversity of animals that were significant to the artists of the Paleolithic. Diverse, indeed, is the zoological community that dwells in the artistic imagination. The imagination draws upon nature but also embellishes and combines elements in fertile and meaningful ways.

Early accounts speculating on the significance of the menagerie painted on cave walls conjectured that they served aesthetic purposes alone—art for art's sake. There is no denying the gorgeousness and technical virtuosity of this art: the famous paintings of Chauvet and Lascaux (ca. 15,000 BC) include some of the most compelling images of all time. But the fact that these pictorial stories were painted and engraved in deep recesses in the rock makes it implausible that they were for aesthetic display only. Theories that argue for a totemic relationship between the artists (and their communities) and the animals depicted seem partial. The images are too various for them to represent mere totemic votives—one might expect some caves to be dedicated to just one animal, but this is not what we find. Theories that argue that these images performed sympathetic magic helpful in the hunt seem reasonable, and yet most compositions have little to do with the hunt.

So what accounts for the production of this art? Clottes believes, controversially, that cave art was associated with the shamanistic practices of hunter-gatherers. Shamanistic practices are various, but the performance of the shaman is central in this belief system. Shamans can project themselves into the (supernatural) world in a way that permits direct connection with powerful natural forces. The shaman can transform into various animal forms, can occupy different states of consciousness often assisted by hallucinogens, and thereby can exercise influence over the elements that determine health and well-being. Animals are a focus of attention in hunter-gatherer life; animal behavior and motivations have the qualities of being both readily accessible to the intellect, in a way that rocks, for example, are not, but also sufficiently different as to seem to belong to another realm from the human one. Besides, animals were (and are) both the source of food and fear; they were an unavoidable fact of

life. In an animistic worldview, everything—plants, pebbles, mountains, stars—are inhabited by spirit; and yet animals are so palpably
imbued with a spirit that transforming into an animal is commonplace in stories from the oldest times. It remains a bedrock of many
contemporary children's stories. For example, when first we make the
acquaintance of Professor Minerva McGonagall from the Harry Potter series, she is a tabby cat: "It was on the corner of the street that he
noticed the first sign of something peculiar—a cat reading a map."[4]

What makes the connection with shamanism plausible is that at
the time that cave art originated, this worldview had spread around
northern Europe and North America. If the connection with shamanistic religion is correct, then the cave artist is a shaman, the
one who at times is depicted as the bird man or the bison sorceress. In a heightened state, shamans leave their body, can at times
become an animal, and join with the Great Spirit that permeates all
of nature. There are scholars who reject the shamanistic explanation
of cave art—all such interpretations are difficult to test; nonetheless,
it seems inarguable that those who labored in the perpetual night of
caves did not do so whimsically or without purpose.

Regardless of what motivated this art, images on rocks from the
Pleistocene tell us about what it was like to be human at a time from
which there is no written record. In his book *Masters of the Planet*
(2012), paleo-anthropologist Ian Tattersall suggests that cave art—
which is a relatively recent cultural manifestation in the history of
a species whose origin extends back millions of years—is helpful in
examining the development of the cognitive style distinctive of the
modern human animal.[5] A facility with symbols—where one thing,
often an abstract thing, substitutes for something else—is a central
factor in human cognitive functioning and, according to Tattersall,
was a principal ingredient in human development. Animals on cave
walls are skillful depictions of the animals that they stand in for.
Many of the art depictions from that period are, however, abstract:

for example, a series of dots clustered in a way that is clearly intentional even though the meaning of the intention is now unclear. For Tattersall, these symbols—both concrete and abstract, however cryptic their meaning—are key for understanding human "mastery" of the planet. Capable of using symbols, artistic as well as linguistic, we live not just in the world as it is given to us, as most animals do, but are capable of imagining alternative futures that humans then have a hand in shaping. Humans have a sort of cognitive fluidity—an ability to manipulate symbols in a dynamic and novel way—that liberates us from the world as it is given to us. We can change the world in unprecedented ways so that it conforms, up to a point at least, to the plans we have imagined for it. This, on the one hand, was the basis, in ancient times, for our survival, but now is arguably the source of our environmental problems. Push the world, and slowly, inexorably, the world pushes back.

The human being is buffeted by large, wild, and ultimately crushing forces. We weather the storm and live but an instant—no one makes it out alive. The shamanistic artist of the Paleolithic paints on the cave wall and, mediated by these symbols, attempts to get a measure of control over those forces that in turn control us. Cave paintings are the first alcove in a gallery that includes all the artistic representations that have entertained, provoked, soothed, and spiritually uplifted us in the millennia since ancient times. *Where the Wild Things Are* is a descendant, brilliant in its own way, and modest in the grand scheme of things, of this antique human tradition of storytelling.

As with cave art, Sendak's illustrations are dominated by animals. Max is surrounded by depictions of seven wild animals in all. Since there is only one of each, the diversity of this community would be considered low: the Shannon diversity is only 0.3. The animals in *Where the Wild Things Are* are to a large extent representational images: one is identifiable as a lion, a goat, a rooster, and so on. But all the animals possess a mixture of anatomical characteristics and cannot be fully categorized. The bull, for example, has human feet, carefully tended by the looks of them. In their fluidity of form, the animals continue that long tradition of painting stretching back to antiquity. But are they not also reminiscent of mythological creatures? The Minotaur of Greek mythology had the head of a bull and the body of a man. Are such animals not the stuff of dreams or wild nightmares?

Max in his wolf suit in the cavern of his bedroom is a portrait of the shaman as a young man. The real shaman is Sendak though. Sendak, with his peculiar access to childhood memory, recalls those fretful moments when we lose self-control and rage against the world. The ambition of cave artists may, in many cases, have been enormous: protecting their entire community from the swirling and potentially annihilating wild elements. Nonetheless, Sendak employs tools comparable to his early artistic and shamanistic ancestors to illustrate how a child can use their imagination to quell a wild tumult within.

Animals dominate in the cave paintings of the Pleistocene, whereas Sendak illustrates entire landscapes. Vegetation, quite remarkably, is almost totally absent in cave paintings but is profuse in *Where the Wild Things Are*. The landscapes in this little book reveal, in rudimentary fashion, something of the relationship between people and the configuration of our natural environment. Which landscapes induce fear; which can comfort us? This claim is based upon the fact that all accomplished landscape art does this. According to geographer Jay Appleton in his landmark study *The Symbolism of Habitat: An Interpretation of Landscape in the Arts* (1990), human responses to landscapes are undeniably culturally informed but are also founded on inclinations inherited from our evolutionary past.[6] We perceive a variety of symbols in any habitat that alert us to the ecological possibilities and perils of that place.

To illustrate his claim, Appleton examined a large suite of landscape paintings. Generally, landscapes that are considered most pleasing contain life-sustaining elements; water is a primary feature that people find positively appealing. Furthermore, Appleton analyzed which elements in landscape paintings elicit pleasure responses and, alternatively, feelings of disquiet. What he found was that landscapes with the largest appeal felicitously combine open vistas alongside representations of shelter. Open vistas in Appleton's terminology represent "prospect"; this is where the spectator can cast an eye about the scene. In contrast, protected recesses in the landscape, in which the viewer is shielded from inspection from elements in the landscape, are termed "refuges."

More often than not, when human figures are incorporated into paintings, they are shown adjacent to shelter. For example, in Rembrandt van Rijn's *Landscape with the Rest on the Flight into Egypt* (1647), a favorite painting of mine in my youth, the Holy Family is shown crouched about a small fire under the trees, a vast dark hilly landscape looming beyond them.

Water is life-giving, and therefore symbolizes in both painting and in natural landscapes the general productivity of a habitat. Head toward the water if you want sustenance. Open spaces symbolize vulnerability to predation. If you must pass through an open landscape, best to do it close to the trees, and best of all know to what refuge you will flee if circumstances call for it.

Landscapes that elicit the more extreme feelings of disquiet contain within them elements of "hazard." Perhaps this is why Caspar David Friedrich's *Wanderer above the Sea of Fog* (*Der Wanderer über dem Nebelmeer*; 1818) is so unnerving. The wanderer is standing on a precipice and stares into the landscape. The wanderer sees all; all sees the wanderer. It's worth comparing this paining with Friedrich's *Chalk Cliffs on Rügen* (*Kreidefelsen auf Rügen*) from the same year, where the figures looking over the landscape are, more conventionally, safely ensconced in a rocky alcove.

The more controversial claim that Appleton makes is that our responses to landscapes are, to some extent, hardwired in us—humans read landscapes, even in artistic depictions, as if their lives depended upon it. In tracing our responses to landscapes back to deep-seated inclinations for survival, Appleton draws upon and expands several lines of thought. The fact that humans have seemingly hardwired biophobic responses to threatening animals like spiders and snakes is a commonplace and obvious parallel. Stephen Kellert and E. O. Wilson's *Biophilia Hypothesis* (1995) posits a complementary and positive inclination for life that can explain the health benefits of being in nature.[7] A last example: biologist Gordon H. Orians proposed his "savanna hypothesis" initially to explain subtle difference in human preferences for trees—arguing that such preferences are rooted in evolved responses to the savannas of Africa, the habitat in which humankind evolved. In his book *Snakes, Sunrises, and Shakespeare: How Evolution Shapes Our Loves and Fears* (2014), Orians expands his analysis to reveal a role for natural selection in shaping our behavioral preferences and emotional responses.[8]

Though the landscapes of *Where the Wild Things Are* are vegetated, they are intimate ones and for the most part without sweeping vistas. But, for all of that, they hold up reasonably well to Appleton's analysis. Once Max's bedroom has become transformed, we see him surrounded by trees like the savanna-originating creature he is. Though he stands beneath overarching branches, Max faces outward from this "refuge" and gesticulates with wolf claws bared at the "prospect" of the great firmament beyond his forest shelter. He sets out on the ocean, surely a hazardous trip. The inherent vulnerability of the ocean is that in open waters we are observable: on the high seas, there is nowhere to hide. Yet in every single illustration where the open ocean is depicted, there is a tree comfortingly placed at the margin of the picture. This no doubt lessens anxiety for the young hominins reading the story. And sure enough, when Max arrives at the opposite shore, he is greeted to his visible alarm by a sea monster, the first of the wild things. On the shore, emerging from the refuge of the forest, are assembled the other wild things. As the adventure with the wild things proceeds—Max is crowned king, the troop engages in a rumpus—the action is sequestered beneath a leafy veil.

Sendak's story is not just a psychological drama—not a small achievement in itself, of course—but it is an illustrated meditation on the dangers with which we flirt when we sally forth into the world. If the world is wild and dangerous, how might we best mitigate those dangers? In the case of Max and the wild things, there is, as we have seen, some shamanistic magic at play; a boy transformed into a wolf quells and masters the beasts. But Max is also an intrepid navigator taking risks where he must, shielding himself from risk where he can. If Appleton is correct, then Max is simply replaying one of the oldest stories there is: a human ventures into the wilderness, survives, and returns to the hearth. Sendak's art, from this perspective, is one that connects the small trauma of a time-out with one of the enduring themes of human stories: how to be human in a wild larger-than-human world.

☾ ⋆
⋆

It's a heavy burden to place on any one children's story, as I have with Sendak's *Where the Wild Things Are*, to ask that it illustrate how children's stories in general might reinvigorate the idea of wilderness, an idea now regarded as suspicious in many environmental circles. In fairness, we might have chosen any number of stories for the task, for it's a rare children's book that does not have a wilderness interlude. But *Where the Wild Things Are* is exemplary in a number of ways. Of course, each story is not every story, and Sendak has a very particular tale to tell—and yet for all the specificity of the story, it plays, as we have seen, with some fairly universal themes. The overarching thought is an old one: a human engages with wild things and in so doing comes into accord with the world and gains a measure of self-mastery. There is, besides, a universal legibility in Sendak's landscapes that tap into something biologically fundamental and evolutionarily ancient within us. Thus when a parent and child snuggle up to read *Where the Wild Things Are*, reading the words aloud and perusing the illustrations, they replicate, in an idiosyncratic contemporary way, an activity that may be as old as the species. Parent and child cogitate, just as the ancients did, upon the idea of wilderness and the wild.

Where the Wild Things Are is best read aloud, and like all stories of this sort, it smuggles into today's culture a once widespread practice that has now become somewhat rare, namely, oral storytelling. New lines of evidence point to the very deep antiquity of myth-making and oral storytelling. A recent approach to the study of individual myths reveals not only how myths spread around the world, but also how many can be traced back to deep prehistory. For example, by comparing widespread versions of the "cosmic hunt" story—where the stars and constellations are imagined as hunters, their dogs, and the game animals that they pursue and kill—anthropologist Julien d'Huy traces this story back to its Paleolithic origin: "A man pursues a deer, and the animal is alive when it turns into the whole Dipper."[9] In contemplating this today, we hear the echo of ancient human voices raised under remote and gleaming night skies.

Children's stories inherit the spirit of antique storytelling not simply in the communal task they perform—bringing a family together at bedtime, as long before a shaman led acolytes into the cave, or families in elder times gathered about the fire. But they also inherit a set of themes: the life of animals, of course, the necessity of encountering wild things in ways that might not always be safe, and the hope of living to tell the tale.

Children's writers are not typically in the business of directly and critically reflecting on conceptual material, though the best ones do so obliquely and devastatingly. Children's stories are important because in them we get a simple and powerful ratification of the idea that wild nature nourishes us, even though it may be occasionally terrifying; we get an acknowledgment that a child's healthy development requires skills in recognizing both the hominess and uncanniness of the world. Children's stories, besides, grapple with the existential task of distinguishing the self from others. In children's stories, there is appreciation that attaining great goals may require overcoming thorny obstacles (sometimes literally thorny obstacles), and a recognition that our aesthetic appetites can be educated: there is beauty in the world even in places that seem inimical to our health. Children's stories affirm not only that the places of wilderness are important—even wilderness's most ardent critics acknowledge this—but that the very idea of wilderness is actually indispensable.

Themes of wilderness in children's stories are not written in response to contemporary debates about wilderness philosophy. How could they be, since storytelling, as I have tried to show here, is antecedent to these debates? Stories old and new confirm that for the human being, there is always a self and a non-self, a hearth and a wider world, the soothing and the fearsome. The idea of wilderness in children's stories articulates, and at the same time amplifies, the vertiginous aspects of the wider world, but, as often as not, these stories provide succor in navigating the terrors of the terra incognito that surrounds the child. Yes, you, too, must leave the fireside, as humans have always done; you, too, must make your way in the world like the Puss in Boots that you are; you must overcome obstacles, encounter fresh wonders, fail, pick yourself up, and maybe even fail again. But you will be rewarded by the beauty of the world as you encounter it, by the love you find along your way, and, yes, by the baubles of success, fleeting though those trinkets may be. Though nature will claim you in the end, and your atoms will be scattered beneath the soil and into the winds, if you've attended well to life's necessary tasks, you will know what it is to have been wild, and you will know what it is to have been free, if only for a few moments.

10

Wild and Grimm Fairy Tales

WILDERNESS ON THE MARGINS

The story is told that after the Roman Empire completed their conquest of Britain, a colonizing vanguard left for Ireland. Upon seeing a troop of wild Irishmen hopping up and down on densely wooded shores, they turned away and Rome forsook its Hibernian ambitions.

There are a number of Irish folktales—especially in the epic tradition—in which the Irish rebuff invaders from overseas. A favorite of mine is "Bodach an Chóta Lachtna" ("The Churl in the Grey Coat"). In this story, a foreign prince sails to Ireland and challenges Fionn and his Fianna—the legendary warriors of Ireland—to a foot race across Ireland.[1] Were the Fianna to resist the challenge or to lose to the prince, they would have to forfeit Ireland. The stakes were high, but, alas, Ireland's great champions were off attending to important matters: hunting no doubt, or composing epic poems, or soliloquizing to the birds of Ireland, or perhaps even playing hurling, the national game played with stick and ball. So Fionn selects a tramp—the bodach, or churl—begirt in a large tattered coat, as Ireland's champion. The prince and the tramp take off and traverse Ireland's great forests and its wild bogs: the foreign prince goes at a great pace; the bodach at a more desultory one, pausing frequently to feast on berries. Through a variety of ruses, the prince maintains his lead, until the last sprint where the churl overtakes him for the win. Enraged, the prince comes at Carl, for this is the bodach's name, with his sword in hand. Carl has just then settled down to a meal of porridge; seeing his vanquished opponent coming for him, he flings a great scoop of the oats at him and knocks off his head. Immediately overcome by remorse, Carl re-adhered the cleaved head, though in his haste he pasted the head on backward.

As the prince retreats to the European mainland from where he came, he must look back at Ireland, this now being the nature of his head. The bodach then revealed himself to the Fianna as none other than Lug, god of sun and storm, come to Ireland's aid in her hour of need.

Other than claims about how those wild men, dancing on the Irish shores, turned around the Roman boats, there is no specific folk-tale tradition explaining how that empire was rebuffed from Ireland. Perhaps Lug came to the rescue once again! One way or another, an empire that had made its way to Britain never managed to colonize Ireland. At the scale of the Roman Empire, wild landscape thus occupies the periphery. Wilderness is the point beyond which even despots fear to travel. Ireland was a wilderness to Rome, but so was North Africa, Armenia, the coastal region of Asia Minor, and so on. It was from here that Rome imported those wild animals: lions, panthers, and bears that were used for the savage practice called *damnatio ad bestias* (execution by beasts).[2] Many early Christians were martyred in this way.

Wilderness is fractal, however, in the sense that the patterns of the wild are also replicated at more local scales and can always be located close to hand. One doesn't have to travel far to experience wilderness. In more ancient times, when human communities were dotted like currants in a bun across wide continental landscapes, wilderness represents those regions just beyond the limits of settlement—any settlement. In the European folk tradition, the forests that separate the villages, towns, and hamlets are wilderness par excellence.

Dense forest is regarded as ambivalent habitat in many stories from around the world. In such forests dwell ungovernable creatures and people. The creatures and, at times, the people had gargantuan appetites and oftentimes an appetite that extended to human flesh.

In keeping with this, the emotional register associated with forest in the fairy tales of the European tradition is largely negative. That this is so may reflect the inevitable fretfulness of toothsome beings in the face of carnivores, imagined and real. But, for all of that, there are indications in the stories at least suggesting that beneath this fretfulness there is something simultaneously alluring about these dangerous landscapes. Perhaps, indeed, being fretful is itself an allure. For why else do we have roller coasters, fast cars, and fascist politicians. Don't go into the forest! And yet, off to the forest we go.

In the English translation of the *Brothers Grimm Fairy Tales* that I use, the word "wilderness" is infrequently used (five times only), although the word "wild" is used over one hundred times.[3] More prevalent still is the word "forest"—in these stories it is a common synonym for wilderness—which is used over three hundred times. In contrast, the word "tame" is rarely used, though "home," "castle," and "garden" are used so often that they collectively add up to about the same number of instances as that of their wilder counterparts. Considering the balance between these tallies, it seems reasonable to claim that fairy tales, at least those of the German tradition, represent an extended meditation on the balance between the hearth and the forested wilderness beyond.

In illustrating how tensions between the domestic and the wild play out in fairy tales, there are a very large number of stories to choose between. To refresh our memory of the general structure of these stories, I comment on just two of them, "Hansel and Gretel" and "Little Snow White." Armed with these and then drawing upon others, we can ask, "What do wild environments in fairy tales signify? What do we learn from them?"

Hansel and Gretel lived at the edge of the forest, the children of a poor woodcutter. Times were lean and there was not enough food to feed the family. The woodcutter's wife—the children's stepmother—suggests to him that he lead the children into the forest, build a large fire for them to sit by, and abandon them there. The woodcutter protests, saying that he could not "abandon them to wild beasts, for they'd soon come and tear them apart in the forest." Yet, despite his grisly forebodings, the woodcutter does *exactly* as he was bidden. The children, having overheard what was to be their fate, conspire to do something about it. Hansel collects little white pebbles and hides them in his pocket.

The following morning the children are led away into the forest. To divert his parents, Hansel glances back at their house and claims to see his little white cat on the roof, but as his parents turn to see the cat, he drops pebbles on the path. The children are then abandoned as they sleep by the large fire that their parents had made in the middle of the forest. When the moon rises, the children walk home, guided by the pebbles. Their return delights their father and consternates their stepmother.

Hunger descends on the family again. Hansel and Gretel are led into the forest once more. This time, under the ruse of spotting his pigeon on the house roof, Hansel lays a trail of crumbled bread to guide them home. But alas, it is the inevitable nature of edible trails that they are consumed by forest creatures. The children still try to strike out for home, but "they soon lost their way in the great wilderness."

The children come to an edible house constructed with bread and cake and windows made of sugar. They commence eating the house. A witch emerges from within and, seeming friendly at first, feeds the children a nutritious and well-rounded meal of pancakes, milk, fruit, and nuts. That night they sleep in beautiful warm beds. Meanwhile the witch, no doubt hungry from her own labors, looks down at the slumbering children and says, "They'll certainly be a tasty meal for you!" They are now captives of the witch. Hansel is locked in a chicken coop and fed lavishly by his sister, who was herself fed on "crab shells."

Hansel, always quick with a ruse, extends a chicken bone when the sight-impaired witch, anticipating, no doubt, handsomely marbled child flesh, checks on the boy's weight gain.

The time comes when the witch is prepared to wait no longer; fattened or not, the boy is to become her dinner. The witch has plans for the girl as well: she is to be baked. However, God inspires Gretel, and she coaxes the witch to show her how to climb into the oven (there is supposedly a loaf in there that needs inspecting). The witch, who up to this point, has been a very canny creature, falls for Gretel's trick. The witch burns to death and quite rightly so! Hansel and Gretel gather up the witch's impressive collection of jewels and pearls and return home, this time with somewhat surprising ease. No need this time for pebbles or a bread trail. Their father had been unhappy since their departure and is now overjoyed to see them. Their stepmother, for good measure, had died in the meantime. There is no mention that she died from grief over the loss of the children; one imagines she did not.[4]

Little Snow White endured wilderness years of her own. Her mother, the Queen (in some versions of the story, she's identified as her stepmother), jealous of the child's beauty, bids a huntsman to take her into the forest to "a spot far from here." There he is to stab her and return to the Queen with the girl's "lungs and liver" as proof that the dread deed has been accomplished. Out of pity for the pleading girl but also "because she was so beautiful," the huntsman cannot carry out his murderous task. He returns to the Queen with the lungs and liver of a boar. The Queen, no naturalist evidently, accepts this as token of the deed accomplished.

Abandoned to her own devices, Snow White runs deep into the forest toward the Seven Mountains region, where she discovers the empty house of the Seven Dwarfs. She eats their food and falls asleep on one of their beds (in fact, she selects the seventh bed that she tried—even after her ordeal, the girl retains her royal standards).

There she is discovered by the small-statured men. "Oh, my Lord! Oh, my Lord!" they exclaim. "How beautiful she is." Choosing not to disturb her sleep, the seventh dwarf shares a bed with one of his companions. This is a truth of fairy tales—indeed, we've seen it many children's stories—the tradition is very pointed on issues of who gets fed, and when they get fed, and who gets to sleep, and where they get to sleep. (Sleep, by the way, is mentioned 139 times in the Grimm Brothers' fairy tales; and eating appears 165 times—a satisfying ratio of these essential activities.)[5]

After listening to her heartrending story, the dwarfs waste no time and spring into action, appointing Snow White their maid. And there, deep in the forest, Snow White cooks, tidies, and launders the little men's clothes. "When we come home in the evening," they generously insist, "dinner must be ready." Snow White settles down to this polygamous-seeming life deep in the forested wilderness. Meanwhile, the Queen's mirror, which is as incapable of fibbing as yours or mine, imparts the doleful news that she, the Queen, is still not the "fairest in the land." Indeed, Snow White is "a thousand times more fair." Trusting the task of killing Snow White to none other than herself, the Queen, disguised as a peddler, calls upon the dwarfs' house selling lace. She laces up Snow White so tight that the girl faints, but the dwarfs returning to see their maid on the floor, revive her. So the Queen returns, this time selling combs. Special combs to be sure, as they are dipped in poison. Again the dwarfs return from their daily labors and revive the poisoned Snow White. One final time the disguised Queen returns to the dwarfs' house, this time with a poisoned apple. When the dwarfs return this time, it seems that Snow White is dead, although her cheeks remain quite rosy. The Queen's ever-truthful mirror confirms that the pretty girl is deceased. In fairness to the mirror, perhaps Snow White's magical slumber took the edge off her beauty. But however quiescent her state, Snow White is certainly alive.

The dwarfs lay out their young hausfrau in a glass bier, and Snow

White's long period of dormition begins. A prince arrives and tries to buy the incorruptible body of the girl. But the dwarfs, honorable beings that they are, instead gift the girl to the Prince. Eventually, the Prince's servants grow weary of carting Snow White around, so one of their number opens the coffin and lifts Snow White into the air. In executing this maneuver, the servant pushes against Snow White's back and dislodges the poisonous apple from her throat. Snow White is "once again alive." Following on from this is, inevitably, a marriage and a death. Snow White and the Prince marry. The Queen is invited to the wedding and puts on a pair of iron slippers that were heated over a stove; she dances herself to death.

When I first started to learn to play the tin whistle, my wife complained that I was playing the same tune over and over again. I wasn't, but to her ear there is only one Irish tune. What the Grimm Brothers' work shows us is not quite that there is but a single German fairy tale, but rather that quite subtle variations on very similar themes can create an almost infinite number of compelling stories. Small manipulations of key ingredients of plot, character, motivation, and environment can produce strikingly different effects. In each fairy tale, the characters differ subtly, their life circumstances differ subtly, their conflicts differ subtly, and the story's resolutions differ subtly. But almost every fairy tale ever told has a hero (humble or exalted), a fierce antagonist (magical or not), an expulsion (out of the home into inhospitable terrain), an ominous threat (with cannibalism or carnivory or without them), an overcoming of arduous circumstances (with or without the assistance of a royal personage), a retribution (with or without boiling oil), and a resolution (with or without a marriage). And yet a fine tale is always greater than the sum of its parts.

The plots of these tales, as we have seen, can be straightforward, even when the plot is macabre. The narrative of "Hansel and Gretel," for example, follows along quite tidily from scene to anxious scene: children are dumped in the forest, captured by a carnivorous crone, the crone is murdered, a family is reunited, and they all live in perpetual wealth, which is to say happily ever after. The plot is sequenced fairly logically. Other fairy tales, however, have a cryptic, indeed convoluted, logic of their own. In "The Twelve Brothers," for example, a king resolves to behead twelve sons so that his thirteenth child, a daughter, will inherit his kingdom. The sons escape and years later their sister locates them and serves them as maid in their cave in the forest. [*So far so good, I suppose.*] The sister then leaves her brothers' cave and picks lilies. [*Fine.*] The lilies are actually her brothers! [*What's this now?*] But then brothers are no longer plucked lilies—they have been transformed into ravens. [*Excuse me, did you say "transformed into ravens"?*] The logic in such a story is not at all a sequential one.

Perhaps it is the case that the fairy tales that remain most popular today are the ones that are more conventionally plotted. Eccentrically plotted stories like "The Twelve Brothers" are less often included in collections. Perhaps these latter tales have been so worn by retelling, that certain parts—those that connect the episodes—have simply been rubbed away over time. For whatever the reason, it's clear that for a story to work, it need not be efficiently designed. What matters is that they delve into consequential themes. In "The Twelve Brothers," it may not matter that the brothers are lilies or even that they then become ravens, for the story gets at deeper and more captivating themes. Realizing that she has turned her brothers into ravens, the sister sacrifices herself first by taking a vow of silence, then by her immolation at the hands of her husband the king, before finally reunited with her estranged siblings, who save her from the flames. Grimm's fairy tales, both popular and neglected, are united by their often being existential meditations on human relationships, and by their evocation of both the environmental setting and the ecological and economic restrictions of such relationships. Collectively, these tales add up to a master class on perseverance, cooperation, loyalty, and overcoming life's trials and tribulations. If, for reasons that I won't presume to judge you on, you happen to identify with the malevolent characters in Grimm fairy tales, perhaps there's something to be learned in these stories about unspeakable ways to die. Perhaps in general we all need to know more about death, even at a tender age.

For all of their variations and idiosyncrasies, the existential questions examined in the tales remain the same. Fairy tales pare life down to its concrete essentials, and each tale is a semaphored transmission on matters of vital concern. The themes of sibling rivalry, of loyalty, friendship, and enmity between people and animals, of human beauty and its absence, and of caregiving and neglect (especially of children) are critical ones. At the core of each tale, then, is the question "What is it to be human?" (Though is this not the core of every great tale?) The themes are economic. They play out in locations domesticated or wild, in landscapes that are familiar or disorienting, and they center on issues of food: starvation or plenty, appetites that are seemly or perverse, and creatures that are human or beastly. What this means for us is that inasmuch as fairy tales are about large emotions and issues of survival in circumstances that are very often harsh, fairy tales are axiomatically environmental tales.

In addition to reflecting the themes of human relations, Grimm fairy tales also manifest the differences between landscapes domestic and wild in concrete ways. This makes them environmental stories par excellence. There is an antagonism in the stories between lands that have been bent to human purpose—the ones that are plowed, tended, and densely settled—and those beyond direct human control. And though death dwells in the towns and villages too, death, in stories at least, choses more pernicious and capricious agents in the wilds. To die in one's sleep in one's own bed in one's little house is more wholesome to contemplate than being torn apart by wild beasts. "Hansel and Gretel," "Little Brother and Little Sister," and "Little Snow White" all reflect upon death by ravenous animals. *Damnatio ad bestias* may have disappeared with other observances of the ancient world, and yet we subject ourselves to a contemplation of the practice whenever we crack open a book of fairy tales.

What characterizes wilderness in a fairy tale is that a hero may visit but the hero may not remain there. Thus the wilderness of fairy tales conforms to the spirit of legislative wilderness.[6] Its permanent residents are the wild creatures, many of them innocuous of course, though many of them menacing, and some of them quite deranged. Named innocuous animals in Grimm fairy tales, those that live in the forest or in lands or waters beyond the limits of the town, are birds (many species), frogs, toads, ants, honeybees, fishes (many species), ducks and other wild fowl, hares, rabbits, deer, mice, hedgehogs, foxes, worms, and the very occasional snail. Lurking in the wilderness also are beasts of fiercer habits: lions, boars, bears, wolves, eagles, whales, snakes, and dragons. Those humans who live in the wildlands in fairy tales are of the suspicious kind: witches, sorcerers, giants, and at least one wild man. These unsavory types make their way in the world by magic, torment, and, with troubling frequency, cannibalism.

Differences between domesticated lands and wildlands are economic. On one side of the divide, the economy of people prevails; on the other side, the economy of nature is paramount. That being said, it is not quite as clear-cut as this. The logic that dominates the human-dominated side of the forest is, of course, the logic of capitalism, but in "Hansel and Gretel," for example, it is clear that forays into the woodland provide economic resources for woodcutter and his family, and serve as a reminder that our most fundamental sources of wealth derive from the other side of the fence. Our woodcutter must select the wood, cut the wood, and prepare it for market by transforming it into a tradable commodity. His failure to make ends meet propels the narrative: his family is starving and this is why he agrees to forfeit his children. But the forest does not give a whit for his or their fate, for this is the remorselessness of the wilds.

Although the economic affairs of larger landscape are more intense on the human-dominated side, it's only on that side that they can fail. Failure on the wild side is just another name for ecology, just as ecology's other name is success. Or to put this another way: living and dying are both ecological terms.

Chronic hunger and thirst are mentioned in several of the stories. A young girl in "The Old Woman in the Forest" whose party is way-laid in the forest and is left alone cries out: "I'm bound to starve to death." A dove who is, in fact, a prince comes to her aid. In "Hansel and Gretel," as we have already seen, it's the woodcutter's failure to feed his family that gets the plot moving. The solution is to dispatch the children to the forest. In "Little Brother and Little Sister," their stepmother's failure to provide for them leads the children into the forest. And later, when that evil person finds them in the forest, she exploits their thirst to lure them to the stream that turns the little brother into a fawn. Hunger, either temporary or profound, is men-tioned in fourteen stories.

Two additional hunger stories should be commented on, however briefly. These are "The Sweet Porridge" and "The Children of Famine." The first has a tangential connection to the forest; the other is a spare meditation on the melancholia of hunger. In "The Sweet Porridge," a mother and daughter are starving. The girl "went out to the forest where she met an old woman." The woman gives the starving girl a small pot. This enchanted pot obeys the instruction "Little pot, cook," by making sweet millet porridge. Once the porridge is done, the pot is given the simple instruction "Little pot, stop," and the pot stops cooking. One day the mother goes out, but forgets to stop the inde-fatigable pot and it overflows, filling first the kitchen, then the house, and so on, "as if it wanted to feed the entire world." When there is only one house left standing, the girl returns and stops the pot. "The Children of Famine" is shorter and more traumatic. A mother and her two daughters are starving. The mother becomes "unhinged and desperate." She says to her children, "I've got to kill you so I can have something to eat." Twice the children thwart their mother-turned-monster. Finally, the children respond to their mother, saying: "We'll lie down and sleep, and we won't get up again until the Judgment Day arrives." They sleep, and their mother departs.

Grimm's fairy tales give us a sustained meditation on our relationship with wild animals. Sometimes these animals, like Hans the Hedgehog, are quite eccentric ones. No short summary of "Hans My Hedgehog" can do the complete insanity of this story justice. A childless couple declare that they "want to have a child, even if it's a hedgehog." A son is born whose upper half is hedgehog and lower half is human. His father buys him bagpipes![7] Hedgehog boy leaves for the forest astride a rooster (who, by the way, wears shoes). In the forest Hans lives in a tree and tends to his flock of donkeys and pigs. His "beautiful music" attracts a king who is lost. The king seems to pledge his daughter to Hans. A second king does the same. Eventually Hans weds—though his bride, quite rightly, is concerned that his quills will damage her. And on his wedding night, he "slips out of his hedgehog's skin," and four men throw the skin into the fire. Hans is now a prince. Improbably, they all live happily (and unpunctured) ever after.

Hans, our hedgehog boy, is a curious hybrid between wild and domesticated. However, more typically in a Grimm fairy tale, the line distinguishing the wild and domesticated is not so confused. On the one side, you have tame animals, domesticated stock, even some exotic creatures, including an occasional elephant and monkey or two. The forest has its own set of beasts. These range from the placid to the abominable. It is fear of wilder animals that creates the greatest anxiety when it comes to the forested wilderness. A wild boar, for example, in "The Singing Bone" causes "great damage throughout the entire country." It prevents everyone from entering into the forest. (It's killed by the simpleton younger brother of the two men who then proceed to beat the simpleton up after he kills the boar—the king had offered his daughter for marriage to the one who killed the boar.) Terms such as the following abound: "torn to pieces by wild beasts" ("Little Brother and Little Sister"); "abandon them to wild beasts" ("Hansel and Gretel"); "the beast had certainly eaten the grandmother" ("Little Red Cap"); "a gruesome beast is sitting in my cave with terrifying fiery eyes" ("Little Magic Table, the Golden Donkey, and the Club in the Sack"); "anyway, he thought the wild beasts in the forest would soon devour her" ("Little Snow White"); "so he turned around and saw a large black beast that shouted 'Return my rose to me, or I'll kill you!'" ("The Summer and the Winter Garden").

In a brilliant, if controversial, essay on the lines of demarcation between wilderness and the domesticated realm, entitled "The Incarceration of Wildness," scholar Thomas Birch writes:

> At the center of Western culture's incarceration of wildness is its prevailing (mis)understanding of otherness as adversarial, as recalcitrant toward the law, as therefore irrational, criminal, outlaw, even criminally insane (like the grizzly bear).[8]

If you want to visit the maximum security facility for wildness—without running the risk of being torn asunder by wild beasts—just read a Grimm's fairy tale.

€ ⋆

To be human in a fairy tale is to struggle, to endure, to relate to others, to flourish if one can, to materially prosper if one can, to marry royalty if one can, and to avenge oneself, because one must, with fire, oil, or by tossing one's enemies to the wild beasts. Fairy tales are existentially and ecologically instructive to children—though one may hope that children don't take false comfort from the prospect of coaxing a corpse back to life with a kiss—because they dramatize the human situation and our environmental circumstances in profoundly material ways. To put this another and more concrete way:

the human dilemmas in fairy tales are set against a background of well-explicated environmental limits and biological realities. Fantastical though they may be, fairy tales do not neglect the sorts of realities that many other stories do.

Everything is connected is a well-known ecological maxim. But a less-known codicil is that some things are more connected than others. For the most part, we conduct our daily business in tame lands. But there are times when one must venture to the periphery. Folk and fairy tales illustrate to children and adults that this can be a fraught business—as the foreign prince discovered in his encounter with the churl—or they can be transformative, as several characters in Grimm's fairy tales discovered after entering the forest and living to tell the tale.

11

"Gollumgate"

The visitor center for the Burren National Park is tucked away on the ground floor of the Clare Heritage Centre in the tiny town of Corofin, county Clare in Ireland. When I dropped by on a June morning a year ago, I was somewhat taken aback to find that stowed away behind the geological information, the botanical guides, and a stuffed and handsomely displayed mountain goat, there was a speculative exhibit on the relationship between the landscape of that region and the work of scholar and novelist J. R. R. Tolkien. The only thing that "Nuala"— let's call her this to preserve her anonymity—the steward working that day, could tell me about its genesis was that "there's a local fella who thinks that Tolkien had gotten the name of Gollum from around here. I don't know if it's true."[1] Gollum is the demented hobbit who was degraded by his lifelong (and long-life) obsession with the One Ring, an evil jewel that is central to the plot of Tolkien's Lord of the Rings trilogy. The text of the exhibit conjectures on possible links between the landscape of the Burren and both the cave in which Gollum was found in the Misty Mountains and the desolate lands surrounding Mordor where Sauron the Necromancer resided.

The landscape of the Burren—a distinctive and extensive area of karst topography in the West of Ireland—was produced by mildly acidic rain falling for an eon on Carboniferous limestone. A small part of this landscape has been designated a national park since 1991. From the center of the Burren, bare blocks of limestone pavement stretch away as far as the eye can see. Between the blocks are deep crevices, called grykes, that provide habitat for a profusion of plants below the nibbling teeth of grazing cattle. The area is scientifically interesting for this diverse plant community, the antiquity of its archaeological finds, and its geological features, including the longest cave system in Ireland.[2]

The story behind the claim that Tolkien was influenced by the landscape of the Burren is this. On four occasions from the late 1940s through the 1950s, Tolkien in his capacity as an Oxford professor served as an external examiner at University College Galway. External examiners are invited to Irish universities to certify that academic standards are being upheld, advise on disputes about borderline students, and perform a variety of other sundry academic tasks. Tolkien and his host in Galway, Professor Murphy, the chair of the English Department, became good friends and traveled around the West of Ireland together. The trips would include excursions to the Burren, where they stayed with Dr. Florence Martyn, a Burren expert of some renown. Assumably, Tolkien was introduced to the Burren's extensive cave system during one of these visits.

Poll Na gColm (rendered into English as Pollnagollum, and translated as "the hole of the dove") is the entrance to a tunnel that threads its way about sixteen kilometers under the Burren limestone. The local lore has it that the name of the cave entrance and the landscape surrounding it inspired Tolkien and influenced the Lord of the Rings trilogy, which he was in the thick of editing at the time. An especially delightful part of this yarn is that Gollum's distinctive swallowing ("Gollum") is reminiscent of the vocalization of rock doves living in the cave entrance. A problem with this theory is that Tolkien's visits to Eire (as he often called the southern Republic of Ireland) occurred long after the creation of Gollum, who first appeared in *The Hobbit*, published in 1937. So there's that. As far as I can establish, there is absolutely no mention of the Burren in Tolkien's letters (nor of counties Clare or Galway). In addition, in a letter dated June 30, 1955, to his American publisher, Houghton Mifflin, Tolkien wrote, "I have spent a good deal of time in Ireland, and am since last July actually a D. Litt. of University College Dublin; but be it noted I first set foot in 'Eire' in 1949 after The Lord of the Rings was finished."[3] It seems like Tolkien was keen to disavow any Irish connection to his creative endeavors.

Perhaps more interesting than conjectures about the influence of any one locale within the Irish landscape and the writing of specific sections of Tolkien's work is the question of the author's relationship with Ireland in general. This is more than just parochially interesting since Ireland was one of the few places outside of Britain to which Tolkien regularly traveled, and the country clearly made enough of an impact on him that he makes frequent references to Ireland in his correspondence.

Though he was a relatively untraveled man, Tolkien visited Ireland quite frequently, starting with his professional visits to Galway in 1949. He expressed some ambivalence about the country, but in his ambivalence about Ireland there seems to be something important. It may indicate that ruminations about Ireland informed, or perhaps at the very least confirmed for him, that a landscape can provoke both light and dark moods.

The ambition motivating the writing of Tolkien's legendarium was to produce a founding mythology for English culture. As Tolkien wrote to Milton Waldman, an influential literary adviser in London, late in 1951: "I hope I shall not sound absurd—I was from early days grieved by the poverty of my own beloved country: it had no stories of its own (bound up with its tongue and soil), not of the quality that I sought, and found (as an ingredient) in legends of other lands." He was familiar enough with the European traditions including Finnish, for which he had a great admiration, but there was nothing in the English tradition that was not "impoverished chap-book stuff." Could Celtic mythology perhaps be a useful foundation for his work? Apparently not. As early as 1937, he wrote to his English publisher Unwin: "I do know Celtic things (mainly in their original languages

Irish and Welsh), and feel for them a certain distaste: largely for their fundamental unreason." It was especially irritating to him when an early reader found *The Silmarillion* (in manuscript form) to have "a certain beauty, but of a 'Celtic' kind irritating to Anglo-Saxons."[4] (In fact, Tolkien returned time and again in his letters to this reader's assessment of *The Silmarillion*—it clearly bothered him quite a bit.)

There is little doubt that Tolkien's disdain for all things Celtic left him with a lifelong suspicion about the Irish language. In his letters in various places, he wrote: "The Irish language I find wholly unattractive," and "I have no liking at all for Gaelic from Old Irish downwards." Besides, Tolkien found the language difficult: "I have always been rather heavily defeated by Old Irish." Despite this, he liked the Irish people well enough, claiming that he was fond of the country "and of (most of) its people."

Of the Irish landscape, Tolkien reserved his most peculiar comments. In the transcript of dialogue between Clyde S. Kilby (a US Tolkien expert), Humphrey Carpenter (Tolkien's biographer), and George Sayer (a mutual friend of Tolkien's and C. S. Lewis's) that took place on September 29, 1979, in Wheaton, Illinois, Sayer shared the following anecdote:

> I've gone for one or two walks with Tolkien, and he did talk to me about natural scenes he visited. One of the things I noticed, which surprised me from the start, was the way in which he regarded certain natural scenes as evil. This came up most strongly after he'd been examining in order—that is to say classifying students in an Irish University according to their achievements in the English language and literature. He described Ireland as a country *naturally evil*. He said he could feel evil coming from the earth, from the peat bogs, from the clumps of trees, even from the cliffs, and *this evil was only held in check by the great devotion of the southern Irish to their religion*. This was a very strange view, and was not one I could even have guessed. (Emphasis mine.)[5]

The statement has been regarded as perplexing by a number of commentators. The anecdote does not show up anywhere else in the works of any of these men; it's confined to this one snippet. Certainly, Tolkien says nothing close to Ireland being "evil" in any of his letters. It may be tempting to dismiss the story as a piece of blarney. But let's not be too hasty: in this assessment of Ireland, there may be an important clue to Tolkien's general understanding of the relationship between living beings and landscapes in all of this. The landscapes of Ireland can be related to in both a positive and negative way; this is the case for the landscapes of Middle-earth.

In a letter that C. S. Lewis wrote to Arthur Greeves (dated June 22, 1930), Lewis recalled that

> Tolkien once remarked to me that the feeling about home must have been quite different in the days when the family had fed on the produce of the same few miles of country for six generations, and that perhaps this was why they saw nymphs in the fountains and dryads in the wood—they were not mistaken for there was in a sense a real (not metaphorical) connection between them and the countryside.[6]

In this largely positive sense, then, a people well familiar with the land are attuned in a vital way to the place: they see things that others may not see. They feel at home there—and something is lost when people move around too much. Tolkien's comments about the natural evil of Ireland is a reflection of this same sensibility, though this time with a negative valence. If a place emanates evil, this too is felt by the people who reside there. In Ireland, local people sense the spirit of the place, but this is not personified as nymphs in the fountains and dryads in the wood. Not all the magical fauna of Ireland is quite so benign—Irish faeries are beasts of more checkered disposition that Tolkien's stately elves, his pastoral hobbits, or his tough-minded but shepherdly Ents. The Irish countryside was, besides, wilder than the ones he was more familiar with at home in England. Perhaps, like the language, the land was "fundamentally unreasonable." In this sense then, Ireland may have seemed "naturally evil." This evil is held in check by "the great devotion of the southern Irish to their religion."

It is undoubtedly the case that the mood of landscapes in Middle-earth, like those of Ireland, can at times "feel evil" and that this evil emanates from "the earth, from the . . . bogs, from the clumps of trees." Just as tranquility reigns in Ireland as a consequence of the devotion of its prayerful community, peace can be restored to Middle-earth, perhaps, through the devotion of the brighter beings of that world. Perhaps, there is something Irish about hobbits, after all.

In an e-mail exchange with the Burren National Park about their Tolkien exhibit, I expressed my doubts about the claim that Gollum's name derived from features of that landscape. Finally, a park representative wrote saying that "perhaps we will never know." Though Gollum assuredly does not come from county Clare, on the question of whether Ireland had a direct influence on Tolkien, it is, I agree, much harder to say.

12

"I Am in Fact a Hobbit"

TOLKIEN AS ENVIRONMENTALIST

Tolkien and the Trees

In a letter to the *Daily Telegraph* newspaper dated June 30, 1972, J. R. R. Tolkien responded to an article entitled "Forestry and Us," which included the following sentence: "Sheepwalks where you could once ramble are transformed into a kind of Tolkien gloom, where no birds sing. . . ." What irritated Tolkien was to see his name used as an adjective that intensified gloom. In his reply, he wrote, famously, that "in all my works I take the part of the trees as against all of their enemies."[1]

Tolkien enjoyed a lifelong relationship with trees and undoubtedly qualifies as an early environmentalist. His mother, Mabel, was his first botany tutor, and according to Humphrey Carpenter, Tolkien's biographer, under her instruction he became quite an accomplished botanical artist, though, apparently, he was more concerned with capturing the feeling of plants rather than their anatomical details.

An attentiveness to the central role that nature plays in shaping the fates of his characters is obvious throughout the Tolkien legendarium. Nature themes are expressed across the work: nature in its quiet affability in the Shire, in its fearsome inhospitality in marsh and mountaintop, in its strange otherness in the forest, and in its fecund diversity in the inventiveness of Tolkien's creatures. For all of his sensitivity to nature in its many manifestations, Tolkien was

not a traditional naturalist: his was, for the most part, a contemplative immersion in the natural world rather than a corporeal one—he
didn't go into nature much! It seems as if the labors that he devoted
to inventing his own world—what Tolkien called his work of "sub-
creation"—afforded him a level of engagement with nature that other
environmental writers find in strenuous cavorting in the wild.

€ ★

J. R. R. Tolkien was born in South Africa in 1892, though his family
moved back to England; after the death of his father, Arthur Tolkien, the family soon moved to a cottage in the small town of Sarehole. At the time the Tolkiens lived there, the cottage was located far
enough outside Birmingham for it to feel like it was in the English
countryside. Tolkien's time in Sarehole allowed him later in life to
claim that he lived his "early years in 'the Shire' in a premechanical
age." Orphaned at thirteen, Tolkien and his brother, who was a couple of years his junior, moved into Birmingham to live with an aunt.
As Carpenter writes in *J. R. R. Tolkien: A Biography* (1977), Tolkien's
"feelings towards the rural life now became emotionally charged
with personal bereavement."[2] In later years he amusingly referred
to himself as a hobbit "(in all but size)." He was hobbit-like in his
habits and inclinations; he liked "gardens, trees and unmechanized
farmlands; I smoke a pipe, and like good plain food (unrefrigerated),
but detest French cooking; I like, and even dare to wear in these dull
days, ornamental waistcoats." And though there is no record of the
opinions of hobbits on French cuisine, the other characteristics are
consistent enough with hobbitish ways for us to reasonably claim
that hobbits, in their turn, are quite Tolkienesque (in all but size).[3]

In a fascinating chapter in his biography of Tolkien, Carpenter
reflects on a series of photographs taken of Tolkien over the years and
observes "the almost unvarying ordinariness of the backgrounds."
Tolkien was "entirely conventional" in the places that he lived, and
even in the places he visited. In the summertime the Tolkien family

left the travails of ordinary life to visit fairly ordinary places on their vacations. And although Tolkien enjoyed driving a car for a bit, not being mechanically inclined, he abandoned this interest before the Second World War. Tolkien rarely joined his friend C. S. Lewis in the strenuous cross-country walks that that writer enjoyed. All of this is to say that the source of Tolkien's environmentalism is not found in an immersion in immense and iconic natural places.

But for all of that, Tolkien was clearly not indifferent to his surroundings. In 1933 he revisited his childhood home in Sarehole and was outraged by what he saw; it had become a "huge tram-ridden meaningless suburb where I actually lost my way." Tolkien went on to remark, "How I envy those whose precious early scenery has not been exposed to such violent and peculiarly hideous change." What Tolkien is expressing here is an excellent illustration of what environmental philosopher Glenn Albrecht calls "solastalgia," a concept we encountered in a previous chapter. Solastalgia is the melancholy mood that descends upon you when a familiar landscape is degraded or destroyed. What is often mistaken for nostalgia in Tolkien's work, a hankering for the past, may actually be solastalgia, a grieving over environmental destruction.

The loss of the British countryside became a point of moderate obsession with Tolkien. In his "I am in fact a Hobbit" letter to scholar Deborah Webster, he complained about the state of Wales. He loved Wales, or at least "what is left of it, when mines, and the even more ghastly sea-side resorts, have done their worst." As his opinions on this matter became ever more entrenched, Tolkien refused to visit woodlands and nature preserves for fear of finding them destroyed. And so, a man whose encounters with nature were already largely cerebral ones retreated to the task of creation of the mirror environment of Middle-earth and the other regions of Eä ("The World that Is," Tolkien's name for the world). A man of Tolkien's imaginative powers may have needed very little in the way of external stimulation to create a persuasive alternative to this world. As he witnessed the destruction of the British countryside, Tolkien became gloomy and apocalyptic. Despite his protestations to the editor of the *Daily Telegraph*, gloom undeniably pervades his sub-creation. Though Tolkien might justifiably claim that he "takes the part of the trees," this does not mean that the tone of the work is relentlessly optimistic; it's not.

€ ⋆

Tolkien didn't spend much time in nature preserves—his several visits to Ireland in the 1950s may have been influential exceptions—nonetheless, the fate of individual trees was an occasional source of concern for him. Early in his life, he witnessed the wanton destruction of a tree and it shook him. He wrote, "There was a willow hanging over the mill-pool and I learned to climb it. It belonged to a butcher on the Stratford Road, I think. One day they cut it down. They didn't do anything with it: the log just lay there. I never forgot that."[4] Outside the Tolkien family home in Oxford, there grew a very large poplar tree. Tolkien loved it but "was anxious about it." The tree had been mutilated but it grew back, not as grandly as before, but Tolkien enjoyed the company of the tree. His Oxford neighbor, Lady Agnew, agitated to have it cut down, for she feared it would fall on her house in a storm. Besides, it cut the sun from her house. Tolkien was in high dudgeon over the matter. He wrote that "any wind that could have uprooted it and hurled it on her house, would have demolished her and her house without any assistance from the tree." "Every tree," he wrote, "has its enemy, few have an advocate."

In contemplating this inclination to hatred of trees, Tolkien observed that "the hate is irrational, a fear of anything large and alive, and not easily tamed or destroyed." Trees, whether growing singly outside his window or in a wooded community, represented not just Tolkien's aesthetic preferences, but also his conception of the wild. Part of the appeal of the wild for Tolkien is its element of the capriciousness; wild nature is something beyond our easy control and resists our attempts to mechanize it. A strong wind, after all, might in the right circumstances hurtle a tree into her ladyship's house.

In Tolkien's anxious reflections about trees, he also had in mind concerns about his own "internal Tree, *The Lord of the Rings*," which, it seemed to him at the time, would never be finished. Would he be unable to complete it, as happened to Niggle, the artist, in Tolkien's short story "Leaf by Niggle" (1945)?[5] In that story Niggle finds himself interrupted in his painting of a canvas of a great tree that is depicted with a forest in the distance. And in darker times, the tree came to represent Tolkien's own mortality. After the death of C. S. Lewis, Tolkien described himself as being like an old tree "that is losing all its leaves one by one: this feels like an axe-blow near the roots."

Fretfulness over the fate of trees in his life spilled over into Tolkien's fiction. The detailed natural history in Tolkien's work is quite remarkable. Tolkien describes dragons, orcs (goblinesque creatures), trolls, wraiths (phantom-like, "undead" beings), birds, beasts in great variety, and insects of all sorts. My favorite of the latter are the Flies of Mordor—naturally, they suck blood—which are marked with a red eye-shape on their backs, each and every one of them. And then there are the trees: beech, birch, holly, and willow are all given elvish names, and play a role in the narrative. Of especial importance are Ents (tree-herds) and Huorns (tree spirits). Ents are a species related to trees and are, besides, like Tolkien, the protectors of trees.

If you were to set aside the adventures concerning rings, malevolent sorcerers, military turmoil, lengthy creation mythology, and so on, Tolkien's fiction would still be celebrated for conceiving the largest ever fictional arboretum.

Trees were beings of special preoccupation for Tolkien. A love of trees was important from the time of his boyhood botanical instruction by his beloved mother and endured in his love of individual trees throughout his life; eventually trees became a metaphor for the growth of his work and the aging of his body. In the legendarium, as in his life, trees are significant individually and collectively.

Trees in their collective form, in forests and woodlands, form a central part of Tolkien's writings on wilderness, the theme we turn to next.

Hobbits in the Wilderness

Tolkien wrote but a single story, but he wrote it well, and it took several volumes, written over the course of a lifetime, to tell; indeed, the author died before the universe that he was creating was fully realized. One might start out as a young child by reading "Leaf by Niggle," *The Hobbit*, and *Farmer Giles of Ham* (1949), then progress to the Lord of the Rings trilogy as a teen reader, revisit these volumes several times as an adult, before progressing to *The Silmarillion* (1977) or other posthumously published titles from the legendarium with advancing maturity (one might even delve into the poetry, or take up the academic work), before dying in the peaceful slumbers of old age, clasping in your frail hands a frayed copy of *Unfinished Tales of Númenor and Middle-earth* (1980).[6]

Tolkien's work alternates between the pastoral loveliness of places like the Shire—where dwelt hobbits—to forested and mountainous wildernesses. These are some of the more formidable wilderness regions created in literature.

For all of that, the word "wilderness" itself is actually seldom used by Tolkien (a mere twenty-one times in the Lord of the Rings trilogy, for example). Indeed, the word is not as frequently used in Britain and Europe as it is in North America. When Tolkien employed it, it invariably refers to desolate places. On some occasions, he used it to refer specifically to regions of unkempt vegetation, to tumbled rock and boulder, and to unpopulated lands. Mountainous wilderness is the most prevalent in kind in the Lord of the Rings trilogy (mainly in reference to the Misty Mountains) (mentioned collectively 569 times). Forests come next (189 times). In addition, these other toilsome habitats are mentioned: marshes (47 times), bogs (10), mires

(5), grasslands (5), and (1 "tumbled") heathland. Even when he does not use the term "wilderness," his meaning is clear: there is an abundance of harsh terrain in Middle-earth.

Tolkien structured most of his adventures as quests in which characters pick their way across vast wildernesses and inhospitable landscapes. Wilderness in the Tolkien sense is connoted by the possibility of encounters with beings, events, and physical circumstances that are inimical to the well-being of a hero. The hero's objective is to endure such encounters and, ultimately, to prevail in the face of such challenges. That is not to say that wilderness does not, in some cases, triumph and repel our characters.

In addition to this sense of wilderness as a challenging place, Tolkien also anticipated a more contemporary definition of that term. He did so by recognizing that a wilderness is not merely an inclement place, but is both a *mood* and an *anticipation* about what lies along the road ahead. This may be what he learned, as we have seen, from his encounters with Irish landscapes.

Consistently across his many volumes, and with increasing intensity, Tolkien finds a way to forewarn his characters of the perils that lie ahead before they strike off into the wilds. A creature living in tumultuous times takes leave of their pastoral home, journeys through formidable landscapes, completes a heroic task, and, though he retires back to domesticity, is irrevocably changed by their experience. Conspicuously, this is Bilbo Baggins's story, and Frodo's, but also with considerable variation, Gandalf's, Strider's, Sam's, Merry's, Pippin's, innumerable elves' and dwarves', and it is the story of humans.

A few instances of wilderness travel in Tolkien's work are worth mentioning.

As the heroes of *The Hobbit*—Bilbo Baggins and his accompanying band of questing dwarves—enter the great forest of Mirkwood, the warnings are stark. In that Third Age of Middle-earth—the period in Tolkien's legendarium when the action of *The Hobbit* and the subsequent trilogy takes place—the vast forest of Mirkwood has fallen under the power of Sauron, a powerful Necromancer. By the time the band passes through it, that forest is breathless, dark, and populated by horrifying beasts. As they set out, Gandalf, the wizard who is patron of their adventure, cautions the company not to stray far from the path. If they were to leave the forest trail, Gandalf says, "it is a thousand to one you will never find it again and never get out of Mirkwood: and then I don't suppose I, or anyone else, will ever see you again." Fair warning!

And yet the company presses on, for they must. Of course, they wander off the path, and the consequences are fateful.

The pattern that Tolkien had pioneered in *The Hobbit*—that of forewarning the characters of what to expect in the wilderness and then confirming their worst suspicious—is one that he intensifies in the Lord of the Rings trilogy.

In *The Fellowship of the Ring* (1954), the first volume of the trilogy and sequel to *The Hobbit*, a lengthy chapter is devoted to the traversing of the Old Forest.[7] This time it is Frodo Baggins—the nephew of Bilbo from whom Frodo had just inherited the One Ring, a piece of jewelry that will determine the fate of Middle-earth—who must pass through a forested wilderness. The ring—a magically powerful one—has attracted some undesirable attention. Thus Frodo must leave the safety of the Shire, the ancestral home of the hobbits, accompanied by his gardener, Samwise Gamgee, and a couple of local hobbit youths, Merry and Pippin. The Old Forest, a woodland formerly of tremendous size, has in the Third Age been reduced to a small fragment adjacent to the Shire. (In this, and in describing similar contractions of the woodlands in his novels, Tolkien expressed his anxiety about the fate of forests in our world.) The greatest mischief there was caused by, of all beings, the trees themselves, some of which were inhabited by seemingly malevolent trees spirits (such trees, though they are not all mischievous, are always brooding; Tolkien names them "Huorns"). The hobbits of the Shire had, some years earlier, been obliged to fight off this forest. This battle was no mere weekend pruning; the hobbits had "cut down hundreds of trees, and made a great bonfire in the Forest."

And yet the hobbits enter the Old Forest, for they must. Let us follow along with them for a while.

"You won't have any luck in the Old Forest," Fatty Bolger, a friend of Frodo's, warns them before they enter. "No one ever has luck in there. You'll get lost. People don't go in there." To this warning, Merry somewhat optimistically retorts: "I have been in several times: usually in daylight of course, when the trees are sleepy and fairly quiet." Already we readers know to expect something unusual: for most of us will never have had concerns about the wakefulness of trees.

Shortly after entering the forest, the hobbits feel anxious. They sense that the forest does not like them. They move on. A branch crashes before them, and the trees appear to close in about them. The forest seems to be listening. Just when the hobbits think they have gotten their bearings, they discover that they are lost. Morning has turned to afternoon. They follow a path that leads along the side of the river Withywindle—a river they have been advised to avoid. The forest gets even denser, even more ominous:

> The hobbits began to feel very hot. There were armies of flies of all kinds buzzing around their ears, and the afternoon sun was burning on their backs. At last they came suddenly into a thin shade; grey branches reached across the path.

The hobbits become drowsy and sit down. One by one they fall asleep—an enchanted dream in that enchanted place. Frodo bends down to drink from the river, and before he knows it, he is in the

water. Beside him, "a great tree-root seemed to be over him and holding him down." Sam drags him from the water. After a time, Frodo
claims, "The beastly tree *threw* me in!" Meanwhile, Merry and Pippin
discover that the cleft in the willow tree against which they lay down
to sleep has closed about them and is beginning to entomb them.
Luckily for them, Tom Bombadil—a very old and complex character,
akin to a god—comes to their rescue. Singing to the willow tree, and
then thrashing it with a branch, Tom Bombadil gets the tree to release
the hobbits. The company then follows Tom out of the Old Forest
and away from immediate danger. They have escaped this wilderness.

Two Ways to Dwell

Alternating motion and stillness, passing through and settling down:
these are the poles of animal existence—whether that animal be a
hobbit, a person, a wizard, or an elf.

Edward S. Casey, a contemporary philosopher, argues that motion
and stasis bracket the dimensions of "dwelling." It's worth pausing to
examine what we mean by that important word. "Dwelling" is one of
those oddities in the English language: words that have *both* positive
and negative connotations, and often having opposing meanings.
As a verb, "to dwell" can have a range of meanings. It can mean "to
remain (in a house, country, etc.) as in a permanent residence" or to
"abide or continue for a time, in a place, state, or condition."[8] From
this we get "places of dwelling," which always sound quite cozy! On
the other hand, to dwell can mean "to lead into error, mislead, delude;
to stun, stupefy." Although this and related meanings are now somewhat obsolete, "dwelling" in this more somber sense can be traced
in its etymology. According to the *Oxford English Dictionary*, the word
"dwelling" comes from the Old English "dwalde," meaning "to lead
astray, hinder, delay; . . . to go astray, err; to be delayed, tarry." It also
has equivalents in Old High German, where "gitwelan" means "to be
stunned, benumbed, torpid, also to cease, leave off, give up." Related is

the Old English word "gedwolen," which has the additional meaning of "gone wrong, [and] perverted." Echoes of this can be heard in suggestions that we do not "dwell on sad news" or on morbid thoughts.

In his fascinating, though undeniably challenging, book *Getting Back into Place: Toward a Renewed Understanding of the Place-World* (1993), Edward S. Casey ruminates on the different ways that embodied creatures, such as you and I, can dwell.[9] Although the philosopher does not specifically include hobbits in his analysis, I think we can safely apply his thinking to these rotund creatures.

Casey distinguishes two forms of dwelling. The first dwelling is "hermetic dwelling," where, with the very wings of Hermes on our heels, we are propelled out of our homes, on into the spaces between them, and out along the dusty highways. For, as Casey writes, Hermes is the "god of roads and of wayfarers." Since ancient times, stories of Hermes depict him as clever, cunning, and dishonest. In *The Homeric Hymn to Hermes*, he is described as "wily and charming, a thief, a cattle-rustler, a bringer of dreams, a spy by night, a watcher at the door. . . ."[10] One of Hermes's roles was to lead the souls of the dead down to Hades. Though Hermes is the "Conductor of Souls" to hell, he could also, in certain circumstances, guide souls back again. For example, after Protesilaus, a hero in Homer's *The Iliad*, was killed in the Trojan War, Hermes returned the dead hero to his wife for only three hours before Protesilaus was returned to the underworld. To dwell with Hermes is to peregrinate, to thread a connection between one place and the next, and, yes, to risk being led astray.

The second form of dwelling is what Casey dubs "Hestial dwelling." This is the dwelling that has us curled up back at the hearth. To dwell hestially is to be at home, and to forgo movement even if only for a time. While the other Greek gods traveled and were venturesome, Hestia remained quietly at home on Mount Olympus. She vowed, besides, to forgo sexual love; as goddess of hearth and home, however, she is revered by all.[11] Hestia is the goddess we venerate when we lie beside our child at night and read them an adventure story. Hestia intensifies the possibility of adventure; her domain is the calm before the excitement begins. Hestia stops us in our tracks.

Casey also discusses dwelling in terms of cities and architecture. Hestial and hermetic dwelling are two aspects of inhabiting the built space of cities—in cities we get from place to place and also stay in place. But the whole wild world, of course, is our home, and the two sides of the (dwelling) coin can be applied at vaster scales that combine both the buildings of the domestic sphere and the natural places beyond the ken of ordinary mortals. Tolkien is the great writer of dwelling from this vaster perspective. He combines in his legendarium the two forms of dwelling but on the scale of Middle-earth in its entirety. Adventures concerning hobbits include periods of hestial dwelling in the Shire and Rivendell (the land of elves), as well as hermetic dwelling in forest, mountain, and in every monstrous wilderness that hobbits must pass through. To dwell hermetically in wilderness requires the cultivation of a special know-how. The hermetic hobbit must acquire a resilience and fortitude, and must, however begrudgingly, make peace with the wilds. The fate of Middle-earth depends upon it. Hobbits do not permanently dwell in wilderness, but some of them, the heroic ones, know it well.

Episodes of traversing wild places, in the dual spirit of Hermes and Hestia, are a staple of children's literature. The migration to and from Narnia by Peter, Susan, Edmund, and Lucy in C. S. Lewis's *The Lion, the Witch and the Wardrobe* (1950) is one example.[12] A strange but fascinating version is to be found in Walter de la Mare's *The Three Mulla-Mulgars* (1910), as the three royal monkeys—Thimble, Thumble, and Nod—traverse Africa in search of their father's land.[13] A very recent addition to the genre is Sara Pennypacker's *Pax* (2016).[14] More hestially inclined stories in wilderness, where the characters dig in to survive, include the robust survival tale *Hatchet* (1999) by Gary Paulsen.[15] Equally compelling are the books from the Little House on the Prairie series by Laura Ingalls Wilder, exploring the lives of the Ingalls family, and the influential tale *My Side of the Mountain* (1959) by Jean Craighead George.[16] So prevalent are such themes in books for children, I challenge you to find a book that does not reflect upon this one way or another.

13

The Tin Woodman's Path of Carnage through the Land of Oz

If you have not tallied the number of creatures the Tin Woodman (or Tin Man, to use his less formal moniker) wantonly slaughtered in L. Frank Baum's beloved classic *The Wonderful Wizard of Oz* (1900), let me help you out by providing a *catalogue raisonné* of the horror.[1]

The Tin Man is, naturally enough, a handy fellow when it comes to clearing a path through a forest; he hacked away at some troublesome branches in the forest that impeded the progress of the little company, which included Dorothy, a girl swept away from Kansas in a cyclone; her dog, Toto; a witless scarecrow; and a cowardly lion. They were making their way to the Emerald City, where dwelt the Wizard of Oz. One can hardly deny a woodman the exercise of his trade.

The killing started innocuously enough, as such things often do. As the company proceeded through the forest, the Tin Man trod on a beetle and killed it. Accidents will happen. The Tin Woodman "wept several tears of sorrow and regret." Not having a heart, the Tin Man vowed to be inordinately careful with creatures and not to be "cruel or unkind to anything." He even went so far as to beg the Cowardly Lion not to kill a deer, fearing that his tears over such a (justified) death would rust his head.

Despite this laudable circumspection in the matter of killing, the death toll started to mount. In the forests of Oz, the company was attacked by Kalidahs, which are monstrous creatures with "bodies like bears and heads like tigers." At the Scarecrow's suggestion, the

Tin Woodman chopped down a living tree to allow the group to cross a ditch. With Dorothy and friends safely over, the Tin Man hacked at the crown of the tree, which was then lying on their side of the ditch. Two Kalidahs fell with the tree and tumbled into the abyss, where they were "dashed to pieces on the sharp rocks at the bottom." I suppose we can chalk this up to quick thinking; after all, the company was under attack.

The Tin Woodman's ax did not lie idle for very long. Dorothy and friends passed through a deadly field of poppies that had a soporific effect on all of them. Both the Cowardly Lion and the girl fell into a deep sleep; the others stumbled out bearing Dorothy, though they left the lion, they think, to his eternal slumbers. Having passed through the field, the Tin Woodman turned to see a great yellow wildcat hurtling over the grass. It was surely chasing something: a gray field mouse as it happened. The Tin Woodman wasted no time and cut the wildcat's head "clean off its body." For emphasis, Baum wrote that the cat "rolled over at his feet in two pieces." One wonders if this might not have been avoided. A cat, even a wild one, might surely have been deflected by other means. But how and ever, in return for the useful murder, the field mouse—no ordinary field mouse, since it was none other than "the Queen of all the field-mice"—organized a work crew that hauled the Cowardly Lion from the poppy field.

By now our Tin Man has fully warmed to carnage. In a later clash with the minions of the Wicked Witch of the West, whom the company pledged to murder, the Tin Woodman went utterly berserk. Seeing the group draw close to her enclave, the Wicked Witch blew upon a silver whistle and gathered her wolves around her. She commanded the beasts to tear the company to pieces. As they approached, the Tin Woodman coolly proclaimed to the company, "This is my fight." His comrades drew behind him, and with his ax whistling the Tin man slew each wolf in turn. Each animal was relieved of its head, and when his bloody fury was sated, forty wolves lay dead in a heap before the tin monster.

Witnessing the complete annihilation of her wolves, the Wicked Witch of the West, reasonably enough, unleashed the wild crows. This time it was the Scarecrow who handled the animals; he caught the King Crow by the head "and twisted its neck until it died." And again, over the course of a morning's work, the Scarecrow slew forty of the birds. Next came the bees, determined to sting to death Dorothy and her barbarous friends. Once again the Tin Woodman drew himself up; the bees did not stand a chance. They shattered their stingers against his metal husk until, dead, they "lay scattered thick about the Woodman, like little heaps of fine coal." The Witch then sent in the flying monkeys. Need I saw more? (I will: they seized the Scarecrow and flung him upon sharp rocks; they did the same to the Woodman, who "lay so battered and dented that he could neither move nor groan." They pulled the straw out of the Scarecrow's clothes and head, then captured the Lion. Dorothy, who had been marked earlier in the story with the Good Witch's kiss upon her forehead, they left unmolested.)

Even still the Tin Woodman's macabre chores lay unfinished. Having recovered from his crushing defeat by the Winged Monkeys, and Dorothy having annihilated the Wicked Witch, the crew took one last ghoulish journey together. In order to consult with Glinda, the Good Witch of the South, about Dorothy's prospects for return to Kansas, they started across the wilderness. Impeding their progress was a hardy gang of fighting trees. These were the "policemen of the forest." As our boorish travelers attempted to enter the forest, the branches of the arboreal guardians bent down, grasped the Scarecrow, and hurled that twiggy fellow to the ground. By now the Tin Woodman—restrained no longer by promises to leave living things unharmed and hardened as he was in the forge of lusty battle—knew exactly what to do. As the tree reached down for him, the Woodman "chopped at it so fiercely that he cut it in two." The tree trembled with pain, and the tin fiend passed beneath it, not without taking one more swipe as a branch reached for Toto the dog.

So, what is the tally: two Kalidahs, a wildcat, forty wolves, countless bees, and a sentient tree. The Tin Woodman went on to become lord of the Winkies: native residents from the western quadrant of Oz. He's out there still no doubt, sharpening his ax. The Tin Woodman is a wilderness hero of the old school.

14

Hunger and Thirst in Suzanne Collins's *Hunger Games*

Wild Life in *The Hunger Games*

Stripped of its love story, its revolutionary politics, its sadistic violence, its acerbic commentary on televised obscenities, its laudable feminist sensibilities, its meditation on self-sacrifice and personal fortitude, and its interrogation of ethics in oppressive times, Suzanne Collins's *The Hunger Games* (2008) is essentially a wilderness adventure.[1] That being said, is not every story, the entire human story included—when stripped of its rarefied politics, its extraneous emotions, and the superficial polish of civilization—essentially a wilderness tale?

Unlike traditional survival tales, bathed as they often are in the sepia tones of nostalgia, *The Hunger Games* is a futuristic story. It takes place in the dystopian nation of Panem, which is the totalitarian state, set in an unspecified future time, that emerged after apocalyptic ecological and military events destroyed North America. Seventy-four years before the beginning of the story, the Capitol of Panem suppressed a rebellion by the thirteen districts that surrounded it. District 13 was supposedly obliterated after the rebellion. In subsequent years, as punishment for the uprising, each of the twelve remaining districts of Panem were expected to select by lottery two "tributes," a boy and girl between the ages of twelve and eighteen, to go to the Capitol to meet in gladiatorial-style combat and fight till only one remained. The (typically one) victor and their family then lived out their subsequent life in relative comfort. The games are played in an arena that is less Coliseum and more like harsh backcountry. This is decidedly not your grandma's wilderness, nor is it a place where only the forces of nature prevail. When the spectators of the Hunger Games' desire for frequent brutal confrontation is insufficiently sated, the Gamemakers can remotely intervene in the arena and, for example, set a conflagration that has all the tributes running for water and into one another's weapon-supplied arms. No one, I suppose, wants to witness a reality show where tributes grub about for food or drink their own urine—I suppose that in this matter, we readers must surely count ourselves among the squeamish spectators. So manipulations of the conditions of the wild arena are frequent and intense. Wilderness in the hands of the Gamemakers of the Hunger Games is both punishment for rebellion and a testing of mettle.

The story follows the fate in the 74th Hunger Games of the two tributes from District 12, which is an impoverished mining district formerly known as Appalachia. One of the tributes is our narrator, sixteen-year-old Katniss Everdeen, who volunteered in place of her younger sister Primrose; the other tribute is Peeta Mellark, also sixteen, the baker's son. The fates of both characters are linked. We witness their selection, preparation, their glamorous pregame presentation in the Capitol, and ultimately the survival struggle of the couple in the arena. Katniss and Peeta become something of a romantic couple. Peeta adopts the strategy with conviction, as he's loved Katniss since they were children; Katniss's affections for Peeta are perhaps more strategic. Our unfortunate couple is aware that if tributes appear sufficiently empathetic or impressive, they might secure sponsors from among the viewers of the Hunger Games. Sponsors may intervene in the games by parachuting in small but often important gifts: medicine and morsels of food, for example. And what in stern times is more likely to appeal to sponsors than youthful ardor? Love in the Hunger Games' arena becomes a survival strategy. Though love might emerge as the winning strategy, nonetheless the tactics that may win the games are founded on Katniss's survival skills. For ever since her father's early death in a mining accident deep beneath the surface of District 12, Katniss has been illegally hunting and gathering in the woods close to their settlement. Long before she ever entered an arena, Katniss has been winning her own hunger games on the home front.

Though it may not have the same snap as *The Hunger Games*, a more accurate title might have been *The Hunger and Thirst Games*. Collins is as attentive as an author can be to the fundamental biological needs of her characters. Being ecologically the creatures that we are, we are consumptive as well as consumable. In the Hunger Games arena, survival requires peerless skills at both finding food and avoiding consumption combined in an advantageous ratio. I should point out that though there are no rules governing behavior in the arena, nevertheless, direct consumption of defeated tributes is seemingly frowned upon. There had been an incident in previous games where a tribute "went completely savage" and made a meal of his foes. However, since cannibalism doesn't make for great TV, the Gamemakers intervened. Nevertheless, one could still benefit in the Hunger Games by possessing enhanced predatory skills as long as one stops short of ingesting human prey.

Thirst is royalty among the human needs. A person will die of thirst long before they die of hunger. Minimal hydration requirements depend upon a range of factors. We lose water to sweat, urine, bowel movements, and so forth, but the extent of these losses depends upon a variety of environmental factors as well as some inherent physiological factors that vary among individuals. Several scholarly sources indicate that the adequate daily intake of water for women is 2.2 liters of water a day and is a little more for men.[2]

As warm-blooded mammals of a moderate mass, we have to eat fairly frequently. There is more variability in human calorific requirements across cultures than there is for human water needs. Calorific requirements per person depend upon age, sex, height, and weight, cultural peculiarities, and individual activity pattern. A young female of Katniss Everdeen's age would require on average 2,300 calories a day, whereas males of Peeta Mellark's age need on average 2,800 calories a day.[3]

A slightly more gruesome way of interrogating the matter of how much food and water is required to sustain human life is to ask how long it would take for a person to die of starvation or thirst. The scientific literature is less precise on this matter than you might think. In one study of hunger striking, prisoners endured from 28 to 40 days. Other studies document that death by starvation can take as long as 73 days. Without water, however, death takes place in 10 to 14 days, though depending on an individual's health, death comes within a few days.[4]

☾⋆

Haymitch Abernathy, the only tribute from District 12 who had ever won the Hunger Games and Katniss and Peeta's reluctant coach for the 74th Hunger Games, has this last piece of advice for the tributes: "Put as put much distance as you can between yourselves and the others, and find a source of water." And if they accomplished this, he counseled that his tributes should try to "stay alive." They should consume first, and then avoid being caught. Therefore, as soon she enters the arena, Katniss reflects, realistically as we have seen in the discussion above, that without water she'd "deteriorate into helplessness and be dead in a week, tops." Her first significant challenge in the arena is to locate a source of water.

A surprising amount of *The Hunger Games* is taken up with Katniss's initial struggle to avoid dehydration and her efforts to find a source of water. (Indeed the theme is taken up at length again in 2009's *Catching Fire*, the second book of The Hunger Games trilogy.)[5] Katniss's first days pass without her finding water, though she discovers that there are game animals in the arena, and so she is able to eat. She finds berries that could provide welcome fluids, but astute natural historian that she is, she suspects them of being poisonous and abandons the tiny fruit. Another day passes. She feels fatigued yet climbs a tree to survey the landscape for water sources. Nothing. By the next day, her head is throbbing and her thinking has become muddled. She tries to weep in frustration but no tears flow. Her legs shake, her heart races, and she falls to the ground: she knows that the end is approaching. Katniss makes patterns in the mud where she lays down to die. And then she realizes that where there is mud, there must be water. Pond lilies grow close by, and there is a pool beneath the flowers. Katniss drinks and is refreshed.

From Katniss's initial expression of concern about dehydration to her success in finding water, seventeen pages elapse (that is about 4.5 percent of the book). Water, drinking, and thirst are mentioned more than one hundred times in *The Hunger Games*. Hunger and food and eating are mentioned almost as frequently. It's hard to imagine another novel intended for relatively youthful readers that devotes such attention to investigating basic human ecological necessities.

Passages devoted to thirst and hunger—of which the example above is just one of several—are immensely significant. This is not only because hunger and thirst are themselves immensely important human needs, but because these episodes allow Katniss to showcase her survival skills. Katniss is attuned to the environment, can read the landscape, knows her plants—the helpful and the malign ones—and is, besides, an accomplished trapper and hunter. Her acumen with a bow and arrow is her greatest asset. The considerable skills that Katniss brings to bear on basic survival are the very ones that also serve her in emerging victorious in the games.

After their minimal biological requirements are met—and we do not learn much of the others' trials, though we know they must have each struggled—the tributes are able to settle down to the grizzly task of annihilating each other. In fairness, Katniss is more the hunted than the hunter of humans in this story. The number of kills directly attributable to her are three out of the twenty-two who die. Just as Haymitch had advised, Katniss has found water and is able to survive. And, of course, love survives, because by using her knowledge of poisonous berries, she threatens the Gamemakers with an ingeniously conceived suicide pact between her and Peeta. The two together win the 74th Hunger Games.

☾ ★
★

Though *The Hunger Games* is set in a wilderness, it is not necessarily a beautiful place. This is not the sublime wilderness of the sort that inspires the nature mystics. One of the few truly beautiful events that occurs is the aftermath of the death of Rue, the elfin twelve-year-old female tribute from District 11 who was speared in a trap by another tribute. Katniss surrounds Rue's body with flowers and sings tenderly to her. But other than this evocative moment, there is little room for beauty in the Hunger Games. Rather, this is the sort of wilderness where one is tested and either found wanting or where one finds within herself what Aldo Leopold, the conservationist, knew: "Wilderness is the raw material out of which man has hammered the artifact called civilization." Katniss knows well this raw material, and thus she survives.

Section Four

Children on Wild Islands

OLD TOM'S ISLAND

Toward the end of his life, "Old Tom," who had spent his early years at sea with the British Navy and later with the Mercantile Marine, washed up on the shore of my hometown of Templeogue and set up camp on the traffic island—a roundabout—near the secondary school. His island was small and vegetated, and was separated from ordinary life by the steady stream of traffic that flowed between Walkinstown, Templeogue, and the southern suburbs, and on into Dublin city center.

The grass on Old Tom's island browned over in the winter, and in springtime and summer, the dandelions and daisies grew among the thick green sward. The island was slightly elevated at the center, and this is where Old Tom pitched his tent, which was really a lean-to comprised of a canvas sheet tied over walls made of boxes.

Once or twice a day Old Tom would leave his island, going to daily mass or setting off around the neighborhood pushing a cart, collecting scraps, and returning to the safety of the island in the evening. No man is an island, surely, and yet Old Tom was island-like. Perhaps, after all, every person is.

While Old Tom lived on his island, no one trespassed, though even when he was moved on, I noticed that only rarely did anyone traverse the island, preferring to cross the roads rather than march across this strange plot of ground. Islands are appealing and uncanny in equal measure.

15

The Why and the What of Islands

Not all islands are wild, of course, but every wild place is an island, surrounded as wildness inevitably is by the well-trafficked and the tame. If a child inclines to the wild, it is to an island, actual or metaphoric, that they should go.

That so many stories for children are set on islands should not surprise us, since islands—by the nature of their isolation, their relative inaccessibility, and the special feelings they evoke—lend an inevitable intensity to a plot. It can be a chore to reach an island; it can also be a chore to leave.

Islands are special places; but is not every story an island of sorts? A story transports us to another world, one that is bordered by discrete beginnings and endings. Books also are islands, crisply defined by the covers of the volume. Is not the reader washed up upon the shores of a book, spat out of the tumult of daily life to lie there awhile coming to grips with the new world in which they inhabit, before righting themselves and hacking away into the interior?

Islands function in the imagination in an ambivalent way. On the one hand, islands are paradisiacal, playing the role, for example, of the dream getaway. On an island one gets away from the rat race and is freed from the demands of ordinary life, and yet once you are on an island, you are trapped with whatever lurks there. In H. G. Wells's *The Island of Dr. Moreau* (1896), for example, Edward Prendick is stranded on a Pacific island with the monstrous Dr. Moreau, who is creating human-animal hybrids via vivisection.[1] Prendick spends his time there surrounded by monsters. In J. M. Barrie's *Peter and Wendy* (1911), on the island of Neverland, the Lost Boys, the pirates, and the "Redskins" hunt each other in a perpetual round, each on the heels of the other, always both the hunter and the hunted.[2] It's rare, in literature at least, for a character stranded on an island not to speculate about what else is on the island.

In what follows, I address the question: What is an island? Why are they so appealing to both biologists and to storytellers? In reading island stories, children get inculcated in the ecology of island life: the intensity of the plot can prepare them for real island encounters. Islands are everywhere.

What *Is* an Island?

The history of many disciplines records our recognition of things assumed the same actually being different, and of things assumed different being the same.[3] And so it is with islands. Although these days the primary definition of an island is "a piece of land surrounded by water," the word was initially used in a less discriminating way, and this is why the word now lends itself to such various uses.

One of the definitions of island—certainly not the primary one—given in the *Oxford English Dictionary* is "a piece of furniture, in a private house or in a museum, library, etc., surrounded by unoccupied floor space." A bookshelf, for example, or a butcher block tastefully centered in the contemporary kitchen. Technical uses of the word can refer to "a small isolated ridge or structure between the lines in fingerprints"—we have islands literally at our fingertips—or "a detached or insulated portion of tissue or group of cells, entirely surrounded by a different structure"—we have islands deep within us. Other definitions of "island," ones that are closer to our more intuitive sense of what a "true island" is, include "an elevated piece of land surrounded by marsh or 'interval' land." Old Tom's roundabout qualifies as an island if the roads of Templeogue can be considered "interval lands."

In the long usage of the word "island," it has, on the one hand, become solidified and surrounded by water; and on the other, "islands" have floated off, so to speak, and become anything surrounded by something that it is not. But let us get concrete and examine the classification of islands. It will help us understand their narrative use in children's stories.

Types of Islands

There is a little tuft of land a few feet seawards of Lettergesh beach in Connemara on Ireland's Atlantic west coast. You can walk out to it and take a perch on its distant shore; sitting there, you can stare out across thousands of miles of open ocean. Exercise a little caution though, for the tide races in quickly here, and during the course of a brief marine reverie, the land that once was safely contiguous with the shore becomes an island.

Several of my students who have visited that beach with me over the years have found themselves marooned on this freshly minted islet. And where moments before the surging of the sea calmed the tumult of their mental tides, it's then they realize that, lost as it is in a private conversation with the moon, the ocean cares not a whit for them. Fortunately, a brief wading through thigh-deep waters gets you back to shore and cools any castaway anxiety.

Tim Robinson, that great chronicler of island life along Ireland's western shores, describes his visits to some of these "intermittent-islands," although the ones he writes about are of a more substantial variety than the islet of Lettergesh. Two of Robinson's islands are inhabited. In "Walking Out to Islands" (1996), he writes: "Sometimes one has to wait for the parting of the waters as for the curtain-up of a play, which wakes high expectations."[4] After this, the timer is set; the duration of your visit is set by the tides.

The shore to which you return from Lettergesh island is itself on the margins of an island. This island, Ireland, has been separated by

an anciently rising post-glacial tide from the neighboring island of
Great Britain. There would have been moments when a dithering
animal, having found itself on Irish soil, could have scampered back
across shallow seas to Great Britain, and then on to, if it cared to,
the continental mainland. Now the ancient land bridges are beneath
the waves, and the shallow waters are gone. The island of Ireland—the
conflict over the autonomy of which has created centuries of political turmoil—in this sense at least, has been free for an epoch.

Islands, Real and Imaginary

Ireland, Great Britain, and the intermittent islet on Lettergesh strand
are what physical geographers call "continental islands." So also, for
example, are the Irish islands of Achill and the Aran Islands, the Scottish islands of Orkney and the Hebrides, the Portuguese islands of
the Azores, the Danish Faeroe Islands, and so on. Indeed, there are
more than three hundred islands off the European mainland larger
than fifty square kilometers. The defining characteristic of continental islands is that they lie on a continental shelf, those shallow
bands of seabed that share a geological history with the continental mainland. Thus the seas around Europe are more sunken valleys
than open ocean.

Continental islands are a frequent setting for children's novels,
such as Kirrin Island in Enid Blyton's *Five on a Treasure Island* (1942)
and the fictional island of Struay in Mairi Hedderwick's Katie Morag
series (starting in 1984).[5] Such islands can generate a sense of insu-
larity, and yet they retain a comforting connection with the mainland. Going over to an island from which characters can come and
go as they please can create a pleasant interlude in the plot, but
when the means of return are eliminated—someone sinking the boat
or stealing oars being the typical ways of stymying a return to the
mainland—this device can alter the register of the story, increasing
the tension or adding terror if this is needed.

In contrast to those islands that are separated from the continent by the shallow seas are those oceanic islands, which were never associated with continents. These islands are the products of deep-sea volcanic eruptions—mounds of lava reaching high enough to protrude above sea level. Oceanic islands often come singly, but not infrequently they are part of archipelagos like the Hawaiian Islands and the Cyclades of Greece, which are dotted across a small area of the ocean. In stories, oceanic islands conjure up a sense of chronic isolation more than continental ones can.

When characters, real or imagined, want to get away from it all, often it's off to an oceanic island they go. The anthropologist and explorer Thor Heyerdahl and his new wife, Liv, set off in their early twenties for Fatu Hiva in the South Pacific to conduct their experiment of getting back to nature. Heyerdahl's book *Fatu-Hiva: Back to Nature* (1974)—which I'd recommend to those adventure-inclined youths not likely to be alarmed by accounts of cannibalism and elephantiasis (a monstrous disease caused by parasitic worms)—reports on the failure of this island escapade.[6] Disease and increasingly hostile natives—one of them, for example, eyes Liv's forearm, describing it as the tastiest part of a woman—chase them off the island. Other familiar oceanic island stories include Robert Louis Stevenson's *Treasure Island* (1883) and William Golding's *Lord of the Flies* (1954).[7]

The continental versus oceanic distinction of islands is the fundamental one. However, in addition, it is useful to note a couple of other types of islands: barrier islands and coral atolls, both of which have immense biological and cultural importance. They are also the setting for several significant stories. Barrier islands form when sediments of sand or gravel accumulate parallel to coastlines, creating narrow strips of land. They are separated from the mainland by a shallow channel, a lagoon. One curious barrier island, North Bull Island, was formed off the coast of Dublin in recent centuries when a plan was drawn up in 1801 by Captain William Bligh, famously associated with mutiny on the HMS *Bounty*, to build a new pier to prevent the silting of Dublin port. Coney Island and Jones Beach near New York City are perhaps better-known examples. Coral atolls and related islands called cays are a rarer type of tropical island. Atolls form from the embers of a volcanic island that has retreated below the ocean surface, and around which a coral reef develops. Reefs enclose a lagoon. A coral island is the setting for Scottish writer Robert M. Ballantyne's aptly named novel *The Coral Island: A Tale of the Pacific Ocean* (1858).[8] This novel famously inspired Golding's *Lord of the Flies*, which is a sort of negative *Coral Island*. Related to atolls are cays, which are small, low tropical islands, composed largely of coral or sand. Theodore Taylor set his survival novel *The Cay* (1969) on this landform.[9]

A final category of island, albeit a strange one, includes imaginary islands. These play an engaging role in the history of children's stories, and yet also play a surprising role in geographic literature. According to Robert Macfarlane, the British admiralty maps of the nineteenth century chart more than two hundred nonexistent islands.[10] A low-lying cloud, an isolated patch of fog, or even the optimism, madness, or the mendacity of some navigators have conjured up nonexistent lands. At least some of these are celebrated in mythology: Hy-Brasil, for example, is an island that was supposed to lie far off the Irish coast. Written about as real by cartographer Angelinus Dalorta in his *L'isola Brazil* (1325), some sailors who managed to land there reported that it was thickly wooded.[11] The imaginary island of Inishmanann—"inis" being the Irish for island, "manann" deriving from the Celtic sea-god Manannaan—close in spirit to the island of Hy-Brasil, is the eponymous Lost Island in Eilís Dillon's 1954 novel.[12] Other famous imaginary islands in children's stories include Neverland, home of Peter Pan, in Barrie's novel *Peter and Wendy*.

Naturalists on Wild Islands

Islands are a privileged habitat in children's stories. Their isolation, novelty, wildness, navigability, and traversable nature make them an appealing setting for many stories. Islands, by virtue of their modest size compared to the continental mainland, are also relatively snug. "Snugness," a feeling of being ensconced and comforted in a small and confined place, is one of the factors that writer Jerry Griswold identifies in his book *Feeling Like a Kid: Childhood and Children's Literature* (2006) as a recurring motif in many successful children's stories. It's as if islands were a landscape designed for a child's imagination.[13]

That islands are a significant habitat for the study of ecological and evolutionary phenomena is, in contrast, somewhat less intuitive to the non-specialist at least. Continental lands, especially in tropical regions, seem to be where all the biological action is. Tropical forests, savannas, and grasslands have received disproportionate, though justifiable, attention from biologists. These habitats are extensive and biodiverse: this, for the most part, is where big fierce animals roam.[14]

Islands occupy only a small fraction of the total landmass on Earth. Setting aside the reasonable contention that all landmasses, including the continents and continental islands like Australia, are inherently island-like (surrounded as they are by oceans), traditional islands—of which there are by some estimates over one hundred thousand in all, many being infinitesimally small—collectively add up to less than 10 percent of the total land area of Earth. Indeed, the top five hundred or so islands by size (ranging from Rothschild Island at five hundred square kilometers to Greenland at 2.166 million square kilometers) collectively make up only 6.5 percent of the Earth's landmass.[15]

Despite their small collective landmass and the undeniable biological importance of continental habitat, especially in the tropics, islands have been accorded attention that is quite considerable compared to their area. Why is this the case? It is because islands have a range of unique properties that recommend themselves to biologists for research. Islands are discrete, having more easily identifiable borders than comparably sized parts of the continental mainland. Once you step into the ocean, you know you've left the island.

In addition to this, islands oftentimes harbor species in distinct combinations. Several islands in an archipelago, each of which may have singular communities of plants and animals, can collectively host an astonishing variety of forms. An ecologist hopping from island to island can thereby investigate strikingly different universes in fairly confined geographical circumstances. In *The Swiss Family Robinson* (1812), Johann David Wyss brings together a most surprising menagerie of animals.[16] On that fictional island, antelopes, bears, cheetahs, dingoes, elephants, giraffes, hippos, hyenas, jackals, kangaroos, leopards, lions, monkeys, peccaries, platypuses, porcupines, rhinos, tigers, walruses, wild boars, wolves, wombats, zebras, and so on are improbably brought together. The bird and plant inventories of the island are equally implausible. While such combinations as Wyss selected are a biogeographic nonsense, islands are, nevertheless, undeniably peculiar, and the spirit of his eclectic biota is laudable.

The relative impoverishment of island communities is oftentimes mirrored in children's stories. In Barrie's *Peter and Wendy*, the inhabitants of Neverland comprise a relatively sparse community, including fairies, birds, the Lost Boys, pirates, mermaids, "Redskins," certain beasts (bears, tigers, flamingoes, and so on), and an occasional gnome, prince, and a small old lady with a hooked nose.

The natural history of islands is summarized in several nonfictional accounts that are accessible to youthful readers. Ones that I especially like include *Islands: Living Gems of the Sea* (2002) by Randy Frahm, *Islands* (1998) by Rose Pipes, and one volume especially relevant for considering the contribution of that most famous of island biologists, Charles Darwin, entitled *Galápagos Islands: Nature's Delicate Balance at Risk* (2000) by Linda Tagliaferro.[17]

Islands are a type of keystone locale, to adopt the language of the late influential experimental ecologist Robert Paine.[18] They are disproportionately represented in children's literature and play an undeniable role in shaping the reveries of childhood. But investigations on and of islands were also integral to formulating our contemporary understanding of how species came into being. More recently, and more ominously, islands have shaped our understanding of how organic forms disappear. Islands are epicenters of species extinction.[19]

This remarkable convergence of a prevalent theme in children's literature and in ecological and evolutionary research should not, however, be over-interpreted. Islands emerge as important in both literatures for fairly distinct reasons. No children's writer, one assumes, writes about islands because they can serve as fruitful experimental replicates for understanding the patterns of nature. Nor might an ecologist choose to study an island because it evokes feelings of comfort, security, and snugness (though they may choose to study it because an island is beautiful—but this is altogether another matter). This caveat against drawing strenuous parallels aside, islands appeal to the literary and scientific imagination alike because they are discrete, contained, manageable, exotic, and quirky. Islands are often wild, often subject to large natural forces, and usually navigable. An island pares things down to their essentials; islands clarify.

Ecologists and evolutionists examine islands in order to determine the forces that shape natural communities. But storytellers oftentimes inform us of how natural patterns appear to their protagonists. They describe what it is like for people to encounter islands with all their insular and discombobulating strangeness. Islands contain and intensify a plot. A significant implication of all of this is that, in the hands of a skilled storyteller, an island story elucidates the island environment. A child may come away from the microcosmic experience of such a book knowing a little more about their relationship with wild forces and more about the world beyond the basic movement of a plot. Stories about islands are a gateway for understanding the nature of islands and the history of our interaction with them and on them. If a child loves an island, the adult they become may value them, and by valuing islands, they may have a disproportionately beneficent impact upon the world. Islands are stepping-stones to the broader world of wild nature.

Islands as a Mood

After the "Famous Five"—Anne, Julian, Dick, George, and Timmy the dog—have returned from one of their early visits to Kirrin Island off England's Dorset coast in Enid Blyton's *Five on a Treasure Island* (1942), Anne makes the following declaration about islands: "Most islands are too big to feel like islands. I mean Britain is an island, but nobody living on it could possibly know it unless they were told. Now this island [Kirrin Island] really feels like one because wherever you are you can see to the other side of it. I love it."

Though we may not want to fully adopt Anne's definition of an island, with its emphasis on the immediate visibility of boundaries, nonetheless, an island should surely feel like an island. If Britain does not feel like an island, it's not clear that Ireland—a smaller country than Britain, to be sure—feels like one either. In ancient times, the Hill of Uisneach in county Westmeath was celebrated as the central point in Ireland. (It's not!) Though on a clear day, you can purportedly see twenty of Ireland's thirty-two counties from Uisneach's peak (182 meters), there is, however, no sight of Ireland's margins from the summit; you would have to be told that the country is an island. Ireland would not qualify by Anne's rather severe island criterion.

Despite Ireland's relatively large interior expanse, the islandness of Ireland is nevertheless part of its national self-identity. To Ireland's writers, the country has long been called the "island of saints and scholars."[20] This self-consciousness about being an island has influenced the literature of the land. Even stories of Ireland's mythological tradition lay stress on the island's geographical separateness. Ireland's literature is also replete with stories about islands off the Irish coasts. Islands off an island are a very special distillate of the very essence of islandness; they are remote even from what already feels remote. Tír na nÓg—the land of perpetual youth, to which Oisín the warrior poet, son of Fionn mac Cumhaill and of Sadhbh (who was a deer—it's a long story) and his fairy princess Niamh traveled—is a mythological island about which several beautiful stories have been told. Hy-Brasil, another imaginary island, is said to lie off Ireland's Atlantic west coast; it, too, appears in several stories and, as we have seen, was even added to many real nautical maps. In the stories, Hy-Brasil becomes periodically visible as the obscuring Atlantic mists rise; even then, being a magical place, the island cannot be reached by ordinary means.

The Irish monks of old—those saints and scholars alluded to above—took to the seas to establish monasteries on lonely islands around the coast. Such voyages, real or apocryphal, are recorded in a type of epic sea tale called an *immram* (plural *immrama*). It's said that the monks would travel to a distant island, stop to see if Ireland could be seen from its highest point, and if it was visible, they would row on. Especially popular since medieval times are stories that retell the feats of St. Brendan the Navigator. *The Voyage of Saint Brendan* (900 AD) is a fantastical account of Saint Brendan's travels.[21] The tradition says that Brendan and his monks traveled to several islands, including the Canary Islands, the Azores, and the island of Madeira; some even claim that he made it to Greenland and perhaps even to North America. *The Voyage of Saint Brendan* shares several features common to all the *immrama*. These include visits to several islands before reaching a final destination (the Island of Promise was Brendan's terminus), accounts of strange islands (Brendan stopped at an island that was actually the back of the whale Jasconius), islands populated by improbable beasts (an island of sheep that are bigger than cattle), islands that provide spiritual comforts (on one they are served magical loaves of bread of "marvellous whiteness"), and—perhaps less marvelous, but nonetheless quite magical—were encounters with volcanoes, icebergs, and so forth. There are several excellent children's versions of this story, including Mike McGrew's *Saint Brendan and the Voyage Before Columbus* (2004).[22]

The *immrama*, legends, tall tales, and spiritual quests are consistent in associating islands with particular moods: islands are mysterious, wondrous, occasionally terrifying, and almost always magical. The association of islands with a peculiar and attractive suite of moods is not exclusive to Britain and Ireland. The legends and fairy tales of the Azores celebrate the magical mood of islands in a lovely fashion. These stories are retold by Elsie Spicer Eells in *The Islands of Magic: Legends, Folk and Fairytales from the Azores* (1922).[23] In her preface, Spicer reminds us that the Azores are often thought to be the mountain peaks of the lost continent of Atlantis. She spent the winter of 1920–21 on the islands recording the stories. My favorite of them are tales of magical deeds. In "The Master of Magic," a young boy assists his father by transforming into a hunting dog. The boy-dog is sold for an enormous price, and then the boy is transformed back to his original state and he returns to his now wealthy father. He then turns himself into a horse and is sold once again, this time to a Great Magician. The lad then becomes a kernel of corn, and the Great Magician transformed into a hen to eat the corn; the corn in turn is transformed into a dog and the boy—now a dog—shook the magician-chicken. In all the hullabaloo, the Great Magician admitted that the boy was "surely a master of magic." The boy then married the magician's daughter. Another story of magic on the Azores may not appeal quite as much to modern sensibilities: in "The Magic Mouthful," a woman is presented with a jar of water by an old woman with the instruction that when her husband scolds her, she should drink of the magic water. She does and avoids being beaten by her husband. Eventually she runs out of the water and searches for the woman, who concedes that the water is ordinary and not magical at all. Swallowing a mouthful prevented her from replying to his scoldings and thereby saved her a beating. The story concludes with the moral: "It is generally known in the Azores that if one does not want to keep up a quarrel it is well to pretend that his mouth is full of water."

The English novelist and poet Lawrence Durrell—brother of Gerald Durrell, whose memoir of the Durrell family's time on the Greek island of Corfu is charmingly recorded in *My Family and Other Animals* (1956)[24]—writes about the special attractiveness of islands to certain people in his *Reflections on a Marine Venus* (1953); he refers to a curious list of diseases, "unclassified by medical science," which include the condition "islomania," a rare "affliction of the spirit." Those who suffer from it find islands irresistible, and the knowledge that they are on an island fills them with "an indescribable intoxication."[25] People suffering from the condition—"islomanes," to use Durrell's term—are putatively descendants of the lost island continent of Atlantis.

We may not all be islomanes, but many of us are sensitive to the magical mood of islands. And children's writers seem to be especially sensitive to the feeling of islandness. Like Enid Blyton's Anne, writers seem to love them.

16

Archmage Ged, Merlin, and Harry Potter and the Training of Wizards and Witches

As they sail toward Selidor, an island on the westernmost fringe of the Earthsea archipelago, the Archmage Ged—the central figure in Ursula K. Le Guin's fantasy series the Earthsea Cycle—conjures up a vision of Gont, the island on which he was born. Ged shares this vision with Arren, his younger companion, who is fated to become the King of Havnor, an island of the Inner Seas. There Arren sees the home of Ogion the Silent, the archmage's early teacher. From the forest that surrounds that home, Ged and Arren look out on "steep, sunlit meadows beneath the rock and snow of the peak, looking . . . along a steep road going down in a green, gold-shot darkness." The wizard says, yearningly, to his younger friend, "There is no silence like the silence of those forests." It is to Gont that Ged eventually returns when, exhausted from his labors in the "Dry Land of the dead," the onetime supremely powerful wizard has lost his magical powers.

The practice of magic, which can be defined as any attempt to influence events or alter the physical nature of things by mystical or supernatural means, is not, of course, a set of practices restricted to islands.[1] But many fictional magicians are associated with islands: Merlin and Harry Potter just being the most obvious. The central claim of this chapter—that magic in children's literature is as often as not built upon a foundation of natural history—applies to sorcerers, witches, and magicians wherever you find them! Shakespeare's witches in *Macbeth* prepare their brew reciting the following ingredients:

Eye of newt, and toe of frog,
Wool of bat, and tongue of dog,
Adder's fork, and blind-worm's sting,
Lizard's leg, and howlet's wing,—
For a charm of powerful trouble,
Like a hell-broth boil and bubble.[2]

Assembling these ingredients requires a mastery not just of the darker arts but a deep knowledge of natural history besides.

This vision of Gont is recounted in *The Farthest Shore* (1972), the third book in the series about the archipelago universe of Earthsea. Other books in the series are *A Wizard of Earthsea* (1968), *The Tombs of Atuan* (1971), *Tehanu: The Last Book of Earthsea* (1990), *Tales from Earthsea* (2001), and *The Other Wind* (2001).[3] All of these books have won literary awards, most notably the Newbery Silver Medal for *The Tombs of Atuan* and the National Book Award for Children's Books for *The Farthest Shore*.

This is a series that, on the one hand, is set in a fantasy landscape but that, on the other hand, takes the detailed physical and cultural environment of islands very seriously. The first words of the lengthy Earthsea Cycle is a reference to the nature of Ged's home island: "The island of Gont, a single mountain that lifts its peak a mile above the storm-racked Northeast Sea, is a land famous for wizards." The Earthsea archipelago is comprised of dozens of islands spread over thousands of square miles. The physical and cultural peculiarities of the islands and the seas that separate them are exploited in full measure in the telling of the story. The landscape is fractured and insular; and the tales of Earthsea alternate between the expansiveness of a quest threading through the open waters that separate far-flung islands and the claustrophobia of the catacombs beneath the island of Atuan. Each island, and we learn about several of them, is distinct: each has its own idiosyncratic culture, and each its own relationship with magic.

When we first meet Ged, the boy—then called Duny—is wild, living on a wild island. His mother is dead, his father is a bronze-smith, and the boy herds goats in the mountains of Gont. He learns his first spells from his aunt, a witch. That spell is acquired accidentally; in copying his aunt's words, he herds goats in a close flock down the mountain. But they huddle so close to him that the boy panics. Seeing his precocious aptitude for spells, the witch calls him into her home to teach him more magic. Hanging from her rafters are herbs set out to dry: "mint, moly, and thyme, yarrow and rushwash and paramal, kingsfoil, clovenfoot, tansy and bay." His aunt teaches him a few additional tricks: he learns, for example, how to coax a snail out of its shell and how to call a falcon from the sky. Though these are small matters, nonetheless knowledge of nature has its power. Ged learns enough of such nature magic to cause a fog to descend about his town when it is attacked by raiders from the Kargad Empire. This feat saves the townsfolk, and it establishes the boy's reputation.

Ged's early prowess has roused the attention of Ogion, who comes down from the mountains to offer Ged an apprenticeship in wizardry. However, the instruction in magic he receives from this powerful wizard proves frustrating to Ged. Ogion teaches him the nature of plants. They see a plant, fourfoil it is called—a fictional plant, unlike most hanging from the rafters in his aunt's home—and Ged asks its use. "None that I know of," replies his teacher. And yet Ogion wants Ged to get to know fourfoil "in all its seasons root and leaf and flower, by sight, scent and seed." For only then will Ged "learn its true name, knowing its being: which is more than its use."

Ged learns his plants. For this is generally a truth in fantasy literature: before extravagant quests, before dragons and gold, before rings of power, before strenuous heroism comes botany. Hobbits farm the Shire, Harry Potter visits the greenhouses with Professor Sprout, and Ged walks the mountains of Gont with Ogion the Silent, learning the uses of plants.

After an incident where Ged overreaches his juvenile power and meets "the shadow"—a premonition of a theme that endures throughout the series—Ogion releases him from his service. The boy goes to Roke Island to attend a school for wizards. If the power-hungry youth thinks that the training will likely be very different on Roke, he is largely mistaken. The foundations of his education remain rooted in natural history. The students on Roke spend days with the Master Herbal, "who taught the ways and properties of things that grow." Other days are spent with the Master Windkey "at the arts of wind and weather." The boys (and they are all boys) sail their boats and create their own "mage-wind" that blows them about the harbor. There were other lessons to be sure: learning the old songs and sleight-of-hand magic; and importantly they take a trip to the Isolate Tower for the winter months with the Master Namer to learn "the lists and ranks and rounds of names." "He who would be Seamaster," the Master Namer tells them, "must know the true name of every drop of water in the sea." Every drop!

In literature, the training of youthful mages like Ged in Le Guin's Earthsea Cycle is more often than not a training in nature-lore. There is a long tradition in Western thought of associating witches and wizards with wilder nature. Perhaps the most famous wizard of all, Merlin—who is associated with King Arthur (although he has a tradition independent of that mythical king)—is drawn in part, according to James MacKillop's *A Dictionary of Celtic Mythology* (1998), from Lailoken, the naked wild man of the woods.[4] According to Nikolai Tolstoy in *The Quest for Merlin* (1985), the character of Merlin may, in fact, be an amalgam of Lailoken, the Welsh bard Myrddin, and the Irish king Suibhne, who, maddened by the din of war, takes flight and lives in the treetops.[5]

When the Wart (a name that is assonant with "Art"), the boy who will become King Arthur, first meets Merlin—or "Merlyn," to use T. H. White's spelling in *The Sword in the Stone* (1938)—the wizard's appearance suggests one who inclines toward natural living. This is how Merlyn is described when first we meet him:

> The old gentleman that the Wart saw was a singular spectacle. He was dressed in a flowing gown with fur tippets which had the signs of the zodiac embroidered all over it, together with various cabalistic signs, as of triangles with eyes in them, queer crosses, leaves of trees, bones of bird and animals and a planetarium whose stars shone like bits of looking-glass with the sun on them. . . . Merlyn had a long white beard and long white moustaches which hung down on either side of it, and close inspection showed that he was far from clean. It was not that he had dirty finger-nails or anything like that, but some large bird seemed to have been nesting in his hair.[6]

A whole chapter of White's novel is devoted to describing Merlyn's abode in the Forest Sauvage. Elements in this scene provide motifs that are repeated time and again in literature concerning wizardly affairs. A "corkindrill" (a mythological reptilian beast) hangs from the ceiling; his shelves are crammed with books propped against each other "as if they had had too much spirits to drink and did not really trust themselves." Various animal trophies hang on the walls, grass snakes squirm in a terrarium, solitary wasps nest, and a beehive opens onto the window; the bees enter and egress into the room as bees are wont to do. Hedgehogs rest on cotton wool, badgers cavort and call out to their master (saying, of all things, "Yik-Yik-Yik-Yik"), drawers are labeled with herb names, and on and on it goes. Indeed, this "and on and on" of mine glides over several pages of detailed description. Merlyn inhabits a veritable museum of natural history.

The Wart meets Merlyn's owl, Archimedes. The owl can talk,

though at first the bird, wisely perhaps, has his doubts about the boy; these doubts are only mollified when the Wart feeds him a mouse. The Wart and Merlyn breakfast together, and in serving them the cutlery and utensils spring to life. The excitement of being in that "most marvelous room" is so much that the boy declares, in wonder, that he must have been "on a quest."

In his education of the Wart, Merlyn eschews formal academics in favor of an immersion in the natural world. He transforms the child into different animals: a perch, a badger, a hawk, an ant, an owl, and a wild goose. The child learns a little from each animal about the exercise of power, and the skills required for kingship. Not all the lessons are benign; for example, a pike, a monster of his kind, informed the Wart that "love is a trick played on us by the forces of evolution." "There is only power," the quasi-Nietzschean pike goes on: "The power of strength decides everything in the end, and only Might is right."

There are other lessons as well that are harrowing though no doubt instructive. A breakout star of Disney's animated version of *Sword in the Stone* (1963) is Madame Mim, who, in the book and movie, takes the form of a crow and plucks an arrow shot by the Wart out of the sky. The movie glides over the fact that Madame Mim is a cannibal; she holds the Wart captive when he mounts a rescue for the arrow. If it were not for a helpful conversation with a goat, a fellow captive of that necromancer, who ran to fetch Merlyn, it would have been the Wart's fate to be dinner and not king of England.

Eventually the Wart is fated to pull the sword from the stone. Since the prophecy was written that "Whoso Pulleth Out This Sword of this Stone and Anvil, is Rightwise King Born of All England," the boy becomes King Arthur, with Merlyn remaining by his side.

Another wizard, perhaps the best known in contemporary fiction, is Gandalf from Tolkien's *The Hobbit* and the Lord of the Rings cycle.[7] Gandalf, a blend of Celtic and Teutonic wizard, is a wanderer and like Merlin possesses powers over nature. However, it is his "cousin," the wizard Radagast, who, in Tolkien's universe, has the most explicit affinity for plants and animals. Of Radagast, Saruman, a leader of the wizards sent to Middle-earth and head of their order, scoffs, "Radagast the Bird-tamer! Radagast the Simple! Radagast the fool!" Yet Gandalf has a more positive view of him and comments, "Radagast is, of course, a worthy Wizard, a master of shapes and changes of hue, and he has much lore of herbs and beasts, and birds are especially his friends."

In Le Guin's Earthsea Cycle, we get a more complete account of the training of a wizard than in most books in this genre. Indeed, Le Guin sees this as a central innovation of the Earthsea novels: "I didn't originate the idea of a school for wizards—if anybody did it was T. H. White, though he did it in single throwaway line and didn't develop it. I was the first to do that."[8]

In amplifying the notion of a wizard's school and in her attention to the pedagogical details, Le Guin no doubt influenced the writing of the most famous of all such wizardly bildungsroman, namely, J. K. Rowling's Harry Potter series (1997–2007). This is not the place to give a detailed account of young Potter's education, but it is worth calling to mind the role that natural history plays even in this less explicitly environmental of magical stories. A glance at the textbooks for first-year students at Hogwarts School of Witchcraft and Wizardry illuminates the orientation of this training. Included are such titles as *One Thousand Magical Herbs and Fungi* by Phyllida Spore and *Fantastic Beasts and Where to Find Them* by Newt Scamander. Students of Hogwarts are also allowed to bring to the school "an owl OR a cat OR a toad." Potter, like Merlyn before him, acquires an owl, naming him Hedwig.

The Potter stories are actually replete with nature references. In addition to the details of the curriculum, the first chapters of *Harry Potter and the Philosopher's Stone* (1997) (released in the United States as *Harry Potter and the Sorcerer's Stone*) describe Harry's curious facility with snakes. He inadvertently releases a large boa constrictor from a zoo. As the animal slides by him, the snake turns to Harry, saying, "Brazil, here I come. . . . Thanksss, amigo." Later, in Diagon Alley when Harry visits Ollivander's wand shop, Mr. Ollivander helps him select a wand of holly with a phoenix feather, a combination of elements found in the wand of Lord Voldemort, who is Harry's principal antagonist in the books. A final reference I'll make in this truncated roster of such events is from the first exchange in the testy relation between Potter and Professor Snape. Snape asks him: "What would I get if I added powdered root of asphodel to an infusion of wormwood?"[9]

A magical education is botany all the way down.

Ursula Le Guin, born in 1929, was the daughter of anthropologist Alfred Louis Kroeber and writer Theodora Kracaw Kroeber Quinn. Alfred Kroeber's academic reputation rested on his ethnographic work on Native American tribes. He was eclectic in his scholarly interests, and books of his such as *Anthropology* (1923; revised edition, 1948), *Configurations of Culture Growth* (1944), *The Nature of Culture* (1952), and *Style and Civilizations* (1957) shaped contemporary anthropology.[10] Theodora Kroeber started to write later in her life and published several engaging books, including *The Inland Whale* (1959), a retelling of nine Native American myths; *Ishi in Two Worlds: A Biography of the Last Wild Indian in North America* (1961); and *Ishi: Last of His Tribe* (1964).[11] During Le Guin's childhood, the Kroeber family split their time between Berkeley during the academic year and summertime on a forty-acre ranch in Napa Valley. This was a stimulating environment, with plenty of visitors—writers, anthropologists, and assorted intellectuals—where Le Guin was exposed to a lot of the ideas that surfaced later in her novels. The rhythms of traditional stories, an attentiveness to mythical belief, and a heightened environmental sensitivity are all evident in the Earthsea novels.

The plots of the Earthsea novels move along at a nice pace; the action is measured, and the drama is intense at times. It always helps to have dragons, especially when these are judiciously employed, as they are in the Earthsea Cycle: after all, a little dragon goes a long way. But there is also a ruminative quality to Le Guin's novels. This quality may explain why it was difficult at first for Le Guin to find her audience. Novels of the Earthsea Cycle are ultimately books about ideas. The ideas that matter most to Le Guin, and those upon which the cycle of books is founded, include feminism, Taoism, and ideas drawn from ecology. It's not necessary, of course, to reduce these disparate philosophies to a single essence, for each thought finds unique expression in Le Guin's writing. Nonetheless, a commonality between these ideas is the notion of balance or equilibrium. A balance between male and female, a balance of action and reflection, a balance between stability and change, and a balance between good and evil. In each case, these dipoles are not as dichotomous as they seem, since each pole in Le Guin's thinking is infused with its apparent opposite. This is what one might call the "Tao of Le Guin."

The greatest expression of these ideas are found in Le Guin's conception of magic. The explication of magic is dispersed across the novels, but we initially encounter its core principles as Ged himself first learns them on the island of Roke. Tiring of working spells of mere illusion, where a wizard temporarily masks an object before it reverts to its original form, Ged asks the Master Hand, one of the nine Masters of Roke, "if I make a pebble into a diamond . . . what must I do to make that diamond remain a diamond? How is the changing spell locked, and made to last?"

The response from the Master Hand is worth quoting at length:

> A bit of the stone of which Roke Isle is made, a little bit of the
> dry land on which men live. It is itself. It is part of the world. . . .
> To change this rock into a jewel, you must change its true name.
> And to do that, my son, even to so small a scrap of the world, is to

change the world. It can be done. . . . But you must not change one thing, one pebble, one grain of sand, until you know what good and evil will follow on that act. The world is in balance, in Equilibrium. A wizard's power of Changing and of Summoning can shake the balance of the world. It is dangerous, that power. It is most perilous. It must follow knowledge, and serve need. *To light a candle is to cast a shadow.* . . . (Emphasis mine.)

In this expression "To light a candle is to cast a shadow" is the essence of both magic's ethics and its ecological significance. Everything is connected to be sure, but it is connected in a nuanced way. We can never only do one thing; every change we impose has ramifications though only rarely do we know the full extent of these changes. It is not light or dark, good or evil—it is always both.[12]

Later it is Ged, by this time the Archmage of Roke, who elucidates the principles of magic to Arren. *The Farthest Shore*, set decades after the action of *A Wizard of Earthsea*, relates events surrounding the waning of the power of magic throughout the archipelago. Even dragons lose their powers of speech. Perhaps there is some evil magic afoot. Arren wonders aloud to Ged if it is some form of pestilence, "a plague, that drifts from land to land, blighting the crops and the flocks and men's spirits?" Ged replies that "a pestilence is a motion of the great Balance, of the Equilibrium itself." By this he means that a pestilence can be seen as something within nature and that "nature is not unnatural." The loss of magic being experienced throughout the archipelago, he speculates, is something altogether different. "This is not a righting of the Balance, but an upsetting of it. There is only one creature who can do that." That would be us, the humans. Moving along with this gloomy thought and resisting Arren's defense, which is stated in the form of an observation of people's reasonable desire to live and therefore the inevitability that they change things, Ged says: "When we crave power over life—endless wealth, unassailable safety, immortality—then desire becomes greed. And if knowledge allies itself with that greed, then comes evil. Then the balance of the world is swayed, and ruin weighs heavy in the scale."

The idea of a "balance of nature" has been demoted in environmental thought in recent years. In fact, even by the time LeGuin was writing the Earthsea books, ecological scientists had largely abandoned the concept as meaningless. As early as the nineteen twenties, Oxford ecologist Charles Elton claimed in his book *Animal Ecology* (1927) that "the balance of nature does not exist, and perhaps has never existed."[13]

But even though the term "balance of nature" is now largely abandoned in the technical literature of ecological science, there remains a conviction among scientists and activists alike that human activity is somewhat exceptional. Undoubtedly, humans are a product of the same natural forces as other creatures; we evolve and, in common with other living beings, we have a relationship with natural resources. To be a living creature is to have an environment, and to have an environment is to both alter and be altered by that environment. Even an amoeba gliding about in the confines of an agar-lined petri dish can do this. To alter an environment is to impose a certain measure of mischief for some creatures (indeed, often the mischief-maker itself) and to provide a boon to some. From this perspective, all organisms are, to some extent, disruptive. But to disrupt a global environment takes a certain tenacity of purpose. Humans may not have set out to do it, and it may have taken an eon to achieve it, but humans might now take some perverse pride in being a geological force, one that transformed a globe.[14]

If we agree with Archmage Ged that craving for wealth, unassailable safety, and immortality, mingled with a technologically cunning know-how, can result in a world catastrophe—and I do—then we might agree that humans are exceptional, and that we can sway the "balance" of the world. As a consequence of our collective impact, "ruin weighs heavy in the scale."

In her suspicion about the role of humans in dimming the power of magic in the world, Le Guin remains a perspicacious environmentalist.

€⋆

Most of the wizards mentioned in my account above are island dwellers, or at least have their roots on islands: Britain, in the case of Merlin, his sources and successors, or hailing from the fictional island universe of Earthsea, in the case of Ged. Their insular origins may be coincidental in some cases. Is Harry Potter, for instance, necessarily English? In the case of Ged, that necessity is more compellingly made. It's not that it would have been inconceivable to weave the plots of Earthsea across continental lands, but Le Guin employs the archipelago to sequester and intensify the action in a variety of ways.

Biologically, islands produce and contain their monsters and their miniatures. As we've seen, islands restrict distribution, and on them are assembled unique constellations of species. Island creatures are often rare. Likewise, those forces that shape populations and determine species' survival and demise are distinctive and often extreme. Ged may have been master of Roke, but to get on or off the islands, he's just another man in a boat on an open ocean (albeit a man with power over the wind). Even dragons—creatures that are most at home in the air and as ungainly on the ground as a swan waddling away from a pond—are confined to their own realm in Earthsea (mainly the islands of "The Dragon's Run" and Selidor).

There may be no balance of nature in the sense of a benign equilibrium that persists as long as humans don't intrude. And yet the action of opposing forces—of colonization and extinction, for example— that prevail on islands is determinative for island beings. Islands are held in precarious equilibrium. All this Le Guin intuits about islands. Unsurprisingly, Le Guin's intellectual hero is Darwin. In an interview with the *Paris Review*, she said: "If I had to pick a hero, it would be Charles Darwin—the size of his mind, which included all that scientific curiosity and knowledge seeking, and the ability to put it all together."[15] It is not coincidental that magic in Earthsea requires a careful command of taxonomy—knowing the name of every drop in the ocean—and is the privilege of those who, like natural historians (that is, like Darwin), know the names of things. Of Darwin, Le Guin in the same interview went on to remark, "There is a genuine spirituality about Darwin's thinking. And he felt it, too." The Earthsea Cycle is the island story par excellence; it is the matchless tale of physical and spiritual equilibrium. Earthsea magic is the magic of a natural world.

17

Is L. T. Meade the *Real* Author of Enid Blyton's Famous Five?

The archives of the Dublin City Library are housed in Pearse Street above the hubbub of the general circulation branch, about half a mile from Trinity College in the center of the city. The room has a pleasant scholarly austerity about it. When I visited these archives, many of the patrons who are scrutinized closely by a vigilant staff before being admitted through a locked gate were, as far as I could tell from the volumes fetched for them from the bowels of the building, researching family histories. After some deliberation about its location in the stacks—the catalog information on the title was incomplete—L. T. Meade's novel *Four on an Island: A Story of Adventure* (1892), which is now quite rare and seldom read, was brought out to me on a cushion.[1] The librarian stood beside me for a moment speculating aloud about my need for gloves while handling the fragile volume. Ultimately deeming them unnecessary, she left me alone with my find.

Is this the book that influenced Enid Blyton's *Five on a Treasure Island* (1942), one of the most enduring novels of childhood in Britain and Ireland in the second half of the twentieth century?[2] Children loved Blyton, their parents, teachers, and librarians, not so much. Some libraries limited checkout of her books to one at a time.[3]

A few days before I visited the library, arriving back in Dublin from the Chicago area, where I now live, I had picked up Blyton's novel, which I remembered as having several helpful environmental references. Although Blyton wrote enthusiastically about nature— her early books include *The Bird Book* (1926), *The Animal Book* (1927), and *Nature Lessons* (1929)—my recollection of *Five on a Treasure Island* was as a sturdy adventure story rather than a bucolic meditation on kids' survival on a wild island.[4] It's a romp where four cousins and their dog gallivant about an island off the Dorset coast, searching for "ingots of gold" and drinking "lashings" of ginger beer.

Island stories are intriguing, as children away from parents' gaze not only get up to high jinks but are often at the mercy of the wilder forces of nature—their own and environmental. Blyton's novel has some pleasant observations on the natural history of Kirrin Island: its rocky inaccessibility, the tameness of its rabbits, the fishing skills of cormorants. I suspect my career choice (a scientist of sorts) derives from a captivation with Uncle Quentin, the irascible scientist, father to Georgina and uncle to her cousins Julian, Dick, and Anne, in Blyton's Famous Five books.

The state of Blyton scholarship is appalling, but *Five on a Treasure Island* has garnered some academic attention because of gender-identity issues.[5] "Tomboy" Georgina, Blyton's most beloved character, prefers to be called George. As Dick says to Anne: "You know she hates being a girl, and having a girl's name." After crying about the sale of Kirrin Island, George, "half-ashamed," exclaims: "I've been behaving like a girl."

Five on a Treasure Island moves briskly. The cousins and their dog Timmy row to the island and witness a wreck being tossed from the bottom of the sea onto rocks during a storm. They investigate and discover that the wreck's gold cargo is buried on the island. Meanwhile, Uncle Quentin unwittingly sells the island to a ne'er-do-well treasure hunter in search of the ingots. Spoiler alert: the kids find the gold and foil the treasure hunters. The end.

And so, a couple of days after rereading it, I tracked down Meade's *Four on an Island* in the archive. I unearthed it only because it has the word "island" in the title; the book is difficult to find. Of Meade's 300-odd books, *A World of Girls* (1886) is one of the few still occasionally read today.[6]

Elizabeth ("Lillie") Thomasina Meade was born in Bandon, county Cork, around 1844. Her father was a Church of Ireland rector. She moved to London with her family in 1847 and died in Oxford in 1914. Although the topics of her widely read books were diverse, the more popular ones were about adolescent girls, often set in schools.

The influence of such novels on later writers, such as Blyton and Angela Brazil, is well established. For example, Meade has a book called *A Very Naughty Girl* (1901), and Blyton has one called *The Naughtiest Girl in the School* (1940), but there is minimal plot overlap.[7] Meade might have also indirectly influenced the Harry Potter series.

Meade's island story concerns English cousins Ferdinand, Isabel, Rachel, and Tony. Their dog Mungo makes five in all. After a storm, the children become stranded off the coast of Brazil. Ferdinand and Isabel ("Bell," as she insists on being called) tame the island. Bell declares: "What a good thing that I was always as much boy as girl!" She fights vicious crabs, wields a hatchet, and thrives in the wild domain. In adapting to island life, the cousins discover a shipwreck on the rocks and investigate.

The plot elements are so undeniably similar to Blyton's island story that it seems probable that the older book inspired the newer one. As well as the plots, there is a curious word similarity between the two. Meade's book refers to a "fishing-smack," common in her day, and fishing-smacks are mentioned several times in *Five on a Treasure Island*, although by the time Blyton wrote, that type of vessel was rare.

To make the bolder claim that Blyton helped herself to characters and plot elements would be difficult. After all, both novels are descendants of Daniel Defoe's *Robinson Crusoe* (1719) and share themes with that very first of all novels.[8] Crusoe was also a victim of a storm at sea and starts his island adventure by ransacking the shipwreck.

That being said, Blyton would have known Meade's work, which was popular when she was a child. Blyton, who was born in 1897, was a voracious reader; at nine she showed off her photographic memory by glancing at a page of a novel and reciting every word to her father. Until she suffered from dementia, shortly before her death, Blyton prided herself on her memory. Describing her creative process to psychologist Peter McKellar, she wrote: "I think my imagination contains all the things I have ever seen or heard, things my conscious mind has long forgotten—and they have all been jumbled about till a light penetrates into the mass, and a happening here or an object there is taken out, transmuted, or formed into something that takes a natural and rightful place in the story."[9] Blyton said that her life experiences "sank down into my 'under-mind' and simmered there, waiting for the time to come when they would be needed again for a book—changed, transmuted, made perfect, finely wrought—quite different from when they were packed away." If Blyton read *Four on an Island*, she wouldn't have forgotten it.

It is possibly for the best if L. T. Meade's book rests in the library archives; it is not a great novel. Neither is Blyton's, by literary standards. But when I returned to Chicago, I reread *Five on a Treasure Island* yet again, enjoying the yarn and bathing in waves of nostalgia.

18

Robinson Crusoe

NOW HERE'S A CANNIBALISM TALE FOR EVERY CHILD

> Here is a good book full of heavy theological doctrine, human character,
> ingenious device, a mine of information on manners, morals, life, which no
> boy will turn from if it is offered between the ages of seven and twelve.
> —Review of *Robinson Crusoe*[1]

Little remarked upon in the literature about Defoe's *Robinson Crusoe*
(1719) is the curious fate of Crusoe's cats. Two cats, both female, are
carried by him from the shipwreck onto the island. One runs away
and Crusoe gives the animal up for dead. The other stays with him.
To Crusoe's surprise, the truant cat returns with three kittens, having bred with one of the island's wild cats.

The first mention of the island's wild cat population occurs early in
Crusoe's narrative. A wild cat sits on his provisions as Crusoe is loading
them from the shipwreck onto the shore. That cat stares directly at him,
and he reports that it looked "as if she had in a mind to be acquainted
with me." When Crusoe points a gun at it, the cat seems unalarmed,
just as young Darwin later discovered was the case for wildlife on
the Galápagos. Such is the unflappability of island fauna. Impressed,
Crusoe feeds the cat, and off it marches back into the island's interior.

The next reported encounter with a wild cat is not quite so cordial.
Crusoe shoots the cat on this occasion and then skins it. The skin, he
reported in his journal, was soft. The flesh, on the other hand, was
"good for nothing." Ominously, Crusoe mentions that he preserved the
skin of every creature he killed. There were, it seems, many such kills.

Crusoe supposed the wild cats on the island to be quite a different kind from European cats. But apparently they breed without difficulty with Crusoe's domestic cat. After these first kittens to issue from a union with the island's fauna, there are to be many more. Crusoe's sanctuary eventually becomes overrun with hybrid cats, and later he is forced "to kill them like vermin or wild beasts, and to drive them from his house as much as possible." After having thus killed "a great many," the cats leave him alone. Nonetheless, the great dispatching of the cats seems to have played on Crusoe's mind quite a bit. He mentions the slaughter on three separate occasions in his journal. On the last occasion when he writes about the feline carnage, he claims the act to have been an obligation. Had he not killed them, he declares dramatically, the cats would have devoured him and all he had.

A curious Noah, Robinson Crusoe is. He rescues two cats from a shipwrecked ark: one of the two remains tame; the other cat goes wild and produces a menace. These two possibilities are, of course, the very ones that face Crusoe himself. Wilderness, after all, can take us to her bosom and nurture the maniacally feral in us, or she can, in somewhat happier circumstances, fashion something sinewy and wholesome out of the soft creature that once we were. Though the point is not developed further in Defoe's novel, it seems likely that Crusoe intuited that his time on the island could have gone two ways. Mirroring his two cats, he could either stay domesticated or have gone wild, thriving, perhaps, even in a monstrous way. Crusoe famously sided with domestication, with civilization. Having made the choice, Crusoe tames the island and dispatches many of its cats.

Robinsonades: The Enduring Influence of Daniel Defoe's Island Story

As we saw in the previous chapter, Enid Blyton, in writing her bestselling children's book *Five on a Treasure Island*, may have inadvertently borrowed themes from L. T. Meade's earlier *Four on an Island*. But

Meade, in her turn, undeniably borrowed from Defoe's *Robinson Crusoe*. The influence of Crusoe is such that the name given to an entire genre of writing about islands—especially when they deal with survival in challenging insular environments or when they contemplate the implications of solitude on a fictional character—is a robinsonade.[2]

Robinsonian themes can be traced through countless later books—not all of them set on islands. Examples include William Golding's *Lord of the Flies* (1954), Jean Craighead George's *My Side of the Mountain* (1959) and *Julie of the Wolves* (1972), Scott O'Dell's *Island of the Blue Dolphins* (1960), and Gary Paulsen's *Hatchet* (1987). Even novels like those in Suzanne Collins's the Hunger Games series (2008–10) are a twist on the theme, though in that series, Katniss Everdeen has a constant supply of awful company in the form of other children who want to kill her in her wilderness arena. She may have preferred a Robinsonian loneliness.

One charming example of the genre is *Abel's Island* (1976) by William Steig.[3] Our Crusoe in this story is an anthropomorphized mouse! A storm carries off Abel's wife's scarf, and Abel impetuously follows after it. He is swept into a river in torrent and becomes stranded on an island in the middle of the river. The current is too swift for him to brave it again, and none of his ingenious plans for escape—ropes made of grass, for example—come to fruition.

And thus our mouse, who is quite a civilized fellow, settles down on his island for the winter. He builds a home in a rotting log and discovers that beneath the veneer of being a civilized mouse, he has all the skills that it takes to survive in tough circumstances. He creates a home, gathers food for the harsh winter, and fights off an owl. All the same, Abel retains some of his civilized instincts. When he defecates, for example, he does so behind a rock, even though no one can see him. He discovers a watch, which he winds and whose ticking, set against the irregular music of nature, provided a "mechanical tempo" that he found he needed in that "wild place."

A mystical side emerges in his thoughts also—just as religious instincts are awoken in Robinson Crusoe. Abel collects feathers of an owl, and planting them in the ground, he utters an incantation over them: "You're in my power / I have your quill!" And he attempts to connect telepathically with his wife, Amanda. A little madness creeps in at the edges though. He talks to himself; he talks to the stars.

Although Abel undeniably becomes a tougher fellow on the island, nonetheless, when he finally escapes the island—by swimming across when the river's waters are at their lowest—he emerges from his ordeal with a new sense of purpose in life. He is intent on being an artist. As he leaves, he looks over at his island: "No wonder he loved it; it was beautiful." He returns his wife's scarf to her.

The strangest Crusoe story of them all can be found in *A Wizard of Earthsea* (1968), the first volume of Ursula Le Guin's Earthsea Cycle. Ged, the wizard, is shipwrecked as he travels the islands that make up the Earthsea universe, and he is thrown by a rogue wave onto the beach of a tiny reef. As he crosses the land that night, he realizes that this "was no island he was on but a mere reef, a bit of sand in the midst of the ocean."

But this reef is inhabited by two people, a sister and brother, who cower when the wizard enters their ramshackle home. He is the first person they have seen in decades. The siblings live on fish, shellfish, and "rockweed." They drink from a brackish-water well. Though nervous of Ged, the old woman is fascinated by him. She shows him a yellowing child's dress, the one she had worn when she was castaway on the reef. Ged guesses correctly that they had been children of a royal house of the Kargad Empire who had been cast off on the island, there to live for the remainder of their years. Before leaving— the couple will not travel with him—Ged transforms their well into one that reliably delivers sweet fresh water. The narrative that ends this story fragment notes: "The hut is gone, and the storms of many winters have left no sign of the two who lived out their lives there and died alone."

☾ ⋆
⋆

Daniel Defoe's *Robinson Crusoe* (1719), or to give it its full title *The Life and Strange Surprising Adventures of Robinson Crusoe of York, Mariner*, the first great English novel, has been recognized as a children's classic, although children were not the intended audience.[4] This success emerged despite the fact that after its publication the novel was widely dismissed by Defoe's contemporaries as having little merit and being more suitable for a "lower class of reader"—or even worse, for children. For example, the satirist Jonathan Swift is typical of Defoe's detractors and referred to Defoe as "the Fellow that was pilloryed, I have Forgotten his Name."[5] In the nineteenth century, things had not much improved for the novel. Of *Robinson Crusoe*, Sir Leslie Stephen—the philosopher, critic, and the first Englishman to ever ski in Switzerland (I tell you this, for what it's worth)—bitingly wrote: "For people who are not too proud to take a rather low order of amusement *Robinson Crusoe* will always be one of the most charming books."

One of the triumphs of more recent criticism of *Robinson Crusoe*, according to Frank H. Ellis in his collection entitled *Twentieth Century Interpretations of Robinson Crusoe* (1969), was that Defoe's book had "been discovered to be a book for adults, even for adults in the twentieth century." It became a trope of twentieth-century reflections on Crusoe for the critic to recall their youthful reading of the book before remarking on their more recent discovery of its portentous themes. James Joyce, for example, greatly admired the novel, though being Joyce, he expressed his appreciation rather acerbically. The story of Crusoe helped explain to Joyce the enigma of "the unlimited world conquest accomplished by that mongrel breed which lives a hard life on a small island in the northern sea."[6] To be clear, that small island is Britain. *Robinson Crusoe* is thus, for Joyce, the true symbol of British conquest, a man who "cast away on a desert island, in his pocket a knife and a pipe, becomes an architect, a knife-grinder, an astronomer, a baker, a shipwright, a potter, a saddler, a farmer, a tailor, an umbrella-maker, and a clergyman." Credit where credit is due, I suppose.[7]

Other critics have remarked sagely on the novel's religious significance, its economic message, its educational value, its moral relativism on the question of cannibalism, and so on. Suitable though the novel assuredly is for sober adult reflection, it is nonetheless time, I think, for *Robinson Crusoe* to be rediscovered as a novel for children. It undoubtedly shaped the childhood sensibility of many intellectual luminaries. Philosopher and economist John Stuart Mill (1806–1873) wrote that *Robinson Crusoe* was the preeminent novel of his childhood and that it "continued to delight me through all my boyhood."[8]

Fundamentally, *Robinson Crusoe* is a ripping yarn: it's a tale of survival under arduous circumstances, replete with stories of encounters with island natives and wild beasts. Crusoe is a practical fellow. He hunts; he domesticates animals; he learns the useful arts; he builds a raft and almost disastrously attempts to leave the island; he conserves his rum; he smokes his pipe; he secures the friendship of Friday—who becomes his acolyte and servant—after having rescued Friday from being eaten by cannibals; he tames parrots; he fights mutineers on a British ship; and after "eight-and-twenty years," he leaves the island and returns to England. Oh, and Crusoe and Friday, after their island adventures, battle famished wolves in the Pyrenees.

If, as early critics complained, all of this is a low form of entertainment, that's probably okay. Children, even some of the relatively sophisticated ones that I know, are, after all, inclined to enjoy a rather low order of amusement.

€ ⋆

Robinson Crusoe is a cannibalism book for every child. The story is told in a plain enough style. So matter-of-fact is its manner that it had often been assumed in the early years after its publication that it was a true account of a stranded sailor, an assumption that was zealously promoted by its publisher. For all of that, it's a rather precocious child, for sure, who can persist in their reading of *Robinson Crusoe*. It's not at all an easy book to break into since it takes a little while for the story to get off the ground. Once it does, however, the plot of *Robinson Crusoe* undeniably moves along at a reasonable clip. This accounts for the fact that there are many excellent abridged versions available for younger souls.

The philosopher and educator Jean-Jacques Rousseau, one of a band of illustrious philosophers who have remarked on the novel, recommended the book to the youthful Émile, his idealized student.[9] *Robinson Crusoe*, Rousseau wrote, is to be "the first book Émile will read; for a long time, it will form his whole library, and it will always retain an honored place." A child can learn from this novel. Rousseau urged readers to dispense with the events before and after Crusoe's time on the island. These, the philosopher observed, are the novel's "irrelevant material." The "irrelevant" material includes an account of Crusoe's youth and his genteel conflicts with his father, who urged upon his son a less adventurous life, promoting, in fact, a sort of pastoral "middle course," one that tacked a little closer to home (advice that many of us might supply to our children). It was advice that Robinson eschewed. Before Defoe gets to the account of Crusoe's marooning on the island, we also get a fulsome account of our hero's first shipwreck, his captivity and enslavement, his escape, his subsequent time as a plantation owner in Brazil, and finally his unseemly days as a slaver, marauding along the West African coast, where he captured and transported human cargo. All of this before his second fateful shipwreck and twenty-eight years of exile on the island.

Let us heed Rousseau's advice, then; let us hack with abandon through the opening section and get right to the novel's insular core. Let's join Robinson Crusoe on the fringes of his island. After his shipwreck Crusoe fights for his life on the island's watery margins:

> Nothing can describe the confusion of thought which I felt when
> I sank into the water; for though I swam very well, yet I could

not deliver myself from waves so as to draw breath, till that wave
having driven me, or rather carried me, a vast way on towards the
shore, and having spent itself, went back, but half dead with the
water I took in.

All of a sudden, Robinson Crusoe is spat out of the brine and up onto
the sand as if born anew. Verily, he crawls up the beach like the first
terrestrial being emerging from its marine origins.

Crusoe stands there on the island's edge, wet, without food or
drink, and without "any prospect before [him] but that of perishing
with hunger or being devoured by wild beasts. . . ." What is to become
of him? Alone, terrified, without provisions, and at the mercy of the
elements and wild beasts, Crusoe's life could have gone in a couple
of directions; these were the opposing fates that befell his cats: one
remaining domesticated, one becoming feral.

Thus, on the one hand, Crusoe, if he possesses the skill, could mod-
ify the island; tame it. On the other hand, the island might irrevocably change him, driving him wild or mad. For this is the fate of many
fictional marooned souls. For example, in Robert Louis Stevenson's
Treasure Island (1883), Ben Gunn after just three years on his island
has "gone crazy in his solitude," the least manifestation of which is
his peculiar craving for toasted cheese.[10] A typical reading of Defoe's
novel concentrates on this former narrative: Crusoe as colonizer, as
world transformer; but there is abundant evidence that the island,
in turn, changes him. It's plausible to expect that after years on the
island, Crusoe has in fact gone completely mad. This is my radical
suggestion—he may not have left the island at all; and his encounters with cannibals, his tutelage of Friday, his collaboration with the
embattled British ship captain, his return to civilization, and finally,
perhaps especially, his battles with ravenous wolves are all figments
of a mind addled by decades of loneliness.

So, let us look at each possible fate in turn. First, Crusoe as island
transformer: in this tale of transformation is the story of humanity

and the environment told in a laudably compressed form. Then we shall examine how the island transformed Crusoe, for this, too, is the story of humankind: as we change our surroundings, the environment makes it mark on us.

Crusoe Transforms His Island

A widely accepted generalization in evolutionary circles is that if evolution were to run its course again, it is unlikely that the same patterns would recur. This is a reformulation of Dollo's law, named for the French-born Belgian paleontologist Louis Dollo, who proposed that "an organism is unable to return, even partially, to a previous stage already realized in the ranks of its ancestors."[11] There's no returning home! And yet Crusoe, in transforming his island, reproduces the economic and ecological history of humankind.[12] His transformation of the island is thus a symbolic reenactment—a recapitulation, to use the language of the evolutionists—of the history of our species compressed into twenty-eight years: long years in the life of one man; vanishingly short in the history of a species.

Crusoe's island life begins, as we have seen, with his emergence from the sea like the first terrestrial creature leaving its marine origins behind.[13] From this point of departure, Crusoe initiates his life in wild and unknown terrain. He (re)domesticates first himself and then domesticates the land, pushing it in to his service. In what follows, I inspect a series of vignettes of Crusoe's life on the island in which he, in essence, seems to reinvent the history of the species. Think of these as being like a series of photographic stills from a vacation album, if one could vacation in an exceedingly lonely part of hell.

Crusoe's first night on the island is a fretful one: ". . . for I was afraid to lie down on the ground, not knowing but some wild beast might devour me." So he scales a tree and sleeps. His mood is a grim one, indeed:

All the remedy that offered to my thoughts at that time was, to get up into a thick bushy tree, like a fir, but thorny, which grew near me, and where I resolved to sit all night, and consider the next day what death I should die; for, as yet, I saw no prospect of life.

The next morning, Crusoe climbs down from the tree as if he were the very first proto-human emerging into the first light of the first day of the human story. He finds himself "more refreshed with it than, I think, I ever was on such an occasion." Thus renewed, he sets about the business of changing his island.

Crusoe initially comes ashore with more or less no belongings: "In a word I had nothing about me but a knife, a tobacco-pipe, and a little tobacco in a box." His first task is to rescue provisions from the shipwreck, which in those first days was still nearshore. He finds plenty of salvageable material—for example, "bread, rice, three Dutch cheeses, five pieces of dried goat flesh . . . and a little remainder of European corn, which had been laid by for some fowls which we brought to sea with us. . . ." In addition, Crusoe brings several tools ashore: "several things very useful to me; as first in the carpenter's stores I found two or three bags full of nails and spikes. . . ." He is well furnished for his subsistence from the ship. "What would I have done without a gun, without ammunition, without any tools to make any thing, or to work with? without clothes, bedding, a tent, or any manner of coverings?" He also possesses "three large axes, and abundance of hatchets (for we carried the hatchets for traffic with the Indians). . . ."

Though it is true that Crusoe, by dint of his own labor, reproduces many of the needful elements of civilization, he does not completely reinvent the means by which these elements could be produced. His reconstruction of civilization is seeded with those remnants supplied by the ship. Some commentators have remarked that this makes Crusoe not just an ingenious laborer, but also a capitalist. Karl Marx wryly noted that "having rescued a watch, ledger, and pen and ink from the wreck, commences, like a true-born Briton, to keep a set of books." Fair enough, but in starting his project of island-living furnished with the technological provisions of the ship, he is, once again, replicating, in a vastly telescoped form, a major pattern of human history. Was not humankind born with tools in hand? Did we not benefit from a generous legacy of pre-human history—our stone tools, older than our species, our braininess the gift of cephalically endowed ancestors? Crusoe did not have to start from scratch; no one human ever did.

In replicating history, Robinson Crusoe becomes a hunter-gatherer first. He develops keen powers of nature observation and notes the existence of herds of goats on the island. His combined natural history skills and acquisition of the requisite hunting skills are described perfectly by Defoe:

> That they were so shy, so subtile, and so swift of Foot, that it was the difficultest thing in the World to come at them: But I was not discourag'd at this, not doubting but I might now and then shoot one, as it soon happened, for after I had found their Haunts a little, I laid wait in this Manner for them: I observ'd if they saw me in the Valleys, tho' they were upon the Rocks, they would run away as in a terrible Fright; but if they were feeding in the Valleys, and I was upon the Rocks, they took no Notice of me, from whence I concluded, that by the Position of their Opticks, their Sight was so directed downward, that they did not readily see Objects that were above them; so afterward I took this Method, I always clim'd the Rocks first to get above them, and then had frequently a fair Mark. The first shot I made among these Creatures, I kill'd a She-Goat which had a little Kid by her which she gave Suck to, which griev'd me heartily.

Faithfully following the human developmental sequence, Robinson Crusoe next becomes a plant domesticator. From the seeds he salvaged from the shipwreck, he eventually "saw about ten or twelve ears come out, which were perfect green barley, of the same kind as our European—nay, as our English barley." And after this, Crusoe becomes pastoralist and goatherd also: "I found that if I expected to supply myself with Goat-Flesh when I had no Powder or Shot left, breeding some up tame was my only way, when perhaps I might have them about my House like a Flock of Sheep." Having this resolve to maintain a flock, he could later report: ". . . in about a Year and half I had a Flock of about twelve Goats, Kids and all; and in two Years more I had three and forty, besides several that I took and kill'd for my Food. And after that I enclosed five several Pieces of Ground to feed them in, with little Pens to drive them into, to take them as I wanted. . . ."

It's not necessary, I think, to relate all the details of Crusoe's industry on the island. All we need to know is that Crusoe has a bona fide genius for domestication. Consider this: "I had never handled a tool in my life; and yet, in time, by labour, application, and contrivance, I found at last that I wanted nothing but I could have made it."

Over his few decades on the island, Crusoe went from frightened potential prey item to world transformer. Within a few years of arriving, he declares: "It was now that I began sensibly to feel how much more happy this Life I now led was, with all its miserable Circumstances, than the wicked, cursed, abominable Life I led all the past Part of my Days." Crusoe had successfully transformed a wild island into a home.

The Island Transforms Crusoe

The first words Robinson Crusoe speaks aloud on his island are addressed to money. There was oodles of the stuff on the shipwreck when he visited to get his initial provisions. "O drug!" he exclaims to the pots of money, "what are thou good for?" Before becoming castaway, Crusoe was undeniably a materialist; during his time there on the island, he remains a materialist. But his later materialism is of a very different stripe. Crusoe speaks sternly to money after the ship-wreck not because he is rejecting wealth; he rejects money because it no longer has present value to him. (He does not, by the way, for-get to bring this money with him when he leaves the island.) For the duration of his stay on the island, Crusoe trades the symbolic value of coin for the tangible value of natural resources. These he trans-forms and imbues with value by dint of his own sinew. Crusoe's sur-vival depends upon his transformation of the island, as we've seen, but the island in its turn transforms him.

For the most part, Crusoe remains on what he refers to as "his side of the island." This is not, in fact, necessarily the more productive side, nor is it even the more pleasant side of the island. It just hap-pens to be the one on which he was washed up upon. The other side of the island has more turtles, more birds, including penguins, and, moreover, is more pleasant! This is the side on which he finds his parrot—which he tames (after he knocked it down with a stick!)—and this is the side on which he secures his first goat. The other side of the island is the one on which he first encounters savages, but more on that in a moment. And after his first trip across the island, he determines never to leave his side for an extended period again. Thus, it is one side of the island that he domesticates—makes his domicile—while the other remains wild.

The transformation of Crusoe by island life occurs in several inter-esting ways. Some changes are amusing and superficial: he takes to wearing animal skins as his civilized clothes disintegrate; he carries an umbrella! Less superficially, his value system changes just as surely as does, very much later, the values of Henry David Thoreau—that more canonical environmental role model—whose very short stay (a mere two years, two months, and two days) in a cabin by Walden Pond has been compared to Crusoe's decades on his island.[14] Though comparisons of Thoreau to Crusoe abound in works of criticism, nonetheless, the critic Archibald MacMechan has the following rea-sonable warning about *Walden*:

The reader who takes up the book with the idea that he is going to enjoy another *Robinson Crusoe* will not be pleased to find that every now and then he will have to listen to a lay sermon, or a lyceum lecture. It is the adventurous, *Robinson Crusoe* part [of *Walden*] that is imperishable.[15]

On the other hand, it would be a poorly forewarned reader, adult or child, who reads *Robinson Crusoe* without expecting—or, indeed, having an appetite for—a fair amount of theology and other weighty topics. For *Crusoe* also, as we have seen, contains a lecture or two on matters of survival. Like all writers of genius, Defoe explicates, for the most part, by "showing" us things, but he does a goodly amount of "telling" as well. The fact is that a substantial part of the narrative is contained in Crusoe's journal, which is both discursive of events and didactic in matters of moral instruction, in equal ratio. In the journal, we learn of the solitary man's acquiescence to the will of God. His religious conversion—his turning to God—comes about slowly, but, considering our theme, it can't be our business here to follow these theological matters in detail.[16] A crucial point, however, is that in his solitude and loneliness, especially, when he feels the vulnerability that comes with being alone and sick (he is feverish when his mind turns to God), Crusoe experiences his religious conversion. Feeling sorry for himself, Crusoe cries out (only the second utterance out loud—after his proclamation to the pot of money—of his stay on the island): "Lord, be my help, for I am in great distress."[17] This, he reports, "was the first prayer, if I may call it so, that I had made for many years." His conversion on the island endures, and he takes up the reading of the New Testament. Crusoe reflects that rather than punishing him for his iniquitous life, God has "dealt bountifully" with him, by bringing him to the island. Though it might appear that he is cut off from the society of other people, the island has become a social place. Crusoe's ruminations are no longer merely with himself; he is thus "conversing mutually" with himself and with "God

Himself." Crusoe asks himself if this is not better than "the utmost enjoyment of human society." The island, long a place of tribulation, has finally redeemed Robinson Crusoe.

I started this chapter with an account of Robinson Crusoe's cats: one goes wild; one remains tame. But let us end the chapter with his domesticated parrots. Crusoe tames several parrots, though only the first of these birds becomes a great talker. The parrot learns to speak his own name. This, then, is "the first word I ever heard spoken in the island by any mouth but my own," writes Crusoe. It is as if, for the very first time, the island talks back to Crusoe, referring first to itself, "Poll," and then it calls out Crusoe's name. A very curious event concerning this parrot occurs that is worth remarking on. It's important because it casts doubt upon the verity of some of the subsequent celebrated events from the narrative: for example, the discovery of cannibals on the islands, the rescue of Friday, and Crusoe and Friday's subsequent departure from the island. Here's what happens.

It is during the sixth year of Crusoe's' residence (or captivity) on his island that he decides to explore it by means of a boat that he made for the purposes of circumnavigating the island's shores. Shortly after he launches himself, he is taken off by the current and begins to regret ever having left shore. When it seems like he will be swept far from his "beloved island" (for it appears beloved to him at the moment that he sees it receding), he has a stroke of good fortune by being caught in a current that returns him safely to shore. He resolves after that to stay on his island. He walks back to a small settlement, his "country house," and falls into a deep sleep. A voice calls out to him in his sleep: "Robin, Robin, Robin Crusoe: poor Robin Crusoe! Where are you, Robin Crusoe? Where are you? Where have you been?"

It won't, I imagine, surprise you that it is his parrot calling out to him. But this surprises Robinson Crusoe greatly. He spends a little time getting over his shock: How did the animal find him there, clear across the island? Second, why does the parrot linger around? The parrot seems overjoyed to see him. Possibly one should not read too much into this episode—though it's undeniably an unusual one—and yet it occurs at a pivotal moment in the plot. After this encounter, Crusoe returns to his own side of the island and does not depart it again for a year. He continues to improve upon his technology and to keep up with his other chores. Yet, in the space of but six paragraphs, we have skipped ahead to the eleventh year of Crusoe's sojourn. Crusoe surveys his domain and gives praise to Divine Providence for what he has carved out of a wilderness. And yet there is undeniably a change in him. He now regards himself as "prince and lord of the whole island." It is he who decides the lives and deaths of his "little family." Poll is now "his favorite" and "was the only person permitted to talk to [him]." Significantly, Crusoe mentions that his dog has grown old and crazy (as indeed, Crusoe himself may have). But Crusoe continues his agricultural enterprises. He grows grapes, which, as raisins, provide "an agreeable dainty" to his diet. One day when he is out checking on his boat—which had for years remained idle where he had left it after the fiasco of being nearly swept away from the island—he makes a discovery that quite shocks him:

> It happened one day, about noon, going towards my boat, I was exceedingly surprised with the print of a man's naked foot on the shore, which was very plain to be seen in the sand. I stood like one thunderstruck, or as if I had seen an apparition; I listened, I looked round me, I could hear nothing, nor see anything; I went up to a rising ground to look farther; I went up the shore and down the shore, but it was all one; I could see no other impression but that one.
>
> I went to it again to see if there were any more, and to observe if it might not be my fancy; but there was no room for that, for there was exactly the very print of a foot—toes, heel, and every part of a foot; how it came thither I knew not, nor could in the least imagine.

Robinson Crusoe, at last, has company, and it famously unhinges him. Fifteen years have passed by without him meeting "the least shadow or figure of any people," until he sees that one footprint. And another two pass in great uneasiness. And then Crusoe discovers the remains of a ghastly feast: "skulls, hands, feet, and other bones of human bodies," in a discarded fire pit. Yet more time passes, and Crusoe remains anxious and melancholic. He ceases some of his labor for fear that the noise will rouse the cannibals; he doesn't fire his gun for the same reason. His mind is preoccupied with nothing but the savages. In one of the more remarkable passages in the book, Crusoe argues that since the cannibals have done him "no injury," it would be wrong of him to condemn them. Eventually, after all those anxious years, he finally spies nine savages on his side of the island. Though considerable plot elements unfold after this discovery, the story moves forward at a great clip. The rescue of Friday, his inculcation into civilized ways, the rescue of Friday's father and a Spanish sailor, the mutiny on a passing English ship, Crusoe's support of that ship's captain, the recapture of the English vessel, the return to England, the recovery of wealth, the fighting of the starving Pyrenees wolves—all move at such breakneck speed that the reader wonders if they are reading an entirely different novel.

Rather than speculating that in creating the rapid-fire action of the conclusion of the story, Defoe was merely wrapping up an already drawn-out tale in a clumsy way, I suggest this alternative reading. The challenges of Crusoe's island had transformed him from dilettante into independent craftsman, from terrified shipwreck victim into farmer and husbandman, and from Godless materialist into an upright and prayerful Christian. But though a person might learn a lot and grow a lot, when thrown upon their own resources, it's quite possible that Defoe knew that solitude such as this would madden a person. Starting with Crusoe's disquiet over his parrot's mystifying discovery of him at a far-flung point on the island, the castaway's anxiety levels increase until he is deranged over his fear of being eaten by savages; Crusoe merely imagines Friday—a miraculous companion pulled from another's jaws. The subsequent mirage includes Crusoe's miraculous escape to England and all the highly improbable events that conclude the novel.

A person may transform an island, but just as surely an island will transform them, and perhaps even destroy them.

19

On Isles Benevolent; on Isles Malevolent

A reader can draw a line in the sand, if I may, in Daniel Defoe's novel, splitting it into two stories. In one, the island has a largely benefi-cent impact on our hero—he is spiritually awakened and recognizes within himself a spirit of resourcefulness. In the other story, Crusoe's bewilderingly long stay on the island provokes within him a deep loneliness that is intensified by fears about cannibals. Latter-day rob-insonades often chose one of these paths over the other, providing us with a redemptive account of being on an island or, alternatively, one where the island awakens horrors that surface when protagonists are isolated from the mainstream and left purely to their own devices.

Even in fictionalized accounts of time spent on a benevolent island, I doubt that the characters would have chosen to be stranded on an island if it were not for the author's assessment that their being castaway would be instructive for readers. But being thus cast onto an island, the experience is portrayed as having some positive conse-quences for the characters. And in turn, the stories edify and delight the reader. In this chapter, we also wash up on inclement shores and observe those circumstances when the outcomes are less wholesome.

☽⋆

Scott O'Dell's *Island of the Blue Dolphins* (1960),[1] his most popular book, is fictionalized history, based upon an account of a woman, Juana Maria, who lived alone for almost twenty years on a remote island, fifty miles off the Southern California coast, in the mid-nineteenth century. She died very shortly after her rescue and return to the California mainland. Her story is a robinsonade, where the plot concentrates on the way in which a lonely human can accommodate herself to the ways of nature. It is an optimistic tale, and yet not a sentimental one. It does not ignore the fact that humans, being social, are injured by isolation, and yet illustrates that other species and the forces of nature can provide a form of solace. The plot manages to capture the magic of island living and provides us with a wilderness adventure, replete with exciting encounters with wild animals. It is also a desperately lonely story. For all of this, *Island of the Blue Dolphins* suggests that a sort of pastoral calm is possible on islands. It describes a life spent in balance with the forces of nature. There is a cautionary tale in all of this. The novel is based upon the biography of the woman who survived her lonely stay on one of the Channel Islands and who died very quickly upon contact with mainland people, as is typically the case when indigenous people make first contact with American settlers.

San Nicolas, called Ghalas-at by its native people, is the most remote of the Channel Islands. It is about three miles wide and nine miles long. The Nicoleño tribe had lived for centuries on the island. After a disastrous encounter with Alaskan Aleuts, hired by the Russian-American Company to hunt sea otters, most of the Nicoleño men were massacred. The island was evacuated by missionaries in 1835, but a young girl was left behind. In some accounts, she dived from the boat as it was leaving the island when she discovered that her child was missing. The child died and the woman survived alone there for twenty years before finally being rescued by Captain George Nidever, a hunter and explorer, in 1853.

By all accounts, the woman had a delightful disposition and was always smiling and singing. She spoke a language that no one could interpret—all other natives of that island having died off—and so the details of her story are hard to verify and are pieced together from the sign language with which she communicated with the missionary padres of Santa Barbara. She died of dysentery seven weeks after her arrival on the mainland. Before she died, she was baptized by the padres, who gave her the Christian name Juana Maria.

Though O'Dell's novel based upon these accounts of the Lone Woman of San Nicholas is often described as a robinsonade, it is actually in many ways the inverse of *Robinson Crusoe*. The central character of the story is a young indigenous woman, Karana, rather than an adult man (a man who was, besides, a slaver before washing ashore on an island). Unlike Crusoe, who was shipwrecked, Karana gets left behind on her island after the ship evacuating her people leaves. Karana has no "Friday" to alleviate her loneliness, although she does make friends, at a distance, with a young girl who comes briefly ashore with a party of Aleuts. However, this encounter serves to intensify her sense of loneliness. And, finally, unlike Crusoe, who survived by dint of his industry and toil, Karana survives by keeping in harmony with the rhythms of the island.

Though this is a tale that emphasizes harmony, the wilds do not give up their bounty without a struggle. Karana's island is paradisiacal, and yet it is not exactly paradise. She has to gather and hunt her food: She clubs seals with rocks to retrieve their meat and sinews; she attempts to kill a sea elephant to get its tusk to serve as a point for her spear; she collects abalone and other shellfish for food; she catches fish; and she forages for plants. She makes a dress of cormorant skin. Overcoming the taboos that prohibited women of Ghalasat from fashioning weapons, she makes a bow and arrow. Using her knowledge of the island and its resources, she creates a new home away from the deserted village where her people used to live.

The island is not without its dangers. For example, her younger brother, Ramo—whose propensity for mischief is what, in O'Dell's version of the story, caused them to be left behind when the island's last remaining population left for the mainland—is killed by wild dogs. Karana, herself, is injured when she gets too close to a fight between two bull sea elephants. An attempt to kill a devilfish—a type of ray—goes badly wrong and again she is hurt. But Karana befriends many animals on the island. She tames two birds belonging to a species that she has not seen before. She rescues an injured otter. But it's her relationship with the wild dogs—the killers of her brother—that is central to the story. Karana vows to avenge herself on these animals after the death of her brother. She hunts down the dogs and leaves the pack leader with an arrow shot deep into his flesh. However, on later discovering him barely alive, she feels sorry for him and saves his life. Rontu, as she names him, becomes her friend.

After this, Karana is no longer quite so lonely. Or perhaps, more complicatedly, she only notices her loneliness after she has Rontu to talk to. The beauty of *Island of the Blue Dolphins* is that it owns up to the existential difficulties of being a person alone in their world—confined, in this case, to an island—and yet reveals the real succor that animals and nature can bring. Encounters with animals lead Karana to the realization that "animals and birds are like people, too, though they do not talk the same or do the same things." By the end of the novel, Karana no longer hunts otter, cormorants, or wild dogs. Without animals, she thinks, "the earth would be an unhappy place." One doesn't need to be a castaway to realize the truth of this.

Golding's Experiments: *Lord of the Flies*

The Walking Dead (serialized from 2003 to the present)—a successful graphic novel written by Robert Kirkman, illustrated by Tony Moore, and subsequently adapted as a popular television program—explores a trope common to many apocalyptic narratives: as civilization unravels during a crisis so also do civilized values. As the forces of mayhem are unleashed—in *The Walking Dead*, for example, the undead consume the living—it is unclear if decency can be maintained. This bleak view, that civilized values are a mere veneer to be swept aside—and pretty easily too—in chaotic times, did not origi-

nate with William Golding. However, *Lord of the Flies* (1954),[2] Golding's first book, was the first to introduce this notion to children. The
novel, which follows the descent of a group of boys who crash-land
onto a tropical island, is frequently recommended to high schoolers.

Those who have spent years in secondary school in Britain or Ireland will have little trouble accepting Golding's novel as a reasonable
conjecture about events that might transpire if a group of schoolchil-
dren were abandoned to their own devices on a tropical island. A useful task while reading the book as an adult is to speculate which character might best represent you! Are you Ralph, the flawed but sensible
leader? Or Piggy, the plump, intellectually capable voice of reason and
civilization? Perhaps you are Jack, who descends into barbarity, bringing his vicious right-hand man, Roger, and a tribe of children along
with him? Perhaps you are Roger, who kills Piggy? You might, however, be Simon, the frail mystic, the nature lover, the seer of visions,
who is murdered by the children as they dance in a frenzy about a fire.
It's possible, of course, that you are one of the "Little 'uns," who "suffered untold terrors in the dark and huddled together for comfort."

William Gerald Golding (1911–1993) knew a thing or two about
children; he was a teacher both before and after the Second World
War. Those years as a teacher included the time he spent writing
Lord of the Flies. In an interview published many years later, in 1982,
he reflected on the major theme of the novel. "My thesis, I believe,
would be this, that you could have taken any bunch of boys from
any country and stuck them on an island and you would have ended
up with mayhem."[3] In speculating about the evil that lurks beneath
the surface of human behavior, Golding was responding to the more
generous visions of humanity that typically characterize adventure
stories involving children. In fact, the characters in *Lord of the Flies*
name some of these. On discovering that they are alone on the island,
Ralph exclaims, " 'It's like in a book.' At once there was a clamor. 'Treasure Island—' 'Swallows and Amazons—' 'Coral Island—.' "

The Coral Island (1858), by Robert Michael Ballantyne (1825–1894), provides a nice example of this optimistic genre.[4] That novel—written in the form of a retrospective narrative by Ralph Rover, who was fifteen at the time—tells the story of three boys shipwrecked on a South Sea island. As the novel opens, Ralph reflects, "I was a boy when I went through the wonderful adventures herein set down." In *The Coral Island*, the three boys, like young Robinson Crusoes, find food and drink, and make their own clothes. They assemble a shelter. The boys make do admirably, and life on their Polynesian island is an idyll. Events take a turn for the worse after they encounter cannibals and, arguably worse still, when they encounter British pirates. Ultimately, with assistance from missionaries, the boys escape, though not before they have converted the cannibal chief to Christianity.

It is hard to imagine that Golding's Ralph would remember his time on a wilderness island as being "wonderful." When help finally arrives in the form of a naval ship, Ralph is being hunted down by Jack's tribe and the island is on fire. The naval officer's diagnosis of the situation as "fun and games" quickly turns to alarm. "No one killed, I hope? Any dead bodies?" he asks. "Only two. And they've gone" is the reply. "Ralph wept for the loss of innocence, the darkness of man's heart, and the fall through the air of a true, wise friend called Piggy." In my recollection of youth, I don't recall a tougher line to read. But the officer turns away in embarrassment and says: "I should have thought that a pack of British boys would have been able to put up a better show than this."

If a thousand small groups of boys had been dropped upon a thousand tropical islands, would each of these "Golding experiments" have resulted in "mayhem"? Is the veneer of civilization so very thin on young boys (or girls, for that matter, though this was not Golding's concern)? Those who grew up in small towns or in discrete suburban neighborhoods, and even those of us—that is, most of us—who endured unsupervised schoolrooms (intense little islands in their own right), will recall that childhood is indubitably a fraught business, particularly when you are left to the mercy of other children. It is hard not to conclude (for is this not the experience of living on our own little islands?) that each "Golding experiment"—albeit by taking a unique path and usually, though not always, with less cataclysmic results—reveals to us that the inculcation of civilized values is hard-won. A troop of youths left to their own devices will not easily reinvent decorum. Happy are those who have forgotten the traumas of childhood; happy are those who emerged with only small scars to show for it. But it is an undeniable truth that outside the ambit of parental supervision—though, sometimes, alas, there too, in what should be absolutely the most secure of recesses—childhood can be a dispiriting affair, especially for those of a sensitive disposition. It's no wonder that the issue of bullying is a staple of children's literature: writers rarely forget their early ordeals. Piggy's suffering at the hands of his tormentors is merely one of many instructive accounts about the anatomy of bullying found in children's literature.

That the particular experiment Golding describes for us in *The Lord of the Flies* ends in homicide and the devastation of the island is, of course, the outcome of an authorial decision. It could have been otherwise had the author chosen it. But that outcome accords with Golding's baleful view that darkness lurks in the human heart. A sensitive reader will have had inklings about the grim conclusion from early on in the story, for Golding gives us several breadcrumbs along the way. Ralph, for example, is a fine boy, but a boy nonetheless, and though he has the qualities of a leader, he is also insecure and blunders too often. Jack, who leads a little flock of hunters (former choristers), is principal architect of the chaos that ensues and might have been reined in under sterner leadership. The flaws of these principal characters are like springs held under tension; the tempo of the tragedy is then set to the ticking of these tensions, resolving, ultimately, in carnage.

In interviews for the rest of his life, Golding held fast to his conviction that civilization was but a varnished and thin bulwark holding back the forces of darkness. Any group of unsupervised boys anywhere would go down in flames. And yet the novel is not set just anywhere. It is set on a tropical island, and that island is not a neutral vessel in which events merely unfold; it plays a part in the events. If we are to read *The Lord of the Flies* as a mechanism over which Golding exerted scrupulous control, we'd be wise to pay attention—more than has been done in the past—to this environment. Golding, like many other novelists who wrote environmentally perceptive books, intuits important things about the relationship between people and the natural world that confirm and expand on theses emanating from the environmental sciences and philosophy.

Golding provides picturesque descriptions of the tropical island. Though the boys don't know exactly where they are, they are consoled by the fact that "the Queen has a big room full of maps and all the islands in the world are drawn there. So the Queen's got a picture of this island." That being said, the boys need more than a monarch's remote familiarity with the island. "I bet nobody's been here before," says Jack. So Ralph, Jack, and Simon traverse the terrain and explore the island. They scramble up a mountain made of pink granite, but the undergrowth of "roots and stems and creepers" arrests their progress. They are exhausted from their efforts; besides something ominous about the adjacent forest, the forest itself "minutely vibrated." The boys heave a rock down the mountainside: it "smashed a deep hole in the canopy of the forest." Moments later they reach the top of the mountain, and looking down they perceive the island in its entirety.

"On either side are rocks, cliffs, treetops, and a steep slope." They look to one side where the descent is tamer, and beyond that they see "the flat of the island," dense green, but drawn at the end to a pink tail of rock. There, where the island peters out in water, was another island: a rock, almost detached, standing like a fort, facing them across the green with one bold pink bastion.

Ralph spreads out his arms at the vista in satisfaction and declares: "All ours."

Each of the three companions goes on to form distinctive, and consequentially different, relationships with the island environment. For one of them, Ralph, the island is a hindrance, a temporary enclosure from which he desires escape (a sentiment shared even more emphatically by Piggy); for another, Jack, it is an opportunity to be who he was always meant to be; and for the third, Simon, it is a temple of sorts in which the inherent sacredness of nature and the depravity of humanity conflicted. In this may be both a history and a future path for our relationships with the environing world.

The island is an obstacle for Ralph to overcome. At a pivotal moment in the plot, when the signal fire has been left to burn out (diminishing the hope of rescue), the frenzy of those boys who became hunters has been mounting, the younger boys have become increasingly fretful over "the beast" (a, hopefully, imaginary malevolent force on the island), and Ralph's authority is being usurped, Ralph walks away by himself to cogitate on the situation. He begins to comprehend why it is so very wearying to live on a wild island. He recalls, mocking himself, his first enthusiastic exploration of the island, for now the problem is crystal-clear to him. On the island, he reflects, "every path was an improvisation and a considerable part of one's waking life was spent watching one's feet." Civilization for Ralph means not having to think about one's footfall on the ground. Nature is all improvisation; civilization is a predictable path where one can lose oneself in thought.

Ralph becomes disenchanted by the island. Piggy—Ralph's loyal, if often disregarded ally—dislikes the island even more. Piggy seems to exist almost outside of nature. The growth of the boys' hair serves Golding's purposes, by not only marking the passage of time but also by indicating the boys' reclamation by nature. Yet Piggy's hair "lay in wisps over his head as though baldness were his natural state. . . ."

This contrasts with the natural vigor of the hair growth of the other boys. Piggy's dependence upon his spectacles (which he has been wearing "since he was three") serves also as an emblem of civilized values. The "specs" are utilized to start the signal fire: the boys' only chance of rescue. Eventually, Piggy's glasses are stolen and the boy is deprived of the ability to even see the island. But it's not clear if he ever really saw that island in the first place. Just in case Golding's point that civilization is perishable was lost on us, Golding has Piggy killed off for good measure—murdered.

Jack's careful attentiveness to the island is in the service of pig hunting. Some of the loveliest but more ominous scenes of the book describe that hunter's growing acumen in the chase. We observe Jack bent over the "humid earth," observing a hint of a trail leading into the forest. He interrogates the slight traces and can "force them to speak to him." The trail goes cold, then he finds droppings and bursts onto a pig run, closer now to his quarry, and then he is throwing a spear. . . . Descriptions of Jack's skills are reminiscent of those concerning indigenous hunters in the field. Barry Lopez, the great American naturalist and writer, describes an indigenous person's reading of landscapes as being like someone who watches a great fire but who, instead of observing just the flames, becomes aware of everything that surrounds the flames:

> My [indigenous] companions would glance off into the outer reaches of that light, then look back to the fire, back and forth. They would repeatedly situate the smaller thing within the larger thing, back and forth. As they noticed trace odors in the air, or listened for birdsong or the sound of brittle brush rattling, they in effect extended the moment of encounter with the bear backward and forward in time.[5]

The undeniably troubling aspect of Jack's ability to discern the subtleties of the hunt is that he ultimately uses these skills to pursue his companions.

The only rival to Jack's knowledge of the island is that of Simon's—the loner, the lover of nature. Just as we read passages of Jack alone on the hunt, we encounter Simon in the depth of the forest. What Simon hunts for is more elusive though. In one especially poignant scene, Simon bends down in a mat of vegetation formed by ferns and the trunk of a fallen tree. He pulls the creepers and bushes over him, and holds his breath. Simon "cocked a critical ear at the sound of the island." He hears the gulls returning to their roosts; he hears the sound of the sea breaking on the distant reefs. A night bloom opens, and he detects their scent taking "possession of the island."

Though Simon has the ethereal bearing of a mystic, he is nonetheless a realist of an important sort. He is the one who realizes that what scares the boys most is not some beast, imagined or real, that lives on the island, but, as he announces to the other boys: "What I mean is . . . maybe it's only us." He struggles to share his intuition. Golding writes: "Simon became inarticulate in his effort to express mankind's essential illness." But then the moment passes. When later Simon stumbles down from the mountain having secured knowledge that what the boys fear most is of a pedestrian and human origin, and not a diabolical one, he is killed before he can make this known.

It has been a tenet of wilderness thinking for more than a century that a natural environment can have a salutatory effect on the human spirit. What Golding implies is that in the correct circumstances—and maybe always when little boys are concerned—it can turn the mind away from civilized values. By all means, ladies and gentlemen, send your children off to a wild island, but don't be so sure it will bring out the best in them.

THE URBAN WILD

During my first winter in Chicago, it snowed like it was never going
to stop. Snow was not an entirely new thing to me. Ireland gets a
dusting of snow every few winters or so. One year in my childhood,
it snowed heavily enough that a gang of us went to the local park to
pelt each other. Trusting the pond that had filmed over with ice to be
safe, my friend Kevin broke through and stood into waist-deep water.
We thought that was pretty funny. And I had survived a brisk winter
in New York City in 1987. In fact, it was that winter in Manhattan
that I experienced my first ice storm. In those days I lived off Times
Square and commuted out to Queen's College, where I was teaching.
The morning of the storm, I left my tiny dormitory room on Forty-
Fourth Street and descended into the urinous stench of the Times
Square subway station. The rats huddled in the warmth of the station
and scattered when the trains rushed in, only to reassemble again
after the trains set off, like birds, greasy and diseased ones, returning to roost after a momentary disgruntlement. By the time I got
onto my train, the ice that had encrusted on my boots had begun to
melt. Not having secured a seat, I held tight to the strap above. As the
train lurched, I started to pirouette on my icy soles. When the train
braked especially hard coming into a station, I spun so vigorously
that I slipped and landed sitting on the lap of an elderly woman. I

thought it amusing; no one else did. The woman glared at me stony-faced. Several sets of eyes flickered listlessly in my direction and then looked away again.

But that's not the story I want to tell here. It was 1999, my first winter in Chicago. The snow was falling hard. I had never known cold like this. I remember wondering if early settlers ever feared that it might never stop snowing, and that the temperatures would continue to plummet until no human could survive it. That first morning of snowfall, the family intrepidly went out for breakfast. The snow was so deep that the heads of our two small boys were below the level of trenches that had been cleared along the sidewalks. It came up above the midriff of my Greek-born mother-in-law, though she gamely moved along, her upper body like the sail of a yacht moving through the foamy Aegean Sea.

Having a novice's excitement about the snow, I set out that afternoon toward Lake Michigan, which was a few blocks away from our apartment. It was midafternoon, and the flakes fell slowly as if they knew that these moments of soft descent are about as good as it gets to be water. I was exuberant—the inclement weather brings out a frontier mannerliness in me. I brought with me a snow shovel in case I could be of some small service to neighbors. Perhaps a car might need digging out; perhaps a sidewalk trench would need fresh attention.

As I reached the lake, the conditions had become blizzard-like. I continued across the park—Chicago has a chain of beachside parks running parallel to the lakeshore and forming a green band that separates water from town—and walked out on the snow that covered the beach in deep drifts. I incautiously walked until I was in a bank of snow so deep that even a very foolish man would be inclined to stop. Stopped there in frigid contemplation, I realized after a few moments that I was no longer confident that I knew which way was the water and which the land.

The buildings had by now slipped away as the snow fell. The afternoon had worn on into a wintry early evening. I was aware that my decisions had now become quite consequential. It seemed completely ridiculous, but it was now possible that I was lost about half a mile from a Starbucks; moreover, it seemed conceivable that I could die out there in a park. I had imagined less ridiculous deaths for myself. Only then did I hear the first of a series of hisses on the snow around me. It was hard to imagine initially what that hiss was. It was as if someone was flinging projectiles in my direction. They fell about me and sank in the snow.

After a few stunned moments, I realized it was the shards of ice coming off the lake. Every time a wave crashed on the ice at the edge of the water, the spray would solidify and come whistling off the lake as daggers of ice. The lake was trying to kill me; the snow was trying to bury me. The danger seemed real enough, but now I knew where the lake was. I started to move, but the snow was so deep it was as if I were in that nightmare where you run and run but can't get away from a weird assailant. Fortunately, however, I'd brought a snow shovel. A few minutes of frenzied digging liberated me.

Once I was back on the sidewalk, I stood under a streetlight, panting hard. The snow was still falling, but lighter now, softer now, and the last big flakes, tumbled from the sky like small sheep gamboling in a cold dark field.

20

The Urban to Rural Gradient of Children's Stories

THE HAPPY PRINCE

If you care to inflict a beautiful tender trauma on your child, by all means read them Oscar Wilde's tale "The Happy Prince" (1888).[1] I read it first about forty-five years ago, and I don't suppose I have truly stopped sobbing ever since. The story is interesting to the urban environmentalist since it features the first and perhaps only anthropomorphized swallow in children's literature. The swallow falls in love with the Happy Prince, a beautiful bejeweled statue that is perched high above the city.

The prince, who in life had been unaware of the human suffering around him, can now see a seamstress fret over her hungry child, a writer working in his garret, a little match-girl who's dropped her wares into the gutter, and all the other calamities that befall the wretched of the city. The prince asks the swallow to postpone his flight to Egypt so as to distribute his jewels to the poor. Each day the swallow tells him a tale of far-off Egypt and each day postpones his departure to warmer climes so he may help the prince. And when the prince's wealth has been disbursed, and he is blind (since his sapphire eyes have been given away), and he is shabby (for his skin had been gold leaf), the swallow says that he will not leave the prince's side. The swallow then kisses the prince upon the lips and dies. Upon the death of the little swallow, the prince's heart breaks within him.

The town councilors notice the body of the bird and throw it in the dust heap, and when the body of the prince is cast into the furnace and his broken heart will not melt, they also throw it upon the heap. When God sends an angel to fetch the more precious things in the city, the angel retrieves the heart and the dead bird.

Wilde's story is, perhaps, of more interest to the moral educator than it is to the ecologist. Its themes of self-sacrifice, compassion, and mercy toward the impoverished are exquisitely told. The swallow, under the benign influence of the Happy Prince, undergoes his beautiful transformation. At first the swallow is concerned only with himself, with his migration away from inclement weather, with his loves, and with stories of exotic luxuries. By the end of the story, he becomes the eyes of the prince and now notices those unfortunates who are in need. Though we cannot doubt that the Christ-like message of mercy toward the poor is uppermost in Wilde's mind when he crafted the tale, nonetheless, he is too fine a writer not to attend to the little details of natural history in executing his story. A swallow persisting during the encroaching winter is unusual. A professor of ornithology notices it and writes about the phenomenon for the newspaper. As the weather gets colder, the swallow's chances of survival are slim. When he dies, it is not empathy that kills him. It is the cold. This is just what might happen to a swallow who stays in a northern city after its fellows have gone.

If you and your child can endure this tale, you will be better people for sure, and it may, besides, attune you to natural history in the city.

☾ ★

The image of urban life in Oscar Wilde's story is bleak. In this story, at least, living in a city is unfortunate for the poor, and morally vacuous for the city's elite. Even after the death of the bird and the discovery of the unmeltable heart of the prince, the politicians fail to discern the marvelous in these items. But why should they? The tiny carcasses of dead birds and scrap metal are commonplace sights in the metropolis. But God sees them, and we, the readers, see them.

In the chapters that follow, I provide an account of some of the best children's stories that concern cities. There is a gradient in attitudes toward the city in children's stories that starts with disgruntlement, runs through tolerance, mildly expressed, and extends in its furthest reaches to celebrations, not of the city, per se, but of the possibility that greening the city will amend its woes. Most stories are to be found at the near end of the spectrum—that is, many children's tales either neglect the cities or paint them in an unflattering light. We will examine this gradient starting with an entire genre that almost fails to notice that cities exist at all: towns are rarely mentioned in nursery rhymes.

21

Antipathy to Urban Life in Nursery Rhymes

Undoubtedly, the reading of nursery rhymes—some silly, some quite profound, and all generally teetering on the brink of insanity—shapes, in their early years, the environmental sensibilities of children. Considering their supposed importance, what should we make of the vast silence of nursery rhymes on important questions concerning urbanization?

Nursery rhymes are regularly preoccupied, in an often healthily irreverent way, with nature. Of the 117 rhymes collected and illustrated by Eric Kincaid in his superb collection *Nursery Rhymes* (1990), all but 23 are set out-of-doors.[1] Fully 43 percent concern animals: dogs, cats, pigs, and hens are especially prevalent. There is one rhyme in which a ship with a well-laden hull is captained by a duck: when the ship moved, this duck, predictably enough, says, "Quack, quack" ("I Saw a Ship A-sailing"). Many nursery rhymes report on very strange human-animal encounters: "Little Miss Muffet" and her spider, for example, or the girl in "Once I Saw a Little Bird," whose ambivalence about the bird hopping on her sill results in it flying away. Other rhymes, ten or so, address encounters with inanimate objects, the weather, and so forth. For example, "One Misty Moisty Morning" remarks on the weather and, by the by, an old man who is clad all in leather; "Twinkle, Twinkle Little Star" and "I See the Moon" concern matters supra-mundane. At least one addresses, if you squint at it, the laudable virtue of family planning: "There Was an Old Woman

Who Lived in Shoe," who, in the opinion of the rhymester at least, had too many children: apparently, she didn't know what to do.

Vegetation, in contrast to animals and inanimate nature, gets short shrift in the ditty canon. By my count in Kincaid's volume, there are only three rhymes specifically devoted to plants (or their fruit): "I Had a Little Nut Tree," "Oranges and Lemons," and "The Hart He Loves the High Wood." However, Kincaid's illustrations more than compensate for the absence of greenery in the text of his collection of rhymes. Just more than half (60 in total) of the rhymes are illustrated with vegetation. Perhaps this just reflects Kincaid's inclination toward green things. Just how much does Kincaid love his plants? On four occasions, he adds a floral motif to wallpaper or on the curtains—Kincaid's work is gratuitously, gloriously botanical! It may be fair to say, though, that greenery is just a given in the universe of rhymes, even if plants themselves do not consume the attention of the rhyme-crafters nor the attention of the children who listen to them. There is an interesting parallel here with the under-representation of vegetation in Paleolithic art, discussed in a previous chapter—so total is the primeval mind's preoccupation with animals, there are no plants there either.

As with plants, the number of explicit references to towns is very low. Nine rhymes out of Kincaid's 117 either refer to specific towns or, more generically, to urban locales, or they reference some aspect of urban life. These are "As I Was Going to St. Ives," "Doctor Foster Went to Gloucester," "How Many Miles to Babylon," "London Bridge," "Oh, the Brave Old Duke of York," "There Was a Girl in Our Town," "This Little Pig Went to Market," "Yankee Doodle Came to Town," and "To Market, to Market." By my count, there are an additional nine rhymes that the narrative makes clear are set in towns of some size. Examples of such rhymes include "Wee Willie Winkie," a rhyme that, if one lingers on it, is the very stuff of nightmares: Wee Willie runs about town in his nightgown yelling at children through their locked doors. Seemingly, he thinks that they should be in bed.

Perhaps we should shrug off the paucity of references to metropolitan life in nursery rhymes as not necessarily a slight to urban living. But unlike what we say for plants, this time Kincaid does not supplement what is missing from the doggerel with illustrations. Very few nursery rhymes are set in the wilderness; "A Man in the Wilderness" is one of the few. Most nursery rhymes are set in rural locations: in the countryside or in hamlets or small towns. Nursery rhymes record the madcap trials and tribulations in the rustic.

Views of big city living don't make the cut.

In trying to come to terms with the absence of urban rhymes, two questions come to mind. Why is it the case? What are the implications? The first is quite easy to answer; the second is a matter for cerebration and is not as easy to answer.

Many nursery rhymes are quite old, and most circulated in oral culture long before being written down. According to *The Oxford Dictionary of Nursery Rhymes* (1955), edited by Iona Archibald Opie and Peter Opie, over 30 percent of nursery rhymes predate 1600.[2] Only 2.3 percent were composed after 1825. The poverty of references to city life should not be surprising since the proportion of the population living in cities and large towns compared to rural locations was a fraction then of what it is today. That any nursery rhymes at all refer to larger towns and cities might, from this perspective, actually impress us.

Over the course of time working on this short chapter, I've asked several of my students to name a favorite rhyme. None could do so without some prompting. I named a few: "Humpty Dumpty," "Baa Baa Black Sheep," "Twinkle, Twinkle Little Star," and "Mary Had a Little Lamb," and these elicited a response. But none could recall more than two or three, and, strangely, none recalled where they heard the rhymes. "Perhaps in band?" one speculated. If rhymes are not in the nursery anymore, perhaps it's just as well: the world of the nursery rhyme is a surreal and occasionally violent one. "Oranges and Lemons," otherwise an innocuous rhyme about church bells, ends:

"Here comes a candle to light you to bed, / Here comes a chopper to chop off your head." Besides, such rhymes describing agrarian life are inscrutable to most children. That being said, these little scraps of nonsense still swirl around in the minds of youths, even if many can't remember how these seeped in, in the first place.

22

Urban Decay

R. CRUMB IN THE NURSERY

Only a reckless guardian would introduce a child at an early stage in their tender development to the work of pornographic cartoonist Robert D. Crumb (b. 1943). R. Crumb, as he signs most of his work, emerged as part of the underground "comix" magazine movement in the 1960s and '70s. For all of the raunchiness of his cartoons—for example, Fritz the Cat, his most famous creation, leads a suave but hedonistic beatnik lifestyle—there are themes in Crumb's writing about urban life that have parallels with those of many environmental texts. Crumb balances an ambivalence about urban life with a nostalgia for untroubled times and bucolic places.

His strip *A Short History of America* (1979) illustrates these two poles of his imagination.[1] Over a series of twelve panels, an open meadow dotted with browsing deer and fringed with dense woodland is gradually transformed to urban blight. Train tracks come first—the "Machine in the Garden," as critic of technology Leo Marx calls this image of nature disturbed by technology[2]—and a tree near the tracks slumps into the woods; a little cabin is built and out in front a tree is planted; telegraphs wires run by the train tracks, the road widens, a fence surrounds the cabin; now other houses festoon the landscape, and the woodlands dwindle; just one tree remains (the one planted outside the cabin). By this time the meadow is a town, and streetcars run down the center of the thoroughfare. In the ninth panel, the last tree is gone. A Texaco sign looms above the little house, which is surrounded by a chain-link fence. Then the cabin itself is no more. Where once there was meadow and woods, and later a modest home, there is a car lot; cars stream up and down the streets, and cars park along the street; the train tracks disappear and make way for more houses. A convenience store (a Stop 'N' Shop) stands where once the little cabin stood. "What next?!!" asks Crumb in conclusion.

Here's a good test of your friends' tolerance for urbanization: at what point in the sequence of pictures do they recoil in horror?[3] If your pals are modern primitives, even the addition of the train tracks and cabin may be despoilments too far. There are those who gravitate to village or small town life, and for such romantic souls, the central panels of Crumb's cartoon may strike a chord. The loss of the woodland strikes really hard though, and when the last tree, the planted one, disappears from the landscape, it would take a flinty heart to still love that place. But perhaps you count such people as your friends; I'm not going to judge you.

If you'd care to assess, or indeed to inform, your child's response to urban decline, and prefer to do so without introducing R. Crumb into the nursery, Virginia Lee Burton's *The Little House* (1942) is a reasonable alternative.[4] The book begins a little further along the urbanization gradient than Crumb does: a little house is already in the scene. Children frolic beneath the canopy, a dog chases a cat up a tree, and birds flit through the air. The little farmhouse is in the middle of busy rural lands: fields are plowed, horses raised, and cows move in and out of the barn. The house endures as the seasons pass, though each day brings new things. At nighttime the city is visible. Where Crumb's text is terse ("What next?!!" is his only comment), Burton provides a pretty accompanying story. After a while the story becomes tinged with melancholy: "The children grew up and went away to the city . . . ," writes Burton, "and now at night the lights of the city seemed a little brighter and closer." And then begins the precipitous decline of the countryside as "horseless carriages" intrude, and smoke belches from the steam shovel that assists in constructing the road. And with the new road come new houses, and a black pall hangs on the horizon. The little house is surrounded by tenements and schools and stores. The house is abandoned. To her credit, at first the Little House wasn't sure if she liked the city or not. But she "missed the fields of daisies and the apple trees dancing in the moonlight." An elevated train is now built right outside the Little House, and a subway system constructed below, and she can no longer tell the seasons nor can she say when it is night or day.

In Crumb's vision, the little house is torn down. Burton, who had started her urbanization gradient one step after Crumb's, extends the sequence beyond his, for she answers the question "What next?!!" One day the Little House is discovered by the great-great-granddaughter of the man who built her. Loving the house, the descendant hoists the house on a trailer and takes it back to the countryside. The final picture shows the contented Little House reinstalled on a hill surrounded by apple trees; it's nighttime and the stars twinkle overhead.

The Little House is unquestionably a delightful picture book. It won the 1943 Caldecott Medal and has long been a children's favorite. No doubt many a rural child has read it over and over again, feeling, as the Little House did before them, the attraction of the big city and yet possessing an anxious heart about what lies at the urban core. Perhaps for some children, the story informs or confirms a resolve to live always in a small town. At the same time, I imagine a young Chicago kid turning the pages of this book seventy-four years after it was published, who hears the "L" train trundling overhead, who sees the bright lights outside their window, who is comforted by the noises of the city, and yet who now, after reading *The Little House*, dreams of a life in places that may no longer be around: there will be no living in a bucolic setting for them. Of such small disappointments is life composed. Perhaps Burton's story elevates and crushes souls to a comparable degree.

Houses for the most part stand in place and the world swirls around them. This is what makes Virginia Lee Burton's *The Little House* an effective story in illustrating urbanization. The Little House was curious about what it might be like to live in the city. She need only wait; the city comes to her. In their relative immobility, trees have the same characteristic. Karen Gray Ruelle's *The Tree* (2008) tells the story of an old elm tree in New York City.[5] The wild land where the seed germinated and the young tree grew becomes a cemetery, a military arsenal, and, as the city evolves around it, an adjacent children's home that was erected and then burned to the ground. Feral pigs foraged the open land of the city, and eventually the land becomes a city park, the park becomes a civil war military base, then a circus ground—and still the city grows, and still the tree grows. The tree is now more than 250 years old.

23

The Escape Artist

With only a small amount of coaxing, biological diversity can increase cities by means of a steady migration in from the periphery. Wildlife follows corridors of green into the city core. Coyotes have been photographed in the business districts of several US cities.[1] As it is with wildlife, so, too, it appears, is it with wildlife in children's stories. The recent "greening" of urban children's literature started with a celebration of nature in suburbia, and this is where we shall start. Two wonderful examples of the genre of suburban environmental stories include Paul Fleischman's *Weslandia* (1999) and Bill Watterson's *Calvin and Hobbes* comic strip (1985–95).[2]

One of the more compromising photos in our family photo album (by which I mean, as do most people these days, that hard drive that is lying around here somewhere) is of a seven-year-old Oisín hogtied on the dining room floor. But let me explain please, Your Honor. Oisín was determined to become an "escape artist." He'd demand that we tie him up, we would demur, he would insist, and then we'd use the belt on his bathrobe as rope and leave him for a few minutes gyrating on the floor trying to shimmy out of his binds. Oisín was no Houdini, for sure, but on a couple of occasions he sprang free. There were also times, the majority, when he would give up and ask to be set loose, which I seem to recall we did in a somewhat timely manner.

I realize now that Oisín may have gotten this idea from a *Calvin and Hobbes* strip (collected in *The Authoritative Calvin and Hobbes*;

1990) where Calvin declares that he is "going to be the next Houdini."[3] Calvin, the six-year-old protagonist, asks Hobbes, his tiger (who is either alive or not depending upon one's vantage point—he's alive to Calvin and that might be all that matters), to tie him to a chair. As he struggles against the ropes, Calvin is called to dinner. He cannot undo the knots. Nor can Hobbes, who slowly thumbs through the Cub Scout manual looking for helpful tips. Eventually, Calvin's father comes to the rescue, and he is baffled by how Calvin got into the predicament in the first place. As the father unties Calvin, Hobbes sits inanimately next to the chair, leaning to one side, as if butter would not melt in his mouth.

The genius of the *Calvin and Hobbes* series is that not only can the strip influence rambunctious children to get up to things they might not otherwise have thought of, as it did with Oisín, but it also reflects, in an idealized form, their world and their youthful preoccupations. This is a child's life as it should be. Calvin's hope, for example, that a snow day will earn him a reprieve on his incomplete homework assignment mirrors every child's hope; his sport with water balloons, slush balls, and toboggan rides across newly fallen snow is theirs; and, if the gods have been even-handed, his fertile imagination should be theirs as well. Though Watterson scrupulously avoided identifying the geographical location of the strip—judging from the amount of snowfall it's somewhere in the Midwest—the setting for this portrait of childhood is inarguably a suburban one. The neighborhood is leafy: there is a ravine nearby, and a woodland is close by their backyard. It is big enough for them to get lost in. On a clear night, Calvin and Hobbes can stand outside, look up at the stars, and reflect upon the existential loneliness of the human condition. Calvin's father works in the nearby city; his mom is a homemaker. These are harassed parents but are tender and loving. Once when Calvin finds a dying raccoon, his mother rushes to the rescue, and though the animal dies in their garage, his father consoles him that the animal was warm and safe as it died. Calvin's life is not entirely without tribulations—

mild bullying, underwhelming scholarly performance, putative monsters under the bed, a stern babysitter, and the occasional scrape or bruise—but these are all manageable. The world that Watterson projects is, in other words, a suburban idyll.

Calvin and Hobbes works in a double fashion: it reflects and inspires. What, then, does the strip reflect and inspire in relation to a role for nature in the life of children? First, and important, Calvin spends a lot of his time out-of-doors (usually voluntarily, although sometimes he is sent out by an irate parent). To confirm my suspicion that Calvin is outside more than is typical of many of his peers, I totted up the number of panels in *The Authoritative Calvin and Hobbes* that depict the duo outside. One thousand forty-four all together. This is 46 percent of the total number of panels. Calvin and Hobbes spend almost half of their time outside, a figure that dwarfs that of the typical child.[4]

Calvin, the precocious environmentalist, has attitudes about human recklessness toward nature that you might expect. "What's this I hear about the greenhouse effect?" he demands of his initially dumbfounded mother in one strip. "Sure, you'll be gone," he continues, "but I won't. Nice planet you are leaving me!" His mother's retort is merely, "This from the kid who wants to be chauffeured any place more than a block away."

In another scene the duo is out in the woods when Calvin comes upon a discarded soda can and fulminates to Hobbes: "Can you believe this? Some idiot tossed garbage here in this beautiful spot?" Extrapolating to the global scale, he continues, his small fist pumping the air, "By golly, if people aren't burying toxic wastes or testing nuclear weapons, they're throwing trash everywhere!" Hobbes, somewhat sanctimoniously, replies that "there are times when it's a source of personal pride to not be human." After a moment's reflection, Calvin sheds his clothes and the pair continue their ramble; Calvin, with clothes bundled under his arm, naked as Adam before the Fall.

Human identity sits lightly on Calvin. He is variously an elephant, a dinosaur, an owl, a bat, a whale, a pterodactyl, a pig, and so on. In one strip Calvin spots a firefly, strains, and looks hopefully over his shoulder. "Your rear hasn't lit, if that's what you are wondering," Hobbes informs him. In another, Calvin creates feathers out of construction paper. He invites an initially reluctant Hobbes to heave him off the ledge of the ravine. "Don't sell the bike shop, Orville," says Hobbes to the injured child, who has crashed far below. In one especially poignant strip, Calvin dresses like a tiger and gets tips from Hobbes on the "Zen" of being a tiger. "You have to think like a tiger," Hobbes says. But neither is quite sure how to proceed. Calvin consults the encyclopedia: "Tigers are secretive and solitary," Calvin learns. Hobbes confirms this and drops a hint that Calvin's parents got Calvin at a flea market. "I've said too much already," Hobbes declares. Then Hobbes stumbles upon a part of the encyclopedia article that shocks him: "It says here we're an endangered species! It says tigers nearly faced extinction and their future remains in doubt." The two friends—a small human and the lanky tiger—side-by-side look forlorn. "That's awful," says Calvin. "I'll say," replies Hobbes. "This explains why I don't meet many babes," Hobbes concludes.

Several types of scenes regularly recur in *Calvin and Hobbes*: for example, sitting under a tree, standing beneath the stars, and so on. These are often the occasion for interesting environmental, indeed existential, exchanges between the friends.

In one strip where the pair sit beneath a tree, Calvin remarks that he loves summer vacation: "I can feel my brain beginning to atrophy already." "Shh . . . ," replies Hobbes already snoozing. But sitting beneath a tree doesn't axiomatically incline Calvin to bucolic thinking. Once, Calvin speculates that happiness comes from the "financial ability to indulge in every kind of excess." For every Thoreauvian inclination in Calvin, there is an equal and opposite hedonistic one. Like all kids, Calvin is at times reluctant to go out-of-doors and often extols the virtues of TV. "I don't like real experience," he starts, and goes on to say, "It's hard to figure out! You never know what's going on!" You don't have any control over events. TV, on the other hand, is preferred because, as he explains, "I like having a narrative imposed on life." Hobbes trips him and says, "Oh good, a farce!"[5]

Calvin and Hobbes go on epic camping holidays with the parents: it usually rains heavily, and his father puts on a brave face and opines about how the experience builds character: "This is what being in the wilderness is all about," he assures them. Calvin is having none of it and grumpily says to Hobbes, "If we live to get home, I'm never going to set foot outside again." And yet, there he is a strip or two later, walking in the autumnal woods, leaves crunching underfoot: "Sometimes it's good to hush up a while and let autumn stick in a few words."

Standing beneath the stars promotes deep thinking. Calvin and Hobbes peer up at the heavens. "We're just tiny specks on a planet particle, hurling through the infinite blackness." Such thinking is, naturally, terrifying, so our duo run for the house to "turn on all the lights."

There is, finally, an apocalyptic strand in Calvin's thinking. In multiple strips we witness Calvin playing in a sandpit. Often such scenes end in disaster, at least for the worlds that he creates there. In one such strip, as he builds castles Calvin reflects upon a city "full of happy, prosperous citizens." He continues, "Alas for the citizenry, the moon has moved closer to the Earth; a tidal wave destroys their homes."

The *Calvin and Hobbes* comic strip is deliberately environmental in its sensibilities. It valorizes the out-of-doors, it castigates environmental recklessness, and it applauds spontaneous play. But for all of that, it is deliberately suburban. Calvin's father works in a nearby urban area, and his parents express the same sorts of stresses and strains that are familiar to every other parent living adjacent to a city. Calvin, Hobbes, and parents live, to be sure, in a very pleasant neck of the woods, but it is not a rural setting. Nature is everywhere: it's time to go out to play.

24

Babar

At the pinnacle of his urban confidence, a suave Babar leans noncha-lantly against the mantel, his back to the mirror. Dressed formally, he crosses one gleaming spatted shoe over the other. He is regaling the Old Lady—his patron—and her friends with stories of the great for-est. A gray-haired lady looks on seemingly edified. One mustachioed gentleman appears to be quite skeptical, another rufous-bearded gent registers perplexity as if he just can't believe what the elephant is telling him. A great forest is clearly one thing to an elephant and, as Babar—recondite storyteller that he is—seems to know, it is quite another thing to conjure up the great forest at a social gathering in a Parisian drawing room.

In *The Story of Babar* (1931), French writer and illustrator Jean de Brunhoff provides us with several snapshots of Babar's urban life: Babar with his clothier, Babar sitting for his photographer, Babar motoring about the city and environs, and Babar paying rapt atten-tion to his professor as the elephant masters arithmetic.[1] From wild beast to assured consumer—in many ways this is the history of humanity—compressed into a few short pages. In the language of urban ecology, Babar the elephant is an urban adapter, that is, one of those species that can tolerate a human presence in dense settle-ments.[2] Coyotes, opossums, and cardinals can serve as examples. Elephants less typically make the roster.

For all of his embracing of urban glitz, Babar has endured a mel-ancholy past. There are times when our dapper pachyderm stands at his window, the shutters flung wide, and weeps for the loss of the frolicsome life that he left behind in the great forest. He weeps for his cousins, for his friends the monkeys, but he weeps most of all for the memory of his poor dead mother. This is a rags-to-riches story, if by rags we mean completely starkers, and if by riches we mean dining out on the Old Lady's dime. Babar had been born into humble circumstances, and as a child of the forest, he gamboled about, quite naked, as the beasts of the forest are wont to do. Young Babar dug in the lakeside sand, bathed in refreshing lake water, and played with friends.

But this jungle Eden was not to last, and Babar's childhood world was to be violently shattered. Imagine the trauma for a young elephant: while he was (oddly, I suppose) riding on his mother's back, a hunter, hidden behind the bushes, shoots at mother and infant. Babar's mother is slain. The elephant calf weeps over her fallen body. In a literature already dense with mothers taken in their prime, this death is one that children often take pretty hard. On the bright side, it comes early in the story and, like ripping off a Band-Aid, once it's done, it's mainly jollity thereafter.

But there's no time for immediate grieving, though, as the hunters give chase to Babar and he flees his forest home. After a few days, the youthful elephant ends up (unaccountably) in a city—presumably Paris. Other than the account of Paddington Bear's arrival at a London railway station—that bear quite oddly showed up after stowing away from "Darkest Peru," as recorded in Michael Bond's *A Bear Called Paddington* (1958)[3]—there are few finer accounts than this of an anthropomorphized animal's grand arrival at the city gates than Babar's. De Brunhoff describes his triumphant ascent into polite society as succinctly as is found in any great Victorian novel.

But Babar's sojourn in the city eventually comes to an end. He is, in the final analysis, an elephant, and elephants are generally not at home in cities. The end of his time in the city is signaled when his younger cousins Arthur and Celeste, for no especially cogent reason, also show up in the city. Wasting no time, Babar springs into action:

he buys them fine clothes; he treats them to good cakes. Eventually, the truant elephants' mothers come looking for the young cousins. Babar makes the difficult decision to return to the forest. As it happens, the former King of the Elephants has died—that unfortunate royal had a mushroom ingestion accident—and Babar, being so well clothed and having such a wealth of experience, is selected as king. King-elect Babar selects Celeste, his cousin, as his elephant Queen— not an uncommon arrangement among royalty, I'm assured. Amusingly, a dromedary is dispatched immediately to fetch bridal clothes for the King and Queen. The animal returned in the nick of time for the nuptials—no doubt, a camel purchasing finery in a Parisian bridal shop creates a small ruckus.

☾ ⋆

For every child snuggling up to listen in on the tender traumas and funny metropolitan dramas recounted in *The Story of Babar*, it seems that there's a Marxist critic scribbling vitriol in the book's margins. "Should we burn Babar?" asked educator Herbert R. Kohl in his 1995 volume of essays on children's literature.[4] Kohl's complaint echoes one already raised in Ariel Dorfman's *The Empire's Old Clothes: What the Lone Ranger, Babar, and Other Innocent Heroes Do to Our Minds* (1983). In setting out his criticism of Jean de Brunhoff's (apparently only seemingly) charming elephant story, Dorfman, a Chilean-American writer, observes: "The year in which this charming tale was written was not once upon a time but 1931. And in case the reader did not already know, it should be added that fifty years ago many countries in Africa—the supposed land of the elephants—had not yet achieved their independence. They were still colonies."[5]

Dorfman's reading of Babar has a charm of its own, and though it's not perhaps a bedtime story, it nonetheless has a certain dreamy plausibility. You don't have to squint too hard to recognize that *The Story of Babar* puts a rather high polish on the project of colonization. Though the hunter's slaughter might have been excessive and a strike against civilized values, did it not, on the other hand, in partial compensation bring Babar into the very bosom of respectable society? Babar replaces the affections of his mother with the ample patronage of the Old Lady. The prelapsarian charms of the great forest are substituted with gaudy acquisitions available (for purchase) in the city. Thus, when Babar returned to the great forest, why *should* it not be him to ascend the throne? After all, he's skilled in arithmetic; he cuts a splendid figure in a suit. But Babar will not be a monarch of the old school. He'll dress the part of the contemporary royal. The leadership in the forest passes from a dullard who perished by eating poisonous fungus to Babar, who will no doubt let them eat exceptionally good cake.

There are those who would clear de Brunhoff of charges of celebrating colonialism, or at least would change the valence of the argument. Far from touting the beneficial charms of the colonial project, surely *The Story of Babar* is taking a mischievous poke at the excesses of colonialism. Babar is clearly a rather preposterous character, not to be taken seriously: so easily seduced by baubles, so mesmerized by progress; and so ready to forget the hunter who murdered his mother. In town he idiotically rides up and down the elevator time and again until the elevator boy politely reminds him that it's time for him to begin to shop. Though he returns to the great forest and is crowned king, surely the animals are merely tugging their forelocks. The animals get it; the new king is an easy tool. The camel is dispatched to the city to fetch the nuptial wear, but not because the camel is enthralled by his new monarch. Rather, he is sent because the animals know how easily this simpleton may be distracted from the tasks of governance. The great forest is now a colony to be sure, replete with their foreign-educated vassal king, but surely this is a small price to pay to keep the even greater excesses of empire at bay. At the end of the story, one older bespectacled elephant is wearing a hat, the very hat that Babar wore on the return journey from the imperial city. To my eye, at least, he is wearing that hat ironically.

Otherwise, you don't see any of the animals of the forest wearing clothes: they remain beautiful, naked, unbowed, and, more or less, uncolonized. These are the animals of the forest. And as the wedding celebrations proceed, the lion dances with the elephant.

In both sides of the spat over the significance of colonial messages in *The Story of Babar*—Babar as inculcating the youth with zeal for the colonial project, or as undermining colonial aspirations by scoffing at it—the city is at best an ambiguous entity. Either the city is the seat of imperial prosperity and power, or it is ground zero for bourgeois triviality. However, there is another lesson about the city in this book, one that doesn't contradict either but rather cuts across them. That message is that the city is an ecological system, perhaps not quite like any other, but certainly one that is open to input and outputs of material and energy. It is a system, besides, in which certain living things thrive: some there by design, and some of them not. And it is besides livable, and it is besides beautiful. This is Babar's "Garden City," about which we need to say a few things.[6]

As Babar arrives at the threshold of the city, he stops in his tracks and stares. "He hardly knew what to make of it," writes de Brunhoff. Two dogs wait by his side, and both look at the elephant as if they hardly know what to make of him! A couple of birds stand on the roadway between the elephant and dogs, but they appear not be looking at the elephant or dogs and look instead at each other, for the concerns of birds are remote from those of an elephant in the great metropolis.

The city before them is densely settled: a lovely yellow building with a turret stands at the corner; a residential building with bright shutters flanks the other side of the street. An automobile and a bus move along the open roadways. The streets are dotted with pedestrians. At the intersections of the city streets stands a statue of a fine-looking gentleman sporting a top hat. He is surrounded by nicely tended trees, five of them in all. This creates a pleasing little green oasis at the city margins.

Babar presses on and soon encounters the dominant animal of this strange system: two humans converse outside the Opera House. Several more trees are there. Another bird, its beak wide open, attends to its remote avian business right there in the thoroughfare. Noticing the attire of the gentlemen, Babar, as nonchalantly nude as Michelangelo's *David*, if not a little grayer, naturally wants some clothes of his own. Off he goes to shop. If our impression of Babar plummets a little at this point, it is surely because a buffoonish attraction to fashion seizes him so swiftly. After all, he's just emerged from a paradisiacal wilderness! But Babar's consumerist stampede through this city is precisely where de Brunhoff's tale becomes most ecological. Babar's clothes, his food—we see Babar and the Old Lady eat a roast at dinnertime; she ladles broth from a tureen, and Babar hoists a glass of wine in his trunk—and all the goods that Babar enjoys depend upon circuits of material that can flow into and out of the city. The ecological material exchange of the city entails both inputs and outputs: food and raw materials must make their way into the city, and waste must be expelled. An elephant turd, in case you don't have this information at your fingertips, weighs up to 5 pounds, and an African elephant produces about 200 pounds of shit a day. If Babar's stay with the Old Lady lasted a full year, the household would have had to deal with in excess of 36 tons of Babar's excrement. One can assume that the Old Lady was happy to see him motor off back to the great forest.

That cities are real ecosystems can be a little hard to see at first. Their artificiality would seem to exclude them from ecological consideration. Ecosystems are defined as a biological community interacting with the abiotic environment in such a way that when energy flows through the system, there are material exchanges among the living, and between the living and the never-alive. To put this less theoretically: in order for a living thing to persist, it requires an energy source (the sun for plants, plants for elephants, and so on), and once energized, living things go into the world to satisfy their material needs. Materially, living beings require carbon, hydrogen, oxygen, nitrogen, phosphorus, sulfur, and a longish trailing edge of dozens of elements. In the ordinary course of our daily lives, we generally perceive individual beings as integrated entities—birds, humans, elephants, rocks, tables, and so on—but when you are wearing your ecosystem ecology hat, these entities are seen as just momentary accretions of elements doing things. To be ecological in your thinking, you should squint at the world, keeping your eye on the streaming of the major elements. Human ecology, and the ecology of anthropomorphized elephants, can thus be summarized: one temporary constellation of oxygen, carbon, hydrogen, nitrogen, calcium, and phosphorus, potassium, sulfur, sodium, chlorine, magnesium, and trace elements, imbued with consciousness, examines another such constellation and proclaims it "Lunch!"

The trick to seeing a city as an ecosystem is to interrogate its boundaries. Those boundaries are rarely confluent with the city walls. After his flight from the great forest, Babar stands looking at the city, but the truth is that he was always already in the city, for the city, from an ecosystem perspective, is not just where the tailor dwells, or where the *bon vivant* sups, or even where the Opera House stands, for the city is the great forest also. To be clear about this: the city, ecologically, is all of its places of consumption (think of Babar's shopping frenzy) but also all the sources for its consumables too. Babar winds up living in the city core, but undoubtedly—and this is a very grim thought—his mother ended up there also. Her feet serve as foot stools, her tusks provide trinkets for polite drawing rooms or provide ivory veneers on piano keys in the Opera House. The hunter who slew Babar's mother was an emissary from the ecosystem's seat of consumption and power dispatched to its productive margins. No doubt Babar's monkey friends will live out their years in the Parisian zoo, the fruits of the great forest will be nibbled from the after-supper fruit platter, and the trees of the great forest will provide lumber for the Old Lady's sumptuously laden dining room table. I stare at the pictures of *The Story of Babar*, and what I see are parts of the great forest atomized and distributed in myriad ways across picturesque bourgeois cityscapes. The critical readings of Babar as a colonial tale seems appropriate from this perspective that I am discussing here, but at the same time, the colonial themes in *The Story of Babar* are a subset of an ecological reading: the colonies are part of the footprint of imperial cities.

The Old Lady gives the elephant an automobile—after all, "she gives him whatever he likes"—and Babar burns hydrocarbons each and every day. We ride along on one occasion. In an illustrated double-page spread, we see Babar, dressed smartly in his motoring gear with matching cravat, driving out into the hinterlands of the city. He drives alongside the river (the river that assuredly carries his annually produced 36 tons of shit out to sea), and we can inspect the urban landscape from this vantage point. A steamer on the river pulls a houseboat behind it; a fisherman stands on a pontoon called *Marie* and hauls a tiny fish from its productive waters. The fields beyond the river form a patchwork of brown and green—plowed and unplowed fields—and cattle graze upon the green. There are chickens on and off the roadway. A goat and a young goatherd stand in the tall grass. Aloft is a hot-air balloon. For those with less leisure time, there is an airplane in the clear sky leaving the city (perhaps it's a hunting party heading to the forest). The lands just outside the city core are harmoniously worked and refashioned to a most laudable degree. These lands also support a generous diversity of wildlife. At least six bird species are depicted: one seems to be a swallow (in his illustrations, de Brunhoff privileges the pretty above the technically accurate, so it can be hard to identify species), and there are also blackbirds, pigeons, and sparrows. Two doves perch in a tree; a kingfisher cavorts over the river. Daisies, several grass species, reeds, and poppies galore festoon the scene. Tree species abound, and shrubs grow on an island in the river and adjacent to its banks. We should note the healthy invertebrate populations in the landscape: these consist of butterflies, ladybugs, ground beetles, a wasp, dragonflies, and one snail. Rounding out the pastoral scene: a steam train chuffs across the bridge over the river in the direction of the city.

The exquisite scene that Babar passes through occupies the middle pages of the book. It's the symbolic core of the story and serves as the measured center point of de Brunhoff's ecological vision. This landscape is neither the unbroken green of the great forest, nor is it the city center. It is, however, adjacent to the city. That a cultivated elephant would chose the urban hinterland for an afternoon spin in his automobile seems quite reasonable. But what's different here compared to suburban environmental themes found in *Calvin and Hobbes*, for example, is that there is no likelihood at all of the sophisticated Babar residing in the burbs. Babar's jaunt merely serves to satiate his bourgeois curiosity—he burns petrol while idly taking it all in. However, the scene affords an opportunity for the ecological reader to get the full measure of the extended global ecosystem as de Brunhoff envisions it.

What we find illustrated across the pages of *The Story of Babar* is an interestingly partitioned ecosystem. The great forest and the city are part of the one entangled system. We can envision a measure of environmental protection in the forest—one that did not, alas, help spare Babar's mother—and a dense human population living in the urban core. Finally, in between the two are the peri-urban areas with their productive though not especially industrialized market farms. De Brunhoff quite extraordinarily and presciently illustrated something that professional ecologists had been formulating during the twentieth century: the model of a so-called compartmental ecosystem. This model is most famously set down in the work of Eugene Odum, the father of American ecosystem ecology. In an often-cited paper called "The Strategy of Ecosystem Development" (1969), Odum envisioned "four compartments of equal area, partitioned according to the basic biotic-function criterion—that is, according to whether the area is (i) productive, (ii) protective, (iii) a compromise between

(i) and (ii), or (iv) urban-industrial."[7] The ecological genius of *The Story of Babar* is that de Brunhoff concretely furnished plans for such an ecologically compartmentalized system. There is one caveat to interpreting *The Story of Babar* as the realization of a realistically balanced ecosystem, however: there is little sign of the industrial production in the book. Where are all those jolly cars produced? Where are the foundries, the cement works, the textile industries, and so on? The only clue—and it's a tiny one—can be found in the illustration of Babar's arrival at the threshold of the city. Beyond the yellow building that we see in this first urban scene, behind the serried ranks of pretty houses, though just before the green hills beyond the metropolis, rises a single smokestack, made tiny in the illustration by a trick of perspective. But it is undeniably there. Close by the smokestack stand two gray buildings, the only gray structures in the scene. Are these factories? If so, then this serves as a tiny reminder that even in de Brunhoff's work—where, as we have seen, the horrors of colonialism are kept out of immediate sight—the dark satanic mills of industrial production must, of necessity, be at work.

Section Six

Learning to Care

AND THE WORLD HUMMED BACK

One of my first jobs as a young zoologist was to catalog the technical papers of the Irish entomologist Dr. Declan Murray. In the collection was a paper that reported a rather unusual incident. A Finnish entomologist was in the field, north of the Arctic Circle, collecting chironomid midges (these are the ones that have antennae like little Christmas trees—you can see them gathering around any light on a summer's evening). In the subzero temperatures, the flies were inactive, and the biologist was in danger of getting hypothermia. He took out his hip flask and had a nip of a fortifying drink. He began, he reported, to sing an old Finnish folk tune. As he did so, he noticed that the flies began to swarm. When he stopped humming, the flies went to the ground. Again he sang, and again the flies arose in response. What he had stumbled upon in those frozen conditions, by virtue of his hypothermia avoidance technique, was that to conserve energy, the male flies only swarmed when the female fly was nearby. His humming reached notes that replicated the wings of the female fly. The entomologist hummed and the world hummed back.

25

Caring for the Rose

ENVIRONMENTAL LITERACY AND ANTOINE DE
SAINT-EXUPÉRY'S *THE LITTLE PRINCE*

If you happen to crash-land on a desert island with your child—let's
say, to soften this traumatic vision, that this crash culminates a beautiful and gently undulating hot-air balloon descent—I hope that your
copy of Antoine de Saint-Exupéry's *The Little Prince* (1943) survives the
incident.[1] Saint-Exupéry, an early aviator, was no stranger to crash
landings in deserts. Indeed, the inspiration for his beloved novella
came, in part, from when, in attempting to break the speed record
for a flight from Paris to Saigon, Saint-Exupéry's aircraft plunged
into the sands of the Libyan desert on December 30, 1935. Saint-
Exupéry and his mechanic, André Prévot, miraculously survived. The
duo endured several increasingly hallucinatory days before being
rescued by a Bedouin nomad who revived the Frenchmen. For all its
gauzy fairy-tale quality, *The Little Prince* is, nonetheless, erected upon
very real sands, and if some find in it an almost unbearable inclination to fatalism and to intimations of mortality, these are also based
upon the concrete realities of Saint-Exupéry's life. Unsurprisingly,
he died relatively young (forty-four) when on July 31, 1944, his recon-
naissance airplane took off from a Corsican airbase and disappeared
into thin air.

Not only is *The Little Prince* one of the few books that upon each
fresh reading resonates for adults and children alike, but it has also
attracted considerable academic attention. To judge from Saint-
Exupéry's dismissal of the geographer occupying a little asteroid in

The Little Prince as being a remote pedant who "does not leave the desk," he would not be all that impressed by his reputation among professors. *The Little Prince* is undeniably a stirring tale, but it is philosophically chewy besides, hence its academic reputation. As you sit beneath the palm tree (recall that you've just survived a traumaless balloon crash and are now on an island) and read the story to your child over and over again, each reading will foster tender and unforgettable moments for both of you. Should it becomes necessary, at some point in the future, for your child to re-create everything important in our world once they leave the island (perhaps your misadventure portends apocalyptic times), *The Little Prince* can provide the blueprints. For this novella contains, in staccato, a complete guide to understanding our responsibilities in caring for the world. And though Antoine de Saint-Exupéry is no ordinary environmentalist, this is a book that clears a path toward comprehensive environmental literacy.

Saint-Exupéry is represented in *The Little Prince* as the aviator who has crashed in the "Desert of Sahara." He is also, to some extent, the little prince too, though the prince is also, in part, modeled on Saint-Exupéry's younger brother, François, who died of rheumatic fever at age fifteen. When the little prince passes from this world and the aviator observes, "He fell gently as a tree falls. There was not even any sound," these were words Saint-Exupéry first wrote in reference to his brother's passing. The little prince—whose romantic entanglements with an inordinately vain, though undeniably intriguing, rose had begun to overwhelm him—travels from his home asteroid, B-612, and winds up on Earth, in the desert, where he appears to the stranded aviator. The aviator has no immediate prospect of rescue and works on his plane while engaging with our extraterrestrial prince.

A centerpiece of the story's charm is its dismissal of adult pretensions and materialistic values. For all of this, it is, of course, written by an adult, and the tension between the little prince's impatience with "grown-ups and their ways" and the fact that this message is filtered through Saint-Exupéry, a grown-up—albeit an idiosyncratic and gifted one—provides the distinctive mood of the work. The novel is nostalgic for lost innocence: innocent ethical values to be sure, but also for unblemished landscapes. It revels in the clarity that the desert brings: a knowledge of the most basic human needs. "It was a matter of life and death for me," says the aviator, who is facing an imminent death by dehydration. Saint-Exupéry is not the first, nor will he be the last, to address the question of what is it to be human, but the question is, as the story illustrates, first and foremost an ecological one.

☾ ⋆

I'll refrain in what follows from rehearsing the story of *The Little Prince*, preferring here to enumerate examples from the book that strike me as especially relevant for a discussion of Saint-Exupéry's engagement with environmental questions. My claim here—and admittedly it is a very grown-up one that no doubt would strike the prince as being of very little consequence—is that taken together these examples add up to a fine introduction to environmental literacy.

We don't have to wait long to establish that the story of *The Little Prince* is nature-inclined. The very first line of the book is this: "Once when I was six years old I saw a magnificent picture in a book, called *True Stories from Nature*, about the primeval forest." The child, destined to be an aviator, creates his first two illustrations in response to *True Stories of Nature*: pictures of a boa constrictor digesting an elephant from the outside (it looks like a hat) and one from the inside. Advised by sensible grown-ups to set aside his artistic interests, the boy eventually chose another profession. He learned to pilot airplanes.

When, years later, we join the aviator now crashed in the desert, he is woken by the little prince, who implores him, "If you please—draw me a sheep!" The prince, though more encouraging of the aviator's art than the grown-ups in his childhood had been, nevertheless critiques the drawings one by one until finally our aviator presents the prince with a picture of a sheep in a box. I must confess that I only see a box furnished with air holes, but it satisfies the prince, who must have noticed the sheep within, for he exclaims: "That is exactly the way I wanted it!"

The desire to have a sheep is not a capricious one on the part of the prince. You see, he needed it to keep the baobab trees at bay. Asteroid B-612 has a baobab problem, and if left unchecked, the "terrible seeds" of this magnificent tree—"Baobab trees are the oldest living things in Africa," a native guide once told the naturalist Peter Matthiessen in *The Tree Where Man Was Born* (1972)[2]—could produce trees so big that they would split the planet into pieces. The problem of "invasive" baobabs illustrates a fundamental axiom of population biology that had been established forcefully by the Reverend Thomas Robert Malthus in his notorious tract, *An Essay on the Principle of Population* (1798).[3] Malthus's essay was excoriated by Karl Marx, who described it as "a libel on the human race," because in it Malthus had expressed doubts about humanity's abilities to keep its population in check and thereby evade squalor. Though Malthus had neglected to mention the baobab problem, nonetheless the kernel of his thinking, that all populations can grow to the point of outstripping available resources, is a cornerstone of environmental thought. Like every great naturalist, the little prince took cognizance of the world around him and saw profound connections where others might just have seen the inexorable growth of a menacing tree.

The key to managing baobabs, as the prince observes, is to attend to the problem early on, for "a baobab is something that you will never, never be able to get rid of if you attend to it too late." In this is the distillation of all sensible contemporary ecological management. It is worth stressing that in the manner in which this principle of management is asserted in *The Little Prince*, one doesn't have to squint to see what's at stake—it's hardly symbolic; it's not cryptic in the least. *The Little Prince* is a veritable instruction manual in good planetary maintenance. To drive home the point, the prince informs the aviator—and obliquely informs those of us interested in ecological management—that for effective land management, "it is a matter of discipline . . . when you've finished your own toilet in the morning, then it is time to attend to the toilet of your planet, with the greatest care."

At this point in the tale, Saint-Exupéry intrudes directly into the story in two important ways. First, to admire his own illustrations of baobabs on a devastated planetlet. ("Why," he asks rhetorically, "are there no other drawings in this book as magnificent and impressive as this drawing of the baobabs?") Second, he endorses the prince's practical message. Speaking directly to children, Saint-Exupéry implores all of his young readers to "watch out for the baobabs."

The little prince is a tenacious questioner. It's true that he does not respond to questions posed to him by others very diligently, nor does he always have answers to his own questions. But such is the natural historian's temperament. The natural historian is one who engages in relentless and passionate inquiry about the world. If the great children's writers like Saint-Exupéry are those who retain a childlike exuberance about the world, it is the natural historian's gift that they retain a childlike persistence in their questioning.

It becomes clear fairly quickly that the prince's ecological intuition about baobabs was no mere lucky guess and that it was the work of a talented ecological thinker. For his next inquiry concerns the impact of generalist predators. The point of departure for this skein of thought starts with his sheep. Recognizing that the sheep may perform a beneficent duty in checking the growth of baobabs, the prince wonders if it will eat other flowers besides. Yes, says the aviator. Will it eat flowers with thorns? Yes, confirms the aviator brusquely, for after all he is working under the fairly unrelenting timetable that death by dehydration imposes. Flowers, he declares, have thorns "just for spite." But the prince doesn't believe him, retorting that flowers "believe that thorns are terrible weapons. . . ."

Ecological monographs have been written on slimmer matters. But since the question is posed: Why *do* plants have thorns? We shall not detain ourselves at length with the often-equivocating answers provided by professors of botany to such questions. But let us pose the question circumspectly as some of our more poetic scientists have done. They ask: "Why is the world green?" If you were a sheep, the whole world might look like a large salad bowl. What's at stake in the question about the greenness of the world is why all this food is unconsumed. Hold a fallen leaf up to the weak autumnal light: the leaf may be largely entire, more or less uneaten; but those small holes where the light streams through are those parts that herbivores have removed from nature's buffet table. For the ecological truth about the world is that plants fight back. Leaves deter their foes with chemicals—crush a cherry laurel leaf, and that delicious toasted almond smell is hydrogen cyanide—and many plants use thorns.

The thorn upon the rose—central to the little prince's concerns —is but one example of plant defense. There is, to give a more gruesome instance, a Chilean bromeliad plant, *Puya chilensis*, that can reach heights of over ten feet, whose flowers have been compared with a medieval mace, and which bears excitingly dangerous barbs. The shrub has been known to ensnare sheep. Not only do its thorns act as a deterrent against browsing this particular Chilean salad, but the plant may enjoy the added benefit of the animal's nutrients after it starves to death in the shrub's thorny embrace. The animal decomposes and its constituents ebb back into the soil and down to grateful roots below.

The prince's interrogation about sheep and baobabs and roses are tremendously ecological. In its own way, the discussion also provides a succinct explication of the problem of biological control: predators introduced to control invasive species don't always do precisely what ecological managers had assumed they would.[4] But the prince's questions are no mere intellectual exercise. There is a deep emotional resonance in this matter for the prince. For when he talks about the rose—that vain blossom deserted on asteroid B-612—he is referring to the love of his life and the greatest source of his emotional distress. Navigating this distress is central to the human psychological drama of the story of *The Little Prince*, which I will have more to say about in a moment.

☾ ✶

In his descent to earth—aided by the migration of a flock of birds— the little prince pays a visit to a series of asteroids on which are exhibited a veritable museum of human follies.

The prince meets a king who commands only what his subjects already have chosen to do, a conceited buffoon who demands the adulation of others, a tippler so ashamed of his drinking that he drinks to forget his shame, a businessman who clearly knows the value of nothing, an assiduous lamplighter on whose planet the days and nights have grown so short that no sooner has he lit the evening lamps than he must extinguish them again, and a geographer who is "too important to go loafing around" and, in the absence of explorers' accounts of his own planet, knows nothing at all about his home. It would be easy enough to discount these escapades as less relevant to the task of appreciating Saint-Exupéry's environmental vision than other aspects of the story. That may be so, and yet each of these vignettes tells us a little about different models of planetary governance. Each asteroid is what is called, in the awkward lingo of contemporary ecology, a "social ecological system."[5] This perspective, a newer one in ecology, argues that the affairs of people are governed by planetary processes, but, in turn, many aspects of ecological functioning is determined by the social behavior of people. The asteroids visited by the little prince are each home to only one person—for each is a lonely place—and these regents and the asteroids they inhabit are ecologically a unit. Each asteroid's inhabitant provides a subtle diagnosis of hubris and human foolishness in the matter of managing a planet: illusions of control, narcissism, shame, calculative thinking, slavish toil, and intellectual engagement remote from any interaction with the world. None of these are based upon an attitude of empathetic care.

We, who live on a planet vaster that any of the asteroids visited by the prince, collectively live in a huge social ecological system, one that extends to the limits of our planet. The planet, in turn—though oftentimes we'd like to ignore it—can constrain us. We are living close to the limits of this social-ecological system.[6] Oftentimes attitudes to planetary affairs on Earth in the face of limits run the gamut from illusions of control and unbridled technological optimism to remote intellectual engagement. Perhaps it is time to recultivate a sense of empathetic care toward our planet. *The Little Prince* can help with this task.

Despite any concerns that you or I might have about our planetary home, the geographer in the story points the prince in the direction of Earth. "It has a good reputation," he says. Compared with the asteroids, Earth has the virtue of vastness. Though it has an impressive human population: two billion at the time Saint-Exupéry was writing his book (well over seven billion now), it, too, seemed a lonely place to our prince. As assiduously as any environmental biologist, Saint-Exupéry lays out the demographic fundamentals. Despite the enormity of its population, the entire population could be squeezed "on a small Pacific islet." The sparseness of human settlement across the face of the globe might seem especially obvious to an aviator. In Saint-Exupéry's award-winning memoir, *Wind, Sand and Stars* (1939)—an odd translation of the French title *Terre des hommes* (Land of humans)—in a chapter entitled "The Plane and the Planet," Saint-Exupéry describes what a pilot sees of the world. Those who travel by road find that it detours, as it must, to those oases that mark the work of civilization.[7] A plane ride provides a more objective view of the world: "We [pilots] discover the essential foundation, the fundament of rock and sand and salt in which here and there and from time to time life like a little moss in the crevices of ruins has risked its precarious existence."[8]

The prince found Earth to be a lonely place. A desert will certainly amplify this sense of loneliness, I suppose. A serpent, with whom our little hero converses, offers, as serpents often will, a dark solution to the prince's problem. He'd help him return to his home place (by ominous means). The prince holds this solution in reserve.

The little prince's encounter with a fox is the intellectual and environmental epicenter of this beautiful tale. The pair meet when our prince is at an especially low point. He has visited a garden "all abloom with roses" and realizes that his rose, on whom he has lavished so much tenderness, far from being the unique creature she claims to be, is, in fact, just one rose among many. The prince lies down and he weeps. Just then a fox, hidden beneath an apple tree, introduces himself to the prince. To alleviate his sadness, the prince urges the fox to play with him. But the fox cannot, for, as the fox informs the prince, he has yet to be tamed. To tame, explains the fox, means to establish ties. When one being tames another, something that seemed to be just a thing indistinguishable from thousands of others becomes individuated. That one being among innumerable other beings becomes *my* being. When, for example, I hear my beloved's step on the stairs, I know it is hers and none other's, and though we might not use the word "taming" for our loved ones, we surely hope that we've established irrevocable ties with them. When the prince tames the fox, it is, says our fox, "as if the sun came to shine on my life."

Since the explicit process of taming another being is unfamiliar to the little prince—the prince, like most of us, I suspect, muddles through when it comes to forging connections with others—the fox is prepared to walk him step-by-step through the procedure. First, know that taming requires patience. You must sit closer to the object of your affectionate attention each day. They will glance sidelong at you, and you will glance at them. Second, establishing a routine is important. If you don't, then the deliciousness of expectation is frustrated. If the fox knows to expect the prince at four in the afternoon, he can start to anticipate the prince's arrival the hour before. When my children were quite little, I'd return from work each day at a somewhat predictable time. They would gather in anticipation at the door and greet me, crying out, "Daddy's home! Daddy's home!" Time being what it is, such moments perish and they never return. Parents take heed!

The prince succeeds in taming the fox, and they establish their ties. But, once again, time being what it is, the day comes when the friends must part. The fox weeps. This is the fox's own fault, remarks the little prince, as he, the prince, had no intention of harming the fox. In response, the fox declares that every time he now sees a wheat field, a field that formerly meant nothing to him, it will remind him of his friend. Being tamed has been good for him. When, at the fox's bidding, the prince revisits the garden abloom with roses, he realizes that his own dear, bewitching, and frustrating rose is *his* rose, against which none of the others could be compared.

In their leave-taking, the fox imparts a secret to his royal friend saying, "It is only with the heart that one can see rightly. What is essential is invisible to the eye." It would be overstating things to say that it is upon this vulpine wisdom that Saint-Exupéry's philosophical reputation rests. And yet there is something undeniably arresting about these phrases. The first sentence is psychologically appealing: it advocates that we pay attention to the stirrings of our emotions. This is, perhaps, what being a child-at-heart means—don't overly complicate things. But, curiously, it is not this sentence that our child-at-heart prince repeats to himself. Rather, to ensure that he remembers the fox's advice, the prince says to himself: "What is essential is invisible to the eye." Here we may have the third lesson of taming: know that the familiar is enriched by that which is not visible. The fox's final "bon mot" is this: "You become responsible, forever, for what you have tamed."

When the aviator learns about the fox's philosophy, he translates it into a little, though thoroughly profound, case study of his own. He brings to mind his childhood home, where there was rumored to be a treasure buried. It was "hiding a secret in the depths of its heart." He goes on to say, "The house, the stars, the desert—what gives them their beauty is something that is invisible."

It's very little of a stretch to see that if the fox's wisdom can extend to the aviator's childhood home, it can also be applied to our planetary one. That we've transformed the planet is undeniable. Earth, especially in the parched reaches of desert and polar caps, sustains, as Saint-Exupéry notes, a sparse human population. Even with today's bloated population of more than seven billion souls, the planet retains its lonelier sections. But the human influence extends almost everywhere, since each person on the planet casts a wide resource shadow over uninhabited spaces—though the wealthy are more shadowy, so to speak, than those who are materially impoverished. Very little of our planet has not been either directly or indirectly influenced by humans; few truly pristine places are left on Earth.

In the scientific community, there is a growing realization that we have tamed, or domesticated, the globe. An influential essay by Peter Kareiva of the Nature Conservancy and his colleagues entitled "Domesticated Nature: Shaping Landscapes and Ecosystems for Human Welfare" makes the case that we live on a fully tamed planet.[9] These scientists argue that the benefits to humankind of a domesticated nature have largely been positive for us. But, even if you are taking a forgiving view, mistakes undeniably have been made, and the Earth is experiencing biodiversity loss, climate change, altered biogeochemical cycles, and all the carnivalesque ecocidal traumas of contemporary times.[10]

To apply the fox's wisdom to the matter of negotiating our relationship with our planetary home, it is useful to start by ruminating on the words that we commonly use when discussing planetary transformation. The word "domesticate"—which is most often used for the process of genetically altering animals and plants so that they better serve our human needs—has its roots in the medieval Latin word *domesticāre*, which means "to dwell in a house." To make a house of the Earth seems benign enough, though no especial mutuality between people and planet is implied. The use of the word "tame" has a slightly different meaning. The word is related to the Latin *domare* and the Greek δαμᾶν, which mean to tame in the sense of to subdue. To tame the Earth is to subdue the Earth.

It is hard to imagine that the processes of domestication—the one-way process of homemaking or taming, in the sense of subduing—are ones of which our fox might approve. As the fox imagines the forging of ties, both the "tamer" and the "tamed" incline toward one another: friends tame each other.

The process of transforming the Earth, especially in recent times, seems to have none of the reciprocity that we saw between the fox and the little prince. This chapter is not the place to critique the entire process by which we have harnessed the Earth for our benefit. After all, my sitting to write that critique would already complicate that critique since specialized professions such as mine, and presumably yours, are products of that bending of the planet to meet our needs in the first place. The very act of writing itself is another product of having civilized the Earth. But even if we were to concede the benefits, if not always the means, of civilization's violent taming of the Earth, surely there is room in our thinking for taking up the fox's advice in a truer spirit.

The word that Saint-Exupéry used in the *Le Petit Prince*—the original French language version of the story—to describe what transpired between the fox and the prince is "*apprivoiser.*" "To tame" is a reasonable translation of "*apprivoiser.*" But whereas "to tame," etymologically, means to subdue, "*apprivoiser*" is a richer and more complex word. "*Apprivoiser*" has as its root the Latin *prīvātus*, which means to deprive, to be bereaved, though it also means to set free. A person, for instance, after holding a political office can become a "private" citizen again and can thus break free from the political state. In this sense the person is set free from the large and chaotic swirling social forces and enters into an individualized state. Taming in the sense of *apprivoiser* makes what we see in the relationship between the fox and prince more transparent. Their friendship brings them into a private relationship and sets them up for the more generalized relationship that usually pertains between one being and another.

Taming involves some pain because it entails a deprivation. Love comes with obligations. The parting of prince and fox brings the fox grief and deprives him of a certain equanimity. And yet he is richer for it since he is also set free to become the fox that he was always meant to be: a fox that now can play with a prince. Taming as *apprivoiser* frees him to see connections that he might not otherwise have seen. The wheat field now has a special beauty for him because he now sees its secret connection with the prince. To be tamed in the sense of *apprivoiser* means that we can now see with our hearts. To love is to see these connections: "What is essential is invisible to the eye." This is the meaning of the fox's philosophy.

To be freed up for a mutual relationship creates an obligation for the other. Both partners in a relationship have been deprived of anonymity, but are compensated by being freed up to be the beings they were destined to be. The fox's parting words to the prince sum this up beautifully and emphatically: "You become responsible, forever, for what you have tamed."

Can we ever tame the Earth in the sense of *apprivoiser*? What would that entail? What we deprive the Earth of seems obvious, but what can we free it up to be? Can we set aside some of its unexplored alcoves, let its mysteries linger like "a secret in the depths of its heart"? If we can, we may discover, in turn, what the Earth frees us up to be.

The Wooing of Earth

René Dubos's engaging book *The Wooing of Earth* (1980) suggests that a relationship with the Earth along the lines suggested by the fox's philosophy of mutual taming described in Saint-Exupéry's *The Little Prince* is, or at least has, been possible.[11] Dubos took the title of his book from Bengali Nobel laureate Rabindranath Tagore's essay "Towards Universal Man" (1961).[12] Reflecting on a railway journey across Europe, Tagore regards that continent as "flowing with richness under the age-long attention of her chivalrous lover, Western humanity." This attention represents, Tagore writes grandiloquently, "the heroic love-adventure of the West, the active wooing of the earth."

Dubos takes up the theme of the wooing of Earth, not with a dewy-eyed dismissal of human devastation of the Earth of which he was well aware, but as might a medical microbiologist, his primary profession. Just as, through knowledge of medical microbiology, humans can improve upon the conditions of their own nature, could humans not also improve upon nature? It *is* possible, he concludes, to "create conditions in which both humankind and the Earth retain the essence of their wildness." This does not happen always, of course, and it cannot happen thoughtlessly: it requires something other than the conversion of wilderness into humanized environments. The key, Dubos writes, is to preserve those natural environments "in which to experience mysteries transcending daily life and from which to recapture, in a Proustian kind of remembrance, the awareness of the cosmic forces that have shaped humankind." In retaining those environments, or elements within those environments, in which to experience "mysteries," there is an echo of the fox's wisdom that the essence of things is invisible to the eye; that mystery is that which the heart can see rightly.

Dubos draws his examples of human improvement of nature from around the globe: the hedgerows of England, continental Europe, and Japan; the wet-rice ecosystem of southern China; the "ingenious" water conservation systems of the Negev desert; the Ghouta orchards of Damascus; the palm groves of Tunis; the oases of Maghreb; the de-desertification of the "Hungry Desert" of Uzbekistan; the conversion of unproductive German and Dutch heathland into thriving farms; the sensitive management of some of the forests of western Europe, for example, the Black Forest in Germany; the maintenance of the "waterways, island groves, and hills" of the "Garden of Perfect Brightness" outside Peking; and on and on. Dubos's examples of wooing the Earth border on a type of fanatic comprehensiveness that is laudable in so concise a volume.

Some of the items to make Dubos's list might strike us these days as involving more ecological sacrifice than can be considered seemly for a process of gentle "wooing." The introduction of the honeybee to North America, one of Dubos's examples, has inarguably had some undeniable benefits, but there were consequential losses of native pollinators that make calculations of trade-offs difficult to assess. More complex still is the reckoning of the costs and benefits of increasing the diversity along the archipelago of Hawaii (which otherwise had a "simple" biota) as a result of deliberate or accidental introduction of species. If Dubos's ambition to show a mutual bending of nature and humanity toward each other seems unfashionable these days, it may be helpful to note that the newly emerging field of cultural landscape ecology is the intellectual offspring of his approach. Cultural ecology recognizes that many landscapes can be shaped by a sometimes harmonious interplay of nature and culture.

What Dubos's work provokes is an awareness that the engagement of the Earth by humans isn't always a burglarizing of nature. This is the essence of vulpine wisdom.

The aviator was dying of dehydration in the desert. "What makes the desert beautiful," the little prince says to him, "is that somewhere it hides a well." And, indeed, the aviator locates this well and lives.

On another occasion the little prince says, "The stars are beautiful, because of a flower that cannot be seen." That flower, his rose, is for the prince the most important thing in the cosmos. Having abandoned her once before because of the complications she created for him, his visit to Earth has taught him how to love her, how to care for her. It is to the rose that one imagines he returns. With the assistance of a snake—they are "malicious creatures," says the aviator—whose bite felled the prince: "He fell as gently as a tree falls." The aviator did not find his body in the next daylight.

There are those rare dreams from which you rise with a new clarity of purpose or a fresh understanding of the world, and though the details of the dream events have burned off like mist from a field on an autumn morning, you are nonetheless a person restored and possessed of a new resolve. *The Little Prince* reads like such a dream, and the reader ever after has a soft determination to care more and to be alert to the mystery of things. An adult reader may also go forward with a clear-eyed awareness of their lover's foibles and yet be determined to love what is unique and marvelous in them. The "dream events" of *The Little Prince* are, somewhat surprisingly, primarily ecological, and yet few readers will recall just how environmentally astute the fable is. However, it should not at all surprise us that the lessons of this story are applicable not just to a vain rose on asteroid B-612, nor even to our own singular loves, but to everything that requires from us our care.

26

What Then Should We Do?

THE LORAX IN THE TWENTY-FIRST CENTURY

If Dr. Seuss had intended the eponymous hero of *The Lorax* (1971) to epitomize the figure of the self-righteous, blustering, and ultimately failed environmentalist, then he succeeded impressively.[1] The strategy that the Lorax deploys to arrest the destruction of the Truffula ecosystem—namely, hectoring, stigmatizing, and shaming the Once-ler, the patriarch of a onetime successful family business—fails dramatically. At the end of the story, the formerly biodiverse Truffula habitat is reduced to a post-apocalyptic wilderness of Grickle-grass. A featherless and forlorn "old crow" wings its way upon the "slow-and-sour" wind above the bleak landscape. He peers down at a boy, who, from my perspective at least, has the ringed eyes of an asthmatic. This boy is to be our hope for the future.

That the Lorax fails should not surprise us. His strategies are precisely the ones that have also routinely failed time and again in protecting ecosystems in the nonfictional biosphere that you and I inhabit. Yet it is already apparent that these demonstrably ineffective tools are the very ones that contemporary progressives hope will be useful in the coming years. A sputtering and fulminating incredulity in response to the environmental proposals will not save the Bar-ba-loots. When they go low, by all means let us go high, but we should not go high-pitched, shrill, sharpish, or bossy! It is time to retire *The Lorax* as a model for environmental advocacy in our times.

The story of *The Lorax* is typically read as a spirited analysis of the rise and fall of a poorly planned business, the corrosive effects of an amplification of technology on a successful cottage industry, the causes and environmental consequences of the rapacious misuse of resources, and, finally, as a steely-eyed analysis of capitalist excess and the utter vacuity of consumer culture. After all, nobody really needs a Thneed. Yet I suspect that you will receive a knitted object these holidays no more or less useless than a Thneed.

The depiction of the disassembly of the Truffula ecosystem under the Once-ler's witless management is without parallel in children's literature. Importantly, Truffula ecosystems are resilient up to a point. The Once-ler harvests the first tree, arduously knits his Thneed, and sells it. All of this has no discernible ecological impact— it's as if a tree just fell in the forest with only the future captain of industry (and the Lorax) there to hear it. Even when the Once-ler's extensive family joins him and Thneed production swings into a higher gear, their business could have been commendably sustainable. The decisive moment for the Truffula ecosystem is when the Once-ler invents his Super-Axe-Hacker. There can be no doubting the Once-ler's ingenuity; however, the introduction of the industrial felling of trees pushes the ecosystem over an ecological threshold. The Bar-ba-loots who are dependent on Truffula fruit are the first animals to be directly impacted. It's admittedly a strange mammal that is so obligately dependent on a single fruit—this is an evolutionary rarity—but this loss illustrates the important ecological principle of food web connectivity. Subsequent ecological losses are driven by the indirect impacts of industrial effluent. The Swomee-Swans are affected by smog: they can't sing and, though the narrative is politely silent on the point, the smog interferes with Swomee-Swan intimate life, disrupting their mating behavior. Gluppity-Glupp and Schloppity-Schlopp from the Thneed factory foul the pond, and so it's curtains for the Humming-Fish. As the Lorax and the Once-ler exchange intemperate words about the situation, they hear the "sickening smack of an axe on a tree." And thus falls the last great Truffula tree. After this the human system quickly unravels, the workers migrate, and Thneeds, too, pass from this world.

Surrounded by the evidence of his own comprehensive failure, the Lorax "lifted himself by the seat of his pants" and he "heisted himself" away from the devastation. Arguably, the Lorax, who is wingless as far as I can tell, is propelled skyward by his own indignant self-righteousness. Perhaps the Lorax was always full of hot air. Why, exactly, did he fail so epically? Let me count the ways.

First, and quite remarkably, the Lorax seems to have an inadequate grasp of how the Truffula ecosystem works in the first place. Like all ecosystems, it seems fairly robust in the face of small perturbations. In nature, trees fall, fruits are seasonal, and populations rise and ebb. And yet the Lorax pops up after the Once-ler fells his very first tree. We have already seen that this had no impact on the ecosystem—Dr. Seuss is clear on this point. Of course, the Lorax may be feigning ignorance about ecosystem ecology for strategic reasons. Perhaps, being a nature ascetic, he tolerates absolutely no use of resources at all.

Second, the Lorax failed to look for any commonality whatsoever with the Once-ler. In their very first confrontation, the Lorax insults the Once-ler. "Sir!" the Lorax proclaims. "You are crazy with greed." Perhaps this is so, and yet the most picturesque description of the delights of that landscape come not from the Lorax, but from the Once-ler. As breathlessly as Sir David Attenborough in his heyday, the Once-ler gushes that "under the trees, I saw Brown Bar-ba-loots frisking about in their Bar-ba-loot suits as they played in the shade and ate Truffula fruits." His rhapsody continues: "From the rippulous pond came the comfortable sound of the Humming-Fish humming while splashing around." But the Lorax does not build on the Once-ler's clear leanings toward nature aesthetics; he is immediately antagonistic. Rather than discussing, say, their shared stake in the beauty of the forest or even the principles of sustainable harvesting, the Lorax starts by insulting the fellow's knitting. Perhaps, of course, there are simply no apt Seussian rhymes for "environmental impact assessment" or "conservation planning"?

Finally, the Lorax claims a form of *locus standi* on behalf of the creatures of the forest. But who appointed him, I ask you? Moreover, his role in the system seems to be more than pure advocacy. He can boss the other creatures about. Of the Bar-ba-loots, he claims, "they loved living here," and yet he declares, "I can't let them stay." Like Noah in reverse, the paternalistic Lorax thus expels the animals from the Truffula forest.

It is hard to avoid the conclusion that if there's a mildly heroic character in the story, it's the Once-ler. Sure in his plutomanical youth, he forgot what it was that he loved about the Truffula trees in the first place. He once found "the touch of their tufts was much softer than silk." He once poetically described their sweet smell as being like "fresh butterfly milk." The Once-ler—a creature of soft habits, boundless ingenuity, and romantic inclination—destroys the very thing he loved. Devastated, he takes to his "Lerkim on top of his store," to nurse his self-inflicted injuries. When the asthmatic child arrives, his wounds are undoubtedly still fresh. But he recognizes in the child, whose watering eyes reminded him no doubt that the land was still in need of healing, a chance for his redemption. He throws a Truffula seed to the boy: the last seed of all! We don't follow the story after this, but can you not see in your mind's eye the fruit of this restorative work? The Truffula trees swaying in a sweet breeze, the song of the Swomee-Swans echoing across the lake full of Humming-Fish. Plump and sated Bar-ba-loots slumber in the shade of the canopy.

The genius of *The Lorax* as a cautionary tale is that it masterfully illustrates a pattern of environmental loss. Its subtlety, perhaps too subtly since the point is often lost on its readers, makes clear that the Lorax is not the fable's hero: his sanctimonious ferocity was never destined to succeed. And though we can justifiably condemn his economic shortsightedness, the Once-ler was always a potential conservation ally.

As we head into the future, we need more than ever to choose a wise way forward. *The Lorax* brilliantly reveals what missteps in advocacy can lead to. By holding the mirror up to the Lorax's fiasco, might we now speculate about a truer, dare I say, winning path? What is needed in light of Dr. Seuss's story is knowledge concerning the limits of resilience of ecosystems where we legislatively permit multiple use, an understanding of the regulatory frameworks available to us that govern resource extraction, a willingness, contra the example set by the Lorax, to stay with, rather than desert, degraded systems, and, above all, a civil attempt to find commonality when it exists. Is it, after all, so hard to imagine a contemporary politician sitting on a deck chair on a Florida beach witnessing a small group of American white pelicans fishing in the waves as the sun sets, and murmuring to himself: "the beauty, oh the beauty"?

Even if the Once-ler—a onetime greedy egomaniac—emerges as the true hero of *The Lorax*, he is not an especially optimistic role model for environmental advocacy. Fortunately, there are several others in children's literature. In Mildred Taylor's superbly moving novella *Song of the Trees* (1975), the Logan family intervenes to prevent their white neighbor, Mr. Anderson, from cutting down trees on their property.[2] The Logan family has to threaten to dynamite the forest to get Anderson and his crew to leave. This strategy may be the port of last call, so to speak. A less drastic strategy is sketched out in Carl Hiaasen's *Hoot* (2002).[3] In that story, Roy Eberhardt, who recently moved to Florida, works with two eccentric friends to halt the construction of a pancake house that threatens a colony of burrowing owls. Though the action is entertaining and the friendships a delight, ultimately the burrowing owls are saved by an investigation of the pancake company's legal compliance. A missing environmental impact statement saves the day. This sort of advocacy is something we can all emulate.

Section Seven

Good Night, Sleep Tight

IN THE TOT LOT

From where I write, I can hear young kids goofing around in the playground beside our house. Glancing over, I see one small boy heap wood chips into the bed of a toy truck and push it across the lot. A cluster of children surrounds a bucket and with small shovels fills it with sand. One of their pals removes some of the sand from the bucket and reinstalls it away to the side of the dig. No one seems to care that he is undoing their work. At the west fence of the lot, a boy and girl, both about four or so, are deep in conversation. The boy's arms are folded, and the girl sits on a tricycle and instructs him on some matter or another; the boy looks incredulous as if he simply can't believe what he is hearing. Another girl runs over to their caregiver sitting on the periphery, leans over her legs, and receives an encouraging pat on the back. The little girl then skips away.

This small troop of children is gently transforming the environment of the tot lot. Small changes to be sure: ones that will be corrected before they leave the playground at the end of the day. The sand will be returned to the small mound to the south of the lot, and the wood chips will all be swept back into place. The toys will be returned to their shelter. The lot restored, the kids leave for the day.

Eventually these childhood games of moving sand about the lot,

of digging and filling in holes, and all those small rearrangements of the land will be games no longer and will be undertaken on a grander scale. The kids will put away childish things, and taking up the implements of adulthood, they will greatly expand their impact.

27

Bookend Conversations

The year I started working on this book, our younger son, Oisín, turned eighteen. On the night of his birthday, my wife and I attended a variety show at his high school for which he was a senior writer. He had not divulged beforehand which sketches he had written, but I correctly guessed most of them. The more absurdist sketches were his. In one, for instance, a math teacher informs a reluctant student about how useful he is likely to find algebra in his future life. We then saw a series of vignettes of the student yelling out increasingly complex algebraic formulae in a variety of improbable circumstances: reviving a choking man and later as leader of the free world. From the margins, the teacher faintly calls: "Trust the equations, Charlie. . . ."

After the show the writers, director, actors, and parents milled about on the stage. My wife snapped a picture of the birthday boy with me. When I look at that picture, I see that Oisín is pulling away from me ever so slightly. He looks like a young man ready to move on to the next thing. I appear melancholy: proud, to be sure, but clearly not ready to let go of our youngster.

I don't plan to detain you any further with an elaborate expression of a father's pride in his children's accomplishments—only the more unfortunate among parents do not share in such sentiments. However, I will say, for the purposes of making a more general point, that both of our children crossed over the threshold into adulthood having acquired along the way good humor, empathy, and an ethical bearing that I find assuring. They will, I hope, bring to their friendships and romantic lives qualities that may elevate when possible, and console when necessary, those around them. Additionally, they both share a gentle comportment with animals, and, though neither is monkishly ascetic, they both have an almost old-fashioned sensibility about material possessions. They are both environmentally literate after a fashion, being aware, I suspect, of the challenges that face their generation, and being aware, also, of some of the tools available to them for wise environmental stewardship.

I helped raise two children. Not an inconsiderable challenge, and yet with just two kids, I can't claim that my attempts at parenting represent a scientifically replicated parenting experiment. Considering the enormous peculiarities of humans—all that variability (there's now over seven billion of us) to use the language of the statisticians—I might have needed to raise hundreds of the little blighters to confidently analyze which of my child-rearing practices worked and which ones didn't. That being said, nurturing children is a form of adaptive management exercise. Each morning a parent should (and most do) wake with the impossible in mind. How can I be a better mom or dad? Or partner, friend, son, or daughter, and so on. And though, undeniably, we are haunted by past failures—and, indeed, we may have failed yesterday—today we can try something new. This book was written with the confidence that there is one thing that I did right: I read to my boys and talked to them about the environmental challenges that we're confronted with. They are in no doubt about what they are facing into.

I've written little in the preceding pages explicitly about the enormity of these environmental challenges. Dispiriting as such conversations are, we need to be clear about them. So, what are they?

Almost a quarter of a century ago, the renowned environmentalist David Orr described a typical day on Earth. On that typical day, he wrote, "humans will add fifteen million tons of carbon to the atmosphere, destroy 115 square miles of tropical rainforest, create seventy-two square miles of desert, eliminate between forty to one hundred species, erode seventy-one million tons of topsoil, add twenty-seven hundred tons of CFCs [chlorofluorocarbons] to the stratosphere, and increase their population by 263,000." Reflecting the severity of the global environmental crisis, Orr concluded that "we have a decade or two in which we must make unprecedented changes in the way we relate to each other and to nature."[1] In the couple of decades since he issued this stern warning, *almost every metric that Orr examined has changed for the worse.* If there have been unprecedented changes since the early 1990s, they have not, for the most part, had salutary implications for the environment.

Recently, I recalculated each of Orr's observations. What is a typical day on Earth like in 2016? First, the good news. Chlorofluorocarbon production is being aggressively phased out. CFCs are volatile organic compounds containing carbon, chlorine, and fluorine that were used as refrigerants and as propellants for aerosol cans. That CFCs damage the Earth's ozone layer, an area of the upper atmosphere where ozone is found in relatively high concentration, was discovered by chemists Sherwood Rowland and Mario Molina, who shared the 1995 Nobel Prize in Chemistry for the discovery. Ozone loss is consequential since it reduces the amount of damaging ultraviolet light reaching the Earth's surface. Since Orr wrote about it, the Montreal Protocol (1987), a treaty that regulates the production of CFCs, has taking effect and both production and distribution of CFCs has, more or less, terminated.

More good news: population growth rate has slowed since the 1990s and continues to slow. In the early 1990s, population growth rate was approximately 1.57 percent, yielding an annual increment to the population of about 227,000 (the historical data I have access to indicates the increment to be a little lower than what Orr reported). The growth rate has dropped, quite considerably actually. It is now at a historical low of 1.060 percent per annum. Now, since the total population size is considerably higher (today it is 7,408,581,320, whereas in 1990 it was a "mere" 5,288,000,000), the annual daily additions of babies remains pretty much the same as it was a quarter of a century ago—215,153.[2]

But the environmental news is more bad than good. Habitat destruction is up, soil abuse is up, species loss is up. And climate change is an omnipresent threat. Thus if today is a typical day on Earth, we will add 24 million metric tons of carbon to the atmosphere, destroy 140 square miles of tropical forest, eliminate dozens of species, and increase the population by 226,000. Current estimates of soil loss suggest that we will deplete the world's topsoil within six decades.

Overwhelming though all of this is, this book is committed to the idea that stories are important in remedying the problem. Not simply because some of these stories inform us about the nature of environmental decline—those that do are important. But just as important is the fact that children's literature can provide a secure foundation in environmental sensibilities.

That reading stories aloud to children is enormously enriching for them is quite obvious to parents. It is an intuition supported by a large body of research in psychology and the social sciences. The insight that reading aloud was a crucial, though often neglected, aspect of early childhood educational success was the subject of Jim Trelease's best-seller *The Read-Aloud Handbook* (1982).[3]

Reading aloud to children adds to a child's vocabulary and cultivates lifelong learning habits. As we have seen in the previous chapters, many of the most beloved children's stories are nature-themed. Thus, the books that parents are reading to their children comprise, often unwittingly, crucial lessons on nature and issues of environmental concern. This presents an unrivaled, though up to now largely untapped, opportunity for parents to promote informed awareness about the natural world in their kids even when they are at a very tender age.

The reading of nature-based stories may stimulate children's wonder and excitement about the natural world, encourage in them an enduring regard for the environment, and promote sensible sustainable practices. In addition, such reading enhances a child's capacity for empathy. That is, children can extend the care they feel for characters in their favorite stories to their pets, to the people who surround them, and to the world in which they live.

As kids grow, the "informal nature curriculum" in the books that are read to them—and those that they later read for themselves— gets more compelling, complex, and challenging. Over the course of childhood, reading those books—both classics and those new favorites that are most often recommended to them—a child can develop a sophisticated and engaged understanding of some of the most important challenges that will confront the globe in the coming years. Climate instability, the species extinction crisis, freshwater depletion, deforestation, and so on are likely to become even more, not less, severe in the generation ahead. Today's children will bear the brunt of these potential calamities, though they can, if they are sufficiently prepared, most certainly contribute to environmental solutions.

To realize the potential of educating children for a dramatically uncertain future, parents do not need to seek out specialized storybooks that were written with nature education in mind. That's because the nature curriculum is already there in favorite stories.

There is, however, a severe impediment to realizing this potential for a truly revolutionary change in environmental education for youngsters. That impediment is the relatively poor state of adult environmental literacy. Despite a professed enthusiasm for promoting an interest in science and a love for nature in their children, many parents simply do not have the sort of confident grasp of the relevant information. The state of many adults' knowledge of both the environmental and life sciences is unfortunately quite low.

This volume addresses this problem by providing parents with a set of tools and a variety of perspectives for stimulating their child's innate curiosity about the natural world and preparing them to face the environmental challenges of the future. The book illustrates where in some of their kid's favorite books delightful and important information about the workings of the natural world can be found. As parents' knowledge grows, they can enhance their children's ability to understand and care for the world around us.

A central contention in this book is that the manner in which children spend their time indoors is as fateful for them and, ultimately, for the planet as is the time they spend in the green and leafy world beyond the threshold of home. Not necessarily more so, but surely not less. Though the manner in which this time is spent will be determined by a variety of factors (each parent will have different priorities), I am especially convinced that time spent reading to children is precious and has enduring implications in the life of a child. Children's books have a very special role in determining a child's sensibility about nature. Almost all books, at least for the very youngest children, have nature themes. That being said, parents are oftentimes environmentally under-informed, so that they cannot respond to their kids' thirst for knowledge beyond the pages of the books they read together. The time that parents, guardians, and teachers spend with children can be immeasurably enhanced if those adults have a full account of the world that faces their children outside the door.

The mismatch between children's attunement to nature and parents' poor preparation to engage them at an appropriate level is perhaps the greatest gap in environmental education, and it is one that my book sets out to close. I tried to avoid being didactic in my readings of selected stories, preferring to show how excavating themes of the pastoral, wildness, and urban nature is possible in stories that are, by and large, familiar to many readers. I have suggested that for readers (parents as well as children) to grow in their environmental literacy, it helps to look for the following in the stories they read: How do characters become attuned and attentive to nature? What is communicated in them about the way nature works? What does the story say about environmental problems and solutions? Does a character learn how to be environmentally responsible in the story? Does a character enhance their ability to solve problems? How much control do the characters have over their fates and the fate of nature? Taken together, these add up to a comprehensive tutorial in environmental literacy.[4]

Specifically, I have suggested in this book that reflective time (often with a book in hand) is as important for a child as active playtime. There is a strong association in books for children between equanimity, peaceful times, and pastoral places. And yet even in the most clement of rural locales, troubles can creep in at the edges. Even the sweetest "happily ever after" cannot permanently stall death. A wilderness, in contrast, can be exciting, and many of the best adventures are set in rugged places. Characters come to terms with themselves and the world in arduous circumstances. Sometimes our hero prevails and emerges the better for these trials. But a wilderness can be maddening and at times it can bring out the maniacal, as it does for the Tin Woodman. Though wilderness, classically, is a place apart from human affairs, wilderness is also a state of mind, as Max discovers in *Where the Wild Things Are*. Islands are a delight, and for storytellers and biologists alike, they are important places. They are locales of magical containment, and they can intensify a plot. They can be isolating and lonely besides. Unlike islands, beloved of ecologists and children's story writers, cities have been a neglected habitat in both traditions. But environmental stories are creeping in at the edge: there are more that are often set in the pastoral of the suburbs, and urban kids' fiction may become a growth industry. Finally, children's stories can help all of us to renew our love of nature. Taking a leaf from *The Little Prince*'s playbook, we might recognize our beautiful responsibility to love the world that we have to some large extent already tamed. To tame can mean to subjugate, but taming can also be done in the gentler sense that Saint-Exupéry meant using the verb *apprivoiser*. We lean toward the Earth, recognize its uniqueness, love it, and care for it.

Stories properly told have no discrete ending: they haunt us beyond the articulation of the final syllable. This may be even more so the case for children where a favorite character from a story can become an integral part of the family. The child who demands the same story, time and time again, imagines this beloved character to be a constant companion. The world created by a great book can open up an opportunity for conversation between adult and child. "Booktalks" are those discussions that encourage a child to read. The term is often used in formal educational settings, but may also be used to describe the conversations that are provoked once the book is closed. I use a more general term, "bookend conversations," to describe those ongoing discussions between parents and their children that both encourage a love of story and that continue dialogue about those characters, events, and themes that come up during story time. There is a growing academic discussion about the value of booktalks, and when and where they are most effective.

Researchers who examine reading aloud to children have shown that having open-ended discussions about the material is crucial to the effectiveness of bedtime stories. According to a 2011 paper by the early education researchers Xenia Hadjioannou of Penn State University and Eleni Loizou of the University of Cyprus: "True booktalks involved interactions that were in many ways reminiscent of the kinds of conversations groups of adult readers have when talking about a book: all participants work together in thinking and trying to make sense of the book through explorations, wonderings, connections, and affective responses."[5]

Parents: Continue to inform yourself about environmental problems, surround your children with the delights of nature, and encourage their attunement to animals and plants. Parents, chat with your children about books.

The picture of Oisín and me on his eighteenth birthday revealed a young man ready to take on the challenges of the world, but also showed my trepidation about letting him go. My pride, though, is that he seems ready. My hope is that despite the challenges ahead that he and his generation will be no less excited by the world they have inherited than were those of any other generation. The challenges that face us need not diminish our sense of the beauty of the world, but rather should sharpen our sense of responsibility toward it and all who live in it.

THE END

Acknowledgments

A number of years ago, when writing a piece on woodlands in Chicago, I noticed that one of them was 100 acres, which sounded somewhat familiar. That essay, without my having planned it, morphed into "The Ecology of Pooh," which was subsequently published by *Aeon* magazine. I owe an enormous debt to Brigid Hains, *Aeon*'s editorial director, for her support of my writing, her advice on that piece, and for publishing a subsequent piece on "Beasts at Bedtime." I am grateful to *Aeon* for the permission to reproduce those essays here.

My editor at University of Chicago Press, Christie Henry, has been a marvel: her support has been constant, her advice has been perceptive, and even when, in a moment of frustration with the manuscript I threatened to burn it and throw myself on the flames, she did not lose her equanimity. I'm not, apparently, the first author to have grown frustrated by a project. My advice to you is don't ever write a book, but if you do, I hope you have an editor imbued with as much genius and good humor as Christie Henry possesses. Thanks also to Erin DeWitt, senior manuscript editor at the Press, for her meticulous work on this project. The comments of two anonymous reviewers selected by the Press were invaluable.

Many thanks to the *Irish Times*, who allowed me to reproduce the essay on the relationship between Libby Meade and Enid Blyton. Thanks also to Abbas Raza, editor of *3QuarksDaily*, who for several years hosted my essays on just about anything I cared to write about.

My colleagues at DePaul University have been unstinting in their support of this project. I have been fortunate to work at an institution that values teaching and the life of the mind in equal measure. My first "boss" at DePaul, Dr. Thomas Murphy, always took the twists and turns of my research interests in his stride. Although he retired before I started on this book, his support over the years was invaluable to me and assured me that I was in the perfect intellectual environment. I would also like to thank my former chair, Dr. Judy Bramble, who supported this odd departure from one of the department's ecologists. She encouraged my teaching a special topics seminar on the subject of the book, and this was very helpful in stimulating ideas. I'd like also to single out for special thanks Dr. James Montgomery ("Monty"), another former chair, and the bedrock of our department. Writing a book while being an academic chair is a challenging business; it would not have been possible without the excellent administrative support of Naomi Leighton and the technical support given to our department by Margaret Workman. Thanks to Dean Gerry Koocher and the College Office of Science and Health, and my previous deans, for their ongoing support of my work. I thank the library staff at DePaul University Library and those at the City of Evanston Public Library.

I have been fortunate enough to have writerly friends who have endured my talking about this work for almost three years now. First, I'd like to thank poets Chris Green and the late Patricia Monaghan, both of whom, several years ago, when I was determined to write for audiences outside my immediate discipline, gave me invaluable advice on some early writing efforts. Their encouragement had more of an impact on me than either might have known. I thank the following friends and colleagues: Hugh Bartling, Christopher Dunn, Richard Engling, James Fairhall, Micheal Gentleman, Randall Honold, William Jordan III, Ming (Frances E.) Kuo, Stephen Murphy, Ron Nahser, Kay Read, Christine Skolnik, Anthony Paul Smith, Dan Stolar, Jeff Tangle, Lauren Umek, Lynne Westphal, Dolores Wilber, Barbara Willard, David Wise, and Paddy Woodworth for friendship and advice over a period of many years. Thanks to my fellow "professors who drink" group: Will McNeill, Rick Lee, and Sean Kirkland. Will McNeill, whose eye for a misplaced comma is without match, gave me useful feedback on several drafts. A special thanks to Gavin Van Horn, who edited a couple of pieces related to this project on his *City Creatures* blog and who has long been a hiking companion along the urban trail.

Some early media interest was encouraging: thanks to Tony Sarabia, host of WBEZ's *Morning Shift,* and to Lori Rotenberk for writing about *Beasts at Bedtime* for *Grist* magazine. I posted a number of drafts of chapters from this book on my Facebook page as notes. The feedback from many dear friends on social media was very helpful— Stanley Cohn, Domenico D'Alessandro, Kathleen Garness, Ric Hudgens, Ming Kuo, and Misha Lepetic led the fray.

It's been my extraordinary good fortune to have taught several generations of inspiring students at DePaul. There are too many to mention in person, but you are all appreciated. I do, however, want to single out Alex Nates-Perez and Katie Kamba, who took a very special interest in this work, and whose insights on this topic contributed to the project in important ways.

My thanks to Kathryn Kysar and Michael Walsh, who invited me to a workshop supported by the Oberholtzer Foundation on Mallard Island, Minnesota, where I drafted the "Wilderness Stories" section of the book. Thanks to Thomas Allen Hanson for illuminating and useful conversations for the duration of that stay.

I wrote and edited a lot of this volume sitting in a window seat of the Brothers K Coffeehouse in Evanston, Illinois. The Brothers Kim—Brian and John—have, over the years, created an affable community of well-caffeinated neighbors. We are all grateful for their hospitality. At the other end of the day, when, exhausted from my labors, I visited either the Local Option on Webster or the Red Lion on Lincoln, I was buoyed up by the comforting environments created by barmen Tony Russomanno and Colin Cordwell.

Writing books is a long and laborious process for a writer but is an extraordinary tedious affair for family members. My boys, Fiacha and Oisín, have endured much: a good half of my text messages to them over the past year have included paragraphs from this book, with requests for feedback. They gave that feedback with verve and good humor. Big thanks to Sarah Heneghan née Horwitz, my daughter-in-law, who provided extensive notes and edits for several chapters. Those chapters were improved immeasurably.

My love of books comes from my parents, Mary and Paddy Heneghan, whom, I'm afraid to say, I've neglected during the writing of this book. Though I have not been a consistent "Skyper" in recent months, I have thought of both of them and appreciated both of them every single day while writing this book. Thanks as well to my siblings: Clare, Anne, Padraic, Maeve, and Paul.

Vassia Pavlogianis, my wife and my beloved, is the sort of person that people call "a force of nature." And if by "force" they mean "love" and if by "nature" they mean "wisdom," I agree. I thank Vassia for her humor, her passion, her insights, and her counsel. She supported this book from start to finish, and I thank her and love her for this.

Notes

INTRODUCTION

1. In E. O. Wilson's *Half-Earth: Our Planet's Fight for Life* (Liveright Publishing, 2016), the naturalist gives an account of sticking his hand into a fire ant nest. In a matter of moments, he received dozens of stings. He cautions against repeating the experiment.

2. I have been helped in innumerable ways by friends on Facebook and other social media who not only shared stories and comments useful for this brief reflection on the beastly inclinations of children, but have been unfailingly helpful in providing feedback as I wrote this book.

3. Ravi Chellam, "Ecology of the Asiatic Lion (*Panthera leo persica*)" (PhD diss., Saurashtra University, Rajkot, India, 1993).

4. Vasant K. Saberwal, James P. Gibbs, Ravi Chellam, and A. J. T. Johnsingh, "Lion-Human Conflict in the Gir Forest, India," *Conservation Biology* 8, no. 2 (1994): 501–7.

5. The poem was first published in William Blake's *Songs of Innocence and of Experience* (1794).

6. Examining the relationship between reading and later environmental attitudes is an emerging field. Clearly reading to children in tandem with encouraging them to get out-of-doors has implications for the emergence of an environmental ethic. See, for example, Paul F. J. Eagles and Robert Demare, "Factors Influencing Children's Environmental Attitudes," *Journal of Environmental Education* 30, no. 4 (1999): 33–37; or more recently Robert Gifford and Andreas Nilsson, "Personal and Social Factors That Influence ProEnvironmental Concern and Behaviour: A Review," *International Journal of Psychology* 49, no. 3 (2014): 141–57.

7. Liam Heneghan, "Studies of Soil Microarthropod Communities Experimentally Manipulated by Chronic Low-Level Nutrient Input, and Their Impact

on Some Ecological Processes" (PhD diss., University College Dublin, 1994).

8. Paul Geraghty, *The Great Green Forest* (Red Fox, 1994).

9. For a full treatment of the concept of "locus of control," see Herbert M. Lefcourt, *Locus of Control: Current Trends in Theory and Research*, 2nd ed. (Psychology Press, 2014).

10. Though I am not reviewing this literature in depth, I have been influenced by many scholarly writers in this discipline, especially the following: Maria Tatar, *Enchanted Hunters: The Power of Stories in Childhood* (Norton, 2009); Seth Lerer, *Children's Literature: A Reader's History from Aesop to Harry Potter* (University of Chicago Press, 2008); Perry Nodelman, *The Pleasures of Children's Literature*, 3rd ed. (Pearson, 2002); Marah Gubar, *Artful Dodgers* (Oxford University Press, 2009); and various volumes by Maria Nikolajeva.

11. Frank B. Golley develops this point well in his book *A Primer for Environmental Literacy* (Yale University Press, 1998).

12. J. K. Rowling, *Harry Potter and the Philosopher's Stone*, Harry Potter: Book 1 (Bloomsbury, 1997).

13. See http://www.nea.org/grants/teachers-top-100-books-for-children.html.

CHAPTER ONE

1. If you care to refresh your memory of these, here is a good account: https://plato.stanford.edu/entries/paradox-zeno/. I had once attempted to convince Mrs. Heneghan that I was immortal, using Zeno as support. We both realize now that I am very mortal.

2. Ben Ross Berenberg, *The Churkendoose: Part Chicken, Turkey, Duck and Goose* (Wonder Books, 1946).

3. Noel Barr, *Ned, the Lonely Donkey: A Story* (Wills & Hepworth, 1954).

4. My favorite versions of these stories are in James Stephens, *Irish Fairy Tales*, illus. Arthur Rackham (Macmillan, 1920). There are several children's versions of these available, though I'd recommend that you read Stephens's versions and then tell a version of your own to your children.

5. J. R. R. Tolkien, *The Hobbit* (George Allen & Unwin, 1937).

6. Richard Louv, *Last Child in the Woods: Saving Our Children from Nature-Deficit Disorder* (Workman, 2005).

7. Samuel Beckett, *The Unnamable* (Faber & Faber, 2012).

8. John Calder's introduction to *The Unnamable* is frequently included in copies of this book, a copy of the text can be found here: https://www.naxos.com/mainsite/blurbs_reviews.asp?item_code=NA533712&catNum=NA533712&filetype=About+this+Recording&language=English.

9. Modern Library, "100 Best Novels," http://www.modernlibrary.com/top-100/100-best-novels/.

10. Max Beerbohm, *Zuleika Dobson; or, An Oxford Love Story* (Heinemann, 1911), 132–37.

11. Jack London, *The Call of the Wild* (Macmillan, 1903).

12. George Orwell, *Animal Farm* (Random House, 2010).

13. Eric Carle, *The Hungry Caterpillar* (Philomel, 1969).

14. Bill Martin, *Brown Bear, Brown Bear*, illus. Eric Carle (Puffin Books, 1984).

15. Marcus Pfister, *The Rainbow Fish*, trans. J. Alison James (North-South Books, 1992).

16. Margaret Wise Brown, *The Runaway Bunny*, illus. Clement Hurd (Harper & Row, 1972).

17. Wilson Rawls, *Summer of the Monkeys* (Doubleday, 1976); Theodore Taylor, *The Cay* (Avon Books, 1970).

18. Gene Myers, *The Significance of Children and Animals: Social Development and Our Connections to Other Species*, 2nd ed. (Purdue University Press, 2007).

19. Vanessa LoBue, Megan Bloom Pickard, Kathleen Sherman, Chrystal Axford, and Judy S. DeLoache, "Young Children's Interest in Live Animals," *British Journal of Developmental Psychology* 31, no. 1 (2013): 57–69.

20. John Newbery, *A Little Pretty Pocket-Book* (1744).

21. Beatrix Potter, *Beatrix Potter: The Complete Tales* (Frederick Warne, 2006); Kenneth Grahame, *The Wind in the Willows*, illus. Ernest H. Shepard (1908; Methuen Children's Books, 1998).

22. Aubrey H. Fine, ed., *Handbook on Animal-Assisted Therapy: Theoretical Foundations and Guidelines for Practice* (Academic Press, 2010).

23. Kevin Coyle, *Environmental Literacy in America* (National Environmental Education & Training Foundation, 2005).

CHAPTER TWO

1. Quotes such as this one—"Everybody needs beauty as well as bread, places to play in and pray in, where nature may heal and give strength to body and soul alike," from *The Yosemite* (1912)—abound in the work of the nineteenth-century naturalists.

2. Henry D. Thoreau, "Walking," in *Collected Essays and Poems* (1861; Library of America, 2001).

3. Journalist Richard Louv writes about these movements in "Leave No Child Inside," *Orion Magazine* 57, no. 11 (2007), https://orionmagazine.org/article/leave-no-child-inside/.

4. Richard Louv, *Last Child in the Woods: Saving Our Children from Nature-Deficit Disorder* (Workman, 2005).

5. See, for example, Roger L. Mackett and James Paskins, "Children's Physical Activity: The Contribution of Playing and Walking," *Children & Society* 22, no. 5 (2008): 345–57; although the links with physical health may be complex: see Richard Larouche, Didier Garriguet, Katie E. Gunnell, Gary S. Goldfield, and Mark S. Tremblay, "Outdoor Time, Physical Activity, Sedentary Time, and Health Indicators at ages 7 to 14: 2012/2013 Canadian Health Measures Survey," *Health Reports* 27, no. 9 (2016): 3.

6. This is confirmed in a number of cases. For example, in her paper "An Investigation of the Status of Outdoor Play," *Contemporary Issues in Early Childhood* 5, no. 1 (2004): 68–80, Rhonda Clements writes: "The mother's play experiences, compared with the child's, clearly indicate that children today spend considerably less time playing outdoors than their mothers did as children. The study reveals several fundamental reasons for this decline, including dependence on television and digital media, and concerns about crime and safety."

7. For an assessment of this evidence, see Andrea Faber Taylor, Frances E. Kuo, Christopher Spencer, and Mark Blades, "Is Contact with Nature Important for Healthy Child Development? State of the Evidence," *Children and Their Environments: Learning, Using and Designing Spaces* 124 (2006); and Louise Chawla, "Benefits of Nature Contact for Children," *CPL Bibliography* 30, no. 4 (2015): 433–52.

8. The relationship between environmental knowledge and conservation ac-

tion is notoriously complex. Jacqueline Frick, Florian G. Kaiser, and Mark Wilson illustrate that only certain types of knowledge inform conservation behavior in their paper, "Environmental Knowledge and Conservation Behavior: Exploring Prevalence and Structure in a Representative Sample," *Personality and Individual Differences* 37, no. 8 (2004): 1597–613.

9. Charles Darwin's *The Voyage of the Beagle: Journal of Researches into the Natural History and Geology of the Countries Visited during the Voyage of HMS Beagle Round the World* reports on his explorations. During those years on the voyage, the naturalist spent more time on land than at sea; by my count, the word "walk" (and words with near meanings) occurs over ninety times throughout the book, the word "sail" (and words with near meanings) occur around fifty times, and finally, as befits an account by a man in the active exploration phase of his career, the word "read" occurs about twenty times. That it occurs at all reminds us that even when he was hoofing around wild parts, Darwin retained some quiet hours for an engagement with books and reports.

10. The notion of "reading the book of nature" is a concept emerging from medieval philosophy which contends that an inspection of nature permits one to have some knowledge of God.

11. A reasonable amount of scholarship has been devoted to racism in children's literature. For example, see Gillian Klein, *Reading into Racism: Bias in Children's Literature and Learning Materials* (Routledge, 2002); Bernice A. Pescosolido, Elizabeth Grauerholz, and Melissa A. Milkie, "Culture and Conflict: The Portrayal of Blacks in US Children's Picture Books through the Mid- and Late-Twentieth Century," *American Sociological Review* (1997): 443–64; Rebecca Harlin and Hani Morgan, "Review of Research: Gender, Racial and Ethnic Misrepresentation in Children's Books: A Comparative Look," *Childhood Education* 85, no. 3 (2009): 187–90.

12. An excellent overview of the immense thicket of terms associated with "environmental literacy" is given by B. McBride, B. Brewer, C. A. Brewer, A. R. Berkowitz, and W. T. Borrie, "Environmental Literacy, Ecological Literacy, Ecoliteracy: What Do We Mean and How Did We Get Here?" *Ecosphere* 4, no. 5 (2013): 1–20.

13. Martin H. Manser, Jonathon Green, Elizabeth McLaren Kirkpatrick, Rosalind Fergusson, and Jenny Roberts, eds., *Bloomsbury Good Word Guide* (Bloomsbury, 1990).

14. I have used the *OED Online* throughout the text of this book. Oxford University Press, http://www.oed.com.ezproxy.depaul.edu. I never write without having a tab for the *OED* open, I recommend this practice to you.

15. http://www.lib.cam.ac.uk/exhibitions/Darwin/bigpics/Albert_Way _caricature.jpg.

16. Some, though not all, of the literature on environmental literacy is geared toward professional training, and much of it toward adult populations. There is less explicitly an environmental literacy for children. This is a growing field. See, for example, Ruth Wilson, *Nature and Young Children: Encouraging Creative Play and Learning in Natural Environments* (Routledge, 2012).

17. Frank B. A. Golley, *A Primer for Environmental Literacy* (Yale University Press, 1998).

18. This is the advice that Sir Peter Medawar also gives in his *Advice to a Young Scientist* (Basic Books, 1979).

19. In *The Spell of the Sensuous: Perception and Language in a More-than-Human World* (Vintage, 1997), David Abram writes, for example, "The alphabetized intellect stakes its claim to the earth by staking it down, extends its dominion by drawing a grid of straight lines and right angles across the body of a continent—across North America, across Africa, across Australia—defining states and provinces, counties and countries with scant regard for the oral peoples that already live there, according to a calculative logic utterly impervious to the life of the land." Elsewhere in that volume, he writes, "In the absence of writing, we find ourselves situated in the field of discourse as we are embedded in the natural landscape; indeed, the two matrices are not separable. We can no more stabilize the language and render its meanings determinate than we can freeze all motion and metamorphosis within the land."

20. Harvey Yunis, ed., *Plato: Phaedrus* (Cambridge University Press, 2011).

21. This is why folklore compilations such as the one by Lady Augusta Gregory, *Visions and Beliefs in the West of Ireland* (1920), are valuable. Such volumes often reveal an immense practical wisdom about the natural world. Of course, much of what gets written down is nonsense: this, for example, is the cure for "yellow jaundice": "If you are attending a funeral, pick out a few little worms from the earth that's thrown up out of the grave, few or many, twenty or thirty if you like. And when you go home, boil them down in a

sup of new milk and let it get cold; and believe me, that will cure the sickness."

22. For a biography of Wallace, see Peter Raby, *Alfred Russel Wallace: A Life* (Princeton University Press, 2001).

TOPOPHILIA

1. From the poem "Christmas" in John Betjeman, *A Few Late Chrysanthemums* (Murray, 1955).
2. See a very brief account here: http://source.southdublinlibraries.ie/handle/10599/8067.

CHAPTER THREE

1. Margaret Wise Brown, *The Runaway Bunny*, illus. Clement Hurd (Harper-Collins, 1942).
2. J. R. R. Tolkien, *The Hobbit; or, There and Back Again* (George Allen & Unwin, 1937), 330.
3. J. R. R. Tolkien, *The Fellowship of the Ring* (George Allen & Unwin, 1954), 283.
4. See *Theocritus*, edited with a translation and commentary by A. F. S. Gow (Cambridge University Press, 1950).
5. *Virgil's Eclogues*, trans. Len Krisak (University of Pennsylvania Press, 2010).
6. This book is a restorative to the soul: Kenneth Grahame, *The Wind in the Willows* (1908; Methuen, 1966).
7. Virgil's *Eclogues* inspired poetic imitators up until Elizabethan times, though contemporary poets only sporadically attempt pastoral poems. As I wrote about this, I found myself sitting in a coffee shop in Evanston, Illinois, beside Josh Corey, the editor of a recent compendium of poems entitled *The Arcadia Project: North American Postmodern Pastoral* (2012). Perhaps the very insistence in this volume on the continued vitality of the tradition simultaneously underscores the fact that the pastoral appeal is exceptional rather than typical for contemporary poets.
8. William Empson, *Some Versions of Pastoral* (New Directions, 1935).
9. It is hard to imagine a child's book that does not employ pastoral themes to some degree. There are, however, some books that ooze with pastoral

themes and others where the pastoral is expressed with considerably less vigor. For example, Roald Dahl's *Charlie and the Chocolate Factory* (Knopf, 1964) is urban, industrial, and entirely shepherdless. Despite its great popularity among its readers, the novel has perplexed critics. One celebrated complaint is that the story is a "fantasy of an almost literally nauseating kind." But for all of that, the book has its green sensibilities and can be read as an assault on gluttony, on greed, even on the excessive viewing of TV. This critique of the perils of an urban life are quite pastoral in their sensibility; certainly they resonate with appeals for environmental sustainability.

10. Chinua Achebe, with John Iroaganachi, *How the Leopard Got His Claws*, illus. Mary GrandPré (Candlewick Press, 2011).

11. Katherine Paterson, *Bridge to Terabithia* (Avon Camelot, 1977).

12. E. B. White, *Charlotte's Web* (Harper and Brothers, 1952).

13. This suggestion of the perpetuity of happiness is doubtlessly a consoling one. According to *The American Heritage Dictionary of Idioms*, by Christine Ammer (Houghton Mifflin, 1997), this "hyperbolic term," "happily ever after," used in fairy tales dates from the mid-1800s.

CHAPTER FOUR

1. A. A. Milne, *The Complete Tales and Poems of Winnie-the-Pooh* (Dutton, 2001).

2. Richard Louv, *Last Child in the Woods: Saving Our Children from Nature-Deficit Disorder* (Workman, 2005).

3. Christopher Milne, *The Enchanted Places* (Dutton, 1975).

4. A good place to start reading contemporary writing on the relation between people and place is the work of Barry Lopez. He has been very productive; a good place to start is this volume: Barry Holstun Lopez, *Vintage Lopez* (Vintage Books, 2004). I had the pleasure of hosting Barry at a couple of readings over the years. The impact of these hours has stayed with me over the years. I thank him here.

5. Stephen R. Kellert and Edward O. Wilson, *The Biophilia Hypothesis* (Island Press, 1995); Yi-Fu Tuan, *Topophilia: A Study of Environmental Perceptions, Attitudes, and Values* (Columbia University Press, 2013); Jay Appleton, *The Symbolism of Habitat: An Interpretation of Landscape in the Arts* (University of Washington Press, 1990); Richard Louv, *Last Child in the Woods: Saving Our Children from Nature-Deficit Disorder* (Workman, 2005).

6. Theodore Roszak, Mary E. Gomes, and Allen D. Kanner, eds., *Ecopsychology: Restoring the Earth, Healing the Mind* (Sierra Club Books, 1995).

7. Glenn Albrecht, "'Solastalgia': A New Concept in Health and Identity," *PAN: Philosophy Activism Nature* 3 (2005): 41.

8. Tim Robinson, *Setting Foot on the Shores of Connemara and Other Writings* (Lilliput Press, 1996).

CHAPTER FIVE

1. I relied on Linda Lear's biography: *Beatrix Potter: A Life in Nature* (Macmillan, 2008); and I also found Margaret Lane's *The Tale of Beatrix Potter: A Biography* (Penguin, 2011) to be useful.

2. Beatrix Potter, *Beatrix Potter's Journal* (Penguin, 2011).

3. Ibid.

4. Graham Greene, *The Lost Childhood and Other Essays* (Eyre & Spottiswoode, 1951).

5. Marc Brown, *Arthur's Nose* (Little, Brown, 1976).

6. Richard Adams, *Watership Down* (Simon & Schuster, 1972).

7. Virginia Hamilton, *The People Could Fly: American Black Folktales* (Knopf, 1985).

8. The quotes are from *Beatrix Potter's Journals* (Penguin, 2011).

9. Linda Lear, *Beatrix Potter: A Life in Nature* (Macmillan, 2008).

CHAPTER SIX

1. I have found Reindert Leonard Falkenburg's *The Land of Unlikeness: Hieronymus Bosch, The Garden of Earthly Delights* (W Books, 2011) very helpful in thinking about this work.

2. I open this discussion of gardens with Eden since the origin of the word "paradise" stems from the Greek *paradeisos*, which gets translated in the Old Testament as "garden." In Latin the same word is *paradisus*. The first paradisiacal garden, in Western culture, was Eden, the story of the creation from Genesis 2:8—"And the Lord God planted a garden in Eden, in the east; and there he put the man whom he had formed." Notice that God "planted" Eden. Even in the very act of creation, this garden was not passively formed —an act of God's imagination—but rather it was produced by toil, by God's labor.

3. When Adam and Eve left paradise, their return was barred by the angels.

4. The *Oxford English Dictionary* says a garden is "an enclosed piece of ground devoted to the cultivation of flowers, fruit, or vegetables; often preceded by some defining word, as flower-, fruit-, kitchen-, market-, strawberry-garden." A secondary meaning given by the *OED* is that of "ornamental grounds, used as a place of public resort," such as a zoological or botanic garden, for example.

5. I found this encyclopedia entry, which I stumbled upon several years ago, to be inspiring and a great introduction to the topic: Stephanie Ross, "Gardens, Aesthetics of," in *Routledge Encyclopedia of Philosophy* (Taylor and Francis, 2002).

6. Mara Miller, *The Garden as an Art* (SUNY Press, 1993).

7. Hegel quoted in David E. Cooper, *A Philosophy of Gardens* (Clarendon Press, 2006).

8. David E. Cooper, in ibid., writes that to ask what a garden is, is to inquire, "What kind of being does a garden have? What sort of entity or object is a garden, compared with, say, other art objects? Is a garden a complex physical entity, say?" Or, if it is a metaphorical entity, when metaphorically we talk of a garden, what does the metaphor imply?

9. Framed in this way, the very relinquishing of control is in itself another form of control. As an example of a practice of exercising control to allow for more spontaneity in the garden, I am particularly enamored of a form of landscape gardening in Britain and Ireland called Robinsonian gardening. In a form of gardening that William Robinson championed in his book *The Wild Garden* (1870), Robinson advocated for untidy edges, a blurring between the garden boundary and the landscape beyond. A Robinsonian garden can host a profusion of native plants, but the effect is artistic rather than wild.

10. Although I don't agree with his conclusion, I nonetheless find Eric Katz's "Further Adventures in the Case Against Restoration," *Environmental Ethics* 34, no. 1 (2012): 67–97, provocative and useful. There Katz writes: "Indeed, I claim even more radically that working in a garden, rather than teaching us about the authentic experience of natural processes, actually furthers the human worldview of domination."

11. Emma Marris, *Rambunctious Garden: Saving Nature in a Post-Wild World* (Bloomsbury USA, 2011).

12. Hans Christian Andersen, *The Complete Hans Christian Andersen Fairy Tales* (Gramercy, 1984).

13. For details about Andersen's life, I have relied on the Jackie Wullschlager's superb biography, *Hans Christian Andersen: The Life of a Storyteller* (University of Chicago Press, 2002).

14. H. C. Andersen, *The Improvisatore; or, Life in Italy* (1835; Ward, Lock, 1897).

15. Jack David Zipes, "Critical Reflections about Hans Christian Andersen, the Failed Revolutionary," *Marvels & Tales* 20, no. 2 (2006): 224–37.

16. The range of services provided to the human economy by nature is discussed in recent literature under the notion of "ecosystems services." See Gretchen Daily, ed., *Nature's Services: Societal Dependence on Natural Ecosystems* (Island Press, 1997). One interesting children's story that can be read as a parable concerning the pathological exhaustion of nature's services is Shel Silverstein, *The Giving Tree* (HarperCollins, 1964). In it a boy exhausts the gifts offered by a long-suffering tree.

17. Frances Hodgson Burnett, *The Secret Garden* (Puffin, 1911); Johanna Spyri, *Heidi: A Story for Children and Those That Love Children* (1881; Ginn, 1899).

18. Roger Ulrich, "View through a Window May Influence Recovery," *Science* 224, no. 4647 (1984): 224–25; Frances E. Kuo and Andrea Faber Taylor, "A Potential Natural Treatment for Attention-Deficit/Hyperactivity Disorder: Evidence from a National Study," *American Journal of Public Health* 94, no. 9 (2004): 1580–86.

CHAPTER SEVEN

1. James Stephens, *Irish Fairy Tales* (Macmillan, 1920), 11–12.

2. My favorite translation is by poet Thomas Kinsella, *The Tain* (Dolmen, 1969).

3. William Allingham, "The Fairies," in *The Oxford Book of English Verse: 1250–1900*, ed. Arthur Quiller-Couch (Oxford, 1919).

4. William Butler Yeats, ed., *Irish Fairy and Folk Tales* (Modern Library, 2012).

5. W. B. Yeats, *The Celtic Twilight* (1893; Cosimo, 2004).

6. John Zneimer, *The Literary Vision of Liam O'Flaherty* (Syracuse University Press, 1970).

7. Rene Dubos, *The Wooing of Earth* (Macmillan, 1980).

8. I once almost got my head stove in by an otherwise fairly equanimous

bullock (steer) in a field in the Irish Midlands who took a sudden fit.

9. Jared Diamond, "The Worst Mistake in the History of the Human Race," *Discover* 8, no. 5 (1987): 64–66.

CHAPTER EIGHT

1. Joe Paddock, *Keeper of the Wild: The Life of Ernest Oberholtzer* (Minnesota Historical Society Press, 2001).

2. Ibid.

3. Roderick Nash, *Wilderness and the American Mind* (Yale University Press, 2014).

CHAPTER NINE

1. Selma G. Lanes, *The Art of Maurice Sendak*, ed. Robert Morton (Abrams, 1980).

2. Jean Clottes, *Cave Art* (2008; Phaidon, 2010).

3. This is one of those occasions where Wikipedia is as good a resource as any: the entry for Shannon diversity is rock-solid: https://en.wikipedia.org/wiki/Diversity_index#Shannon_index.

4. J. K. Rowling, *Harry Potter and the Philosopher's Stone* (Bloomsbury, 1997).

5. Ian Tattersall, *Masters of the Planet: The Search for Our Human Origins* (Macmillan, 2012).

6. Jay Appleton, *The Symbolism of Habitat: An Interpretation of Landscape in the Arts* (University of Washington Press, 1990).

7. Stephen R. Kellert and Edward O. Wilson, *The Biophilia Hypothesis* (Island Press, 1995).

8. Gordon H. Orians, *Snakes, Sunrises, and Shakespeare: How Evolution Shapes Our Loves and Fears* (University of Chicago Press, 2014).

9. Julien d'Huy, "A Cosmic Hunt in the Berber Sky: A Phylogenetic Reconstruction of Palaeolithic Mythology," *Les Cahiers de l'AARS* 15 (2013): 93–106. There is an nice summary of d'Huy's work here: Julien d'Huy, "Scientists Trace Society's Myths to Primordial Origins," *Scientific American*, December 2016. Thanks to Julien d'Huy for helpful comments on an early draft of this chapter.

CHAPTER TEN

1. This is a nice English version of the story; it differs a little from the one I learned at school. "Bodach an Chota-Lachtna / The Clown with the Grey Coat: A Fenian Tale," *Irish Penny Journal* 1, no. 17 (October 24, 1840): 130–32, https://www.jstor.org/stable/30001137?seq=1#page_scan_tab_contents.

2. Caroline Wazer, "The Exotic Animal Traffickers of Ancient Rome," *Atlantic*, March 30, 2016.

3. I have used the following translation exclusively throughout this book: Jacob Grimm and Wilhelm Grimm, *The Original Folk and Fairy Tales of the Brothers Grimm: The Complete First Edition* (Princeton University Press, 2014).

4. Donna Jo Napoli has an excellent retelling of the story where the witch is portrayed more sympathetically in *The Magic Circle* (Penguin, 1995).

5. The numbers vary slightly depending upon the translation one uses and depends, quite naturally, upon the comprehensiveness of the collection.

6. The Wilderness Act of 1964 gives the following definition of wilderness: "an area where the earth and its community of life are untrammeled by man, where man himself is a visitor who does not remain."

7. Since I've mentioned bagpipes on a couple of occasions in a slightly disparaging way, in compensation let me encourage you to listen to some Irish bagpipe music. The uilleann pipes were on the verge extinction several decades ago, but they have come roaring back, so to speak. My current favorite youthful pipers are Blackie O'Connell (see https://www.dubhlinnband.com/band) and Fiachra O'Regan (see http://www.fiachrapipes.com/).

8. Thomas H. Birch, "The Incarceration of Wildness," *Environmental Ethics* 12, no. 1 (1990): 3–26.

CHAPTER ELEVEN

1. Many thanks to the staff of the Burren National Park who entertained several e-mails from me about the exhibit. I recommend you drop by the park as well as the visitor center in nearby Corofin.

2. See Gordon D'Arcy, *The Natural History of the Burren* (Immel, 1992).

3. J. R. R. Tolkien, *The Letters of J. R. R. Tolkien*, ed. Humphrey Carter with Christopher Tolkien (Houghton Mifflin Harcourt, 2014).

4. J. R. R. Tolkien, *The Silmarillion*, ed. Christopher Tolkien (Houghton Mifflin, 1977).

5. The original reference is *Minas Tirith Evening-Star* 9, no. 2 (January 1980): 15–16; see http://sacnoths.blogspot.com/2010/01/tolkien-on-ireland-part-two.html.

6. Thanks to Ric Hudgens for bringing this letter to my attention. It is reproduced here: https://mlanders.com/2014/02/17/c-s-lewis-on-j-r-r-tolkien-the-strength-of-the-hills-is-not-ours/.

CHAPTER TWELVE

1. Humphrey Carpenter, *J. R. R. Tolkien: A Biography* (Houghton Mifflin Harcourt, 2014).

2. Ibid.

3. Letter to Deborah Webster (who wrote her doctoral dissertation on Tolkien and C. S. Lewis), October 25, 1958, in J. R. R. Tolkien, *The Letters of J. R. R. Tolkien*, ed. Humphrey Carter with Christopher Tolkien (Houghton Mifflin Harcourt, 2014).

4. Carpenter, *Tolkien: A Biography*.

5. J. R. R. Tolkien, "Leaf by Niggle" (Trinity Forum, 1975).

6. J. R. R. Tolkien *Unfinished Tales of Númenor and Middle-earth* (Houghton Mifflin Harcourt, 2012); J. R. R. Tolkien, *The Silmarillion*, ed. Christopher Tolkien (Houghton Mifflin, 1977).

7. J. R. R. Tolkien, *The Fellowship of the Ring* (Allen & Unwin, 1954).

8. "dwell, v.," *OED Online* (Oxford University Press), http://www.oed.com.

9. Edward S. Casey, *Getting Back into Place: Toward a Renewed Understanding of the Place-World* (Indiana University Press, 1993).

10. The quote is reprinted in J. March, "Hermes," in *Dictionary of Classical Mythology* (Oxbow Books, 2014).

11. J. March, "Hestia ('Hearth')," in ibid.

12. C. S. Lewis, *The Lion, the Witch and the Wardrobe* (HarperCollins, 1950).

13. Walter de la Mare, *The Three Mulla-Mulgars*, illus. Dorothy P. Lathorp (Knopf, 1910).

14. Sara Pennypacker, *Pax* (HarperCollins, 2016).

15. Gary Paulsen, *Hatchet* (Simon & Schuster, 1999).

16. Jean Craighead George, *My Side of the Mountain* (Dutton, 1959).

CHAPTER THIRTEEN

1. L. Frank Baum, *The Wonderful Wizard of Oz* (George M. Hill, 1900).

CHAPTER FOURTEEN

1. Suzanne Collins, *The Hunger Games* (Scholastic, 2008).
2. Peter H. Gleick, "Basic Water Requirements for Human Activities: Meeting Basic Needs," *Water International* 21, no. 2 (1996): 83–92.
3. Peter L Pelleti, "Food Energy Requirements in Humans," *American Journal of Clinical Nutrition* 51, no. 5 (May 1990) 711–22.
4. "How Long Can a Person Survive without Food?" *Scientific American*, November 8, 2004.
5. Suzanne Collins, *Catching Fire* (Scholastic, 2009).

CHAPTER FIFTEEN

1. H. G. Wells, *The Island of Dr. Moreau* (Heinemann, Stone & Kimball, 1896).
2. J. M. Barrie, *Peter and Wendy* (Hodder & Stoughton, 1911).
3. To give examples of this phenomenon: In some older traditions, humans were thought very different from other animals. The radical implication of Darwinian thought was to reveal the shared nature of all animals, ourselves included. On the other hand, Aristotle, for philosophical reasons rather than biological ones, classified whales and other cetaceans as being closely related to fish. They are not.
4. Tim Robinson, *Setting Foot on the Shores of Connemara & Other Writings* (Lilliput Press, 1996).
5. Enid Blyton, *Five on a Treasure Island* (1942; Hodder Children's Books, 1991); Mairi Hedderwick, *Katie Morag and the Two Grandmothers* (Random House, 1997).
6. Thor Heyerdahl, *Fatu-Hiva: Back to Nature* (Doubleday, 1974).
7. Robert Louis Stevenson, *Treasure Island* (Cassell, 1883); William Golding, *Lord of the Flies* (Faber and Faber, 1954).
8. Robert Michael Ballantyne, *The Coral Island: A Tale of the Pacific Ocean* (1858; Thomas Nelson and Sons, 1884).

9. Theodore Taylor, *The Cay* (Scholastic, 1969).

10. Robert Macfarlane, "Water, Water, Everywhere," *Guardian*, April 24, 2009, https://www.theguardian.com/books/2009/apr/25/islands-archipelago -book-review.

11. Angelinus Dalorto, *L'Isola Brazil* (Genoa, 1325).

12. Eilís Dillon, *The Lost Island* (1954; New York Review Children's Collection, 2006).

13. Jerry Griswold, *Feeling Like a Kid: Childhood and Children's Literature* (Johns Hopkins University Press, 2006).

14. This classic and accessible account of ecology is still worth reading: Paul A. Colinvaux, *Why Big Fierce Animals Are Rare: An Ecologist's Perspective* (Princeton University Press, 1979).

15. Thanks to Oisín Heneghan, who tracked down all the data for this paragraph.

16. Johann David Wyss, *The Swiss Family Robinson* (1812; Oxford Paperbacks, 1991).

17. Randy Frahm, *Islands: Living Gems of the Sea* (Creative Education. 2002); Rose Pipes, *Islands* (Raintree Steck-Vaughn, 1998); Linda Tagliaferro, *Galápagos Islands: Nature's Delicate Balance at Risk* (Lerner Publications, 2000).

18. The keystone species concept was introduced by Robert Paine in "A Note on Trophic Complexity and Community Stability," *American Naturalist* 103, no. 929 (1969): 91–93.

19. Dov F. Sax and Steven D. Gaines, "Species Invasions and Extinction: The Future of Native Biodiversity on Islands," *Proceedings of the National Academy of Sciences* 105, supplement 1 (2008): 11490–97.

20. Apparently the phrase was written down first by Archbishop John Healy in *Ireland's Ancient Schools and Scholars* (1893), though it may date to some greater antiquity. See "Island of saints and scholars," in *Brewer's Dictionary of Irish Phrase and Fable*, ed. S. McMahon and J. O'Donoghue (Chambers Harrap, 2009).

21. John Joseph O'Meara, *The Voyage of Saint Brendan: Journey to the Promised Land*, vol. 1 (Dolmen Press, 1978).

22. Mike McGrew, *Saint Brendan and the Voyage Before Columbus*, illus. Marnie Saenz Litz (Paulist Press, 2004).

23. Elsie Spicer Eells, *The Islands of Magic: Legends, Folk and Fairy Tales from the Azores* (1922; HardPress, 2016).

24. Gerald Durrell, *My Family and Other Animals* (1956; Penguin UK, 2006).

25. Lawrence Durrell, *Reflections on a Marine Venus: A Companion to the Landscape of Rhodes* (1953; Open Road Media, 2012).

CHAPTER SIXTEEN

1. See I. Niehaus and I. Niehaus, "Magic," in *Encyclopedia of Social and Cultural Anthropology*, 2nd ed. (Routledge, 2009).

2. William Shakespeare, *The Tragedy of Macbeth* (Classic Books Company, 2001).

3. Ursula K. Le Guin, *The Farthest Shore* (Atheneum, 1972); *A Wizard of Earthsea* (Parnassus Press, 1968); *The Tombs of Atuan* (Atheneum, 1971); *Tehanu: The Last Book of Earthsea* (Atheneum, 1990); *Tales from Earthsea* (Harcourt, 2001); *The Other Wind* (Harcourt, 2001).

4. James MacKillop, *Dictionary of Celtic Mythology* (Oxford University Press, 1998).

5. Nikolai Tolstoy, *The Quest for Merlin* (Little, Brown, 1985).

6. T. H. White, *The Sword in the Stone* (Collins, 1938).

7. Of Gandalf, Tolstoy wrote in *The Quest for Merlin*: "Like Merlin, Gandalf is a magician of infinite wisdom, and power; like Merlin, he has a sense of humor, by turns impish and sarcastic; and, like Merlin, he reappears at intervals, seemingly from nowhere, intervening to rescue an imperilled universe."

8. Ursula K. Le Guin, "Art, Information, Theft, and Confusion," http://www .ursulakleguin.com/Note-ArtInfoTheftConfusion-Part2.html.

9. J. K. Rowling, *Harry Potter and the Philosopher's Stone* (Bloomsbury, 1997).

10. Alfred L. Kroeber, *Anthropology: Biology and Race* (Harcourt, 1923); *Configurations of Culture Growth* (University of California Press, 1944); *The Nature of Culture* (University of Chicago Press, 1952); *Style and Civilizations* (Cornell University Press, 1957).

11. Theodora Kroeber, *The Inland Whale* (University of California Press, 1959); *Ishi in Two Worlds: A Biography of the Last Wild Indian in North America* (University of California Press, 1961); *Ishi: Last of His Tribe* (Parnassus Press, 1964).

12. This is what is known as Garrett Hardin's law of ecology: "We can never do merely one thing."

13. Charles S. Elton, *Animal Ecology* (1927; University of Chicago Press, 2001).

14. P. J. Crutzen popularized the notion of the Anthropocene in a paper entitled "The 'Anthropocene,'" in *Earth System Science in the Anthropocene: Emerging Issues and Problems*, ed. Eckart Ehlers and Thomas Krafft (Springer, 2006), 13–18. For an interesting philosophical account of the implications, see the work of Timothy Morton—start with *The Ecological Thought* (Harvard University Press, 2012).

15. John Wray interview, "Ursula K. Le Guin: The Art of Fiction No. 221," *Paris Review* 206 (Fall 2013).

CHAPTER SEVENTEEN

1. L. T. Meade, *Four on An Island: A Story of Adventure*, illus. W. Rainey (W. & R. Chambers, 1892).

2. Enid Blyton, *Five on a Treasure Island* (1942; Hodder Children's Books, 1991).

3. For good accounts of the Blyton phenomenon, see S. G. B. Ray's *The Blyton Phenomenon: The Controversy Surrounding the World's Most Successful Children's Writer* (Deutsch, 1982); David Rudd, *Enid Blyton and the Mystery of Children's Literature* (St. Martin's Press, 2000); Barbara Stoney, *Enid Blyton: The Biography* (History Press, 2011).

4. Enid Blyton, *The Bird Book* (George Newnes, 1926); *The Animal Book* (George Newnes, 1927); *Nature Lessons* (Evans Brothers, 1929).

5. There are, of course, several biographical accounts of Blyton, but what scholarship that exists on her work, though insightful, is meager compared to her influence. For useful commentary on the Famous Five series, see, for example, David Rudd, "Five Have a Gender-ful Time: Blyton, Sexism, and the Infamous Five," *Children's Literature in Education* 26, no. 3 (1995): 185–96.

6. L. T. Meade, *A World of Girls* (Grosset & Dunlap, 1886).

7. L. T. Meade, *A Very Naughty Girl* (W. & R. Chambers, 1901); Enid Blyton, *The Naughtiest Girl in the School* (George Newnes, 1940).

8. Daniel Defoe, *Robinson Crusoe*, Norton Critical Edition, ed. Michael Shinagel (Norton, 1994).

9. See Barbara Stoney, *Enid Blyton: The Biography* (History Press, 2011).

CHAPTER EIGHTEEN

1. Review of *Robinson Crusoe,* by Daniel Defoe, *North American Review* 190, no. 649 (December 1909): 845.

2. For a useful short account of this genre, see B. L. Hanlon, "Robinsonnade [*sic*]," in *The Cambridge Guide to Children's Books in English,* ed. V. Watson (Cambridge University Press, 2001).

3. William Steig, *Abel's Island* (1976; Macmillan, 2013).

4. Daniel Defoe, *Robinson Crusoe,* Norton Critical Edition, ed. Michael Shinagel (Norton, 1994).

5. Frank Hale Ellis, ed., *Twentieth Century Interpretations of Robinson Crusoe: A Collection of Critical Essays* (Prentice Hall, 1969).

6. *Norton Critical Edition of Defoe's Robinson Crusoe,* ed. Michael Shinagel (Norton, 1994). This volume provides an excellent sampling of the critical literature on *Robinson Crusoe.*

7. Ibid.

8. John Stuart Mill, *Autobiography* (Severus Verlag, 2014).

9. Jean-Jacques Rousseau, *Émile; or, On Education,* trans. Allan Bloom (Basic Books, 1979).

10. Robert Louis Stevenson, *The Annotated Treasure Island,* ed. Simon Barker-Benfield, illus. Louis Rhead (Fine & Kahn, 2014).

11. "Evolution: Ammonites Indicate Reversal," *Nature* 225, no. 5238 (1970): 1101–2.

12. My favorite account of cultural transformation of humans is Allen W. Johnson and Timothy K. Earle, *The Evolution of Human Societies: From Foraging Group to Agrarian State* (Stanford University Press, 2000).

13. See the delightful account of the terrestrializing of animal life by Jane Gray and William Shear, "Early Life on Land," *American Scientist* 80 (1992): 44456.

14. Henry David Thoreau, *Walden, and Other Writings* (Modern Library, 1950). For a good account of parallels between Crusoe and Thoreau, see Marek Paryz, "Thoreau's Imperial Fantasy: Walden versus Robinson Crusoe," in *The Postcolonial and Imperial Experience in American Transcendentalism* (Palgrave Macmillan, 2012), 99–121.

15. Archibald MacMechan, "Thoreau," in *The Cambridge History of English and American Literature: An Encyclopedia in Eighteen Volumes,* ed. by A. W. Ward et

al. (G. P. Putnam's Sons, 1907–21) vol. 16, chap. 10.

16. See, for example, Martin J. Greif, "The Conversion of Robinson Crusoe," *Studies in English Literature, 1500–1900* 6, no. 3 (1966): 551–74.

17. After the monologue with money and his crying out to God, the remaining statements recorded in *Robinson Crusoe* as being uttered aloud were after he rescued his acolyte, Friday.

CHAPTER NINETEEN

1. Scott O'Dell, *Island of the Blue Dolphins* (Houghton Mifflin, 1960).

2. William Golding, *Lord of the Flies* (Faber and Faber, 1954).

3. James R. Baker, "An Interview with William Golding," *Twentieth Century Literature* 28, no. 2 (1982): 130–70, doi:10.2307/441151.

4. Robert Michael Ballantyne, *The Coral Island* (T. Nelson & Sons, 1858).

5. Barry Lopez, "The Invitation," *Granta* 133 (November 18, 2015), https://granta.com/invitation/.

CHAPTER TWENTY

1. Oscar Wilde, *The Happy Prince and Other Tales* (Duckworth & Company, 1913).

CHAPTER TWENTY-ONE

1. Eric Kincaid, *Nursery Rhymes* (Brimax Books, 1990).

2. Iona Archibald Opie and Peter Opie, eds., *The Oxford Dictionary of Nursery Rhymes* (Clarendon Press, 1951).

CHAPTER TWENTY-TWO

1. Reproduced in Bill McKibben, *American Earth: Environmental Writing since Thoreau* (Literary Classics of the United States, 2008).

2. Leo Marx, "The Machine in the Garden," in *The Green Studies Reader: From Romanticism to Ecocriticism* (Routledge, 2000): 104–8.

3. A common critique of this work is that Crumb writes native peoples out of history, but to my ecologist's eye, the opening landscape is not, whatever

the artist intended, pristine nature. It resembles, rather, an indigenously managed system.

4. Virginia Lee Burton, *The Little House* (Houghton Mifflin, 1942).

5. Karen Gray Ruelle, *The Tree*, illus. Deborah Durland DeSaix (Holiday House, 2008).

CHAPTER TWENTY-THREE

1. David Schultz, "Coyotes in the City: Could Urban Bears Be Next?" NPR, October 5, 2012, http://www.npr.org/sections/thetwo-way/2012/10/05/162300544/coyotes-in-the-city-could-urban-bears-be-next.

2. I do not provide a lengthy reading of Paul Fleischman, *Weslandia*, illus. Kevin Hawkes (Candlewick Press, 2002). I recommend it to you nonetheless, for this short picture book performs the subtle miracle of summarizing the history of anthropological theorizing about the emergence of culture and civilization in the space of thirty-two wonderfully illustrated pages. When Wesley cultivates "swist" (a crop plant that blows into his yard), the novelty of the story is not that he creates a civilization but that he manages to be the first to do so in a suburban backyard.

3. Bill Watterson, *The Authoritative Calvin and Hobbes* (Andrews McMeel Publishing, 1990).

4. As little as 5 percent of time outside has been reported in some studies: e.g., Verity Cleland, David Crawford, Louise A. Baur, Clare Hume, Anna Timperio, and Jo Salmon, "A Prospective Examination of Children's Time Spent Outdoors, Objectively Measured Physical Activity and Overweight," *International Journal of Obesity* 32, no. 11 (2008): 1685–93. Of course, we don't typically see too many panels of Calvin sleeping; nonetheless, it's fair to say he spends a disproportionate amount of time outside.

5. Bill Watterson, *The Days Are Just Packed* (Andrews McMeel Publishing, 1993).

CHAPTER TWENTY-FOUR

1. Jean de Brunhoff, *The Story of Babar: The Little Elephant* (Random House Children's Books, 1960).

2. See, for example, Jari Niemelä and Jürgen H. Breuste, *Urban Ecology: Patterns, Processes, and Applications* (Oxford University Press, 2011).

3. Michael Bond, *A Bear Called Paddington,* illus. Peggy Fortnum (Houghton Mifflin, 1960).

4. Herbert R. Kohl, *Should We Burn Babar?: Essays on Children's Literature and the Power of Stories* (1995; New Press, 2007).

5. Ariel Dorfman, *The Empire's Old Clothes: What the Lone Ranger, Babar, and Other Innocent Heroes Do to Our Minds* (Pantheon, 1983), 14.

6. Ebenezer Howard, *Garden Cities of To-morrow,* ed. F. J. Osborn (MIT Press, 1965).

7. Eugene P. Odum, "The Strategy of Ecosystem Development," *Science* 164 (April 18, 1969): 262–70.

CHAPTER TWENTY-FIVE

1. Antoine de Saint-Exupéry, *The Little Prince* (Reynal & Hitchcock, 1943).

2. Peter Matthiessen, *The Tree Where Man Was Born* (1972; Penguin Classics, 2010).

3. Thomas Robert Malthus, *An Essay on the Principle of Population; or, A View of Its Past and Present Effects on Human Happiness* (1798; Reeves & Turner, 1888).

4. The history of the cane toad, introduced to Australia only to become an ecological menace, is but one example of this phenomenon. See Christopher Lever, *The Cane Toad: The History and Ecology of a Successful Colonist* (Westbury Academic and Scientific Publishing, 2001).

5. For a very accessible account of this interesting new perspective, see Brian Walker and David Salt, *Resilience Thinking: Sustaining Ecosystems and People in a Changing World* (Island Press, 2012).

6. This perspective has been around for some time; see, for example, William R. Catton, *Overshoot: The Ecological Basis of Revolutionary Change* (University of Illinois Press, 1982). For a more recent perspective on planetary limits, see Will Steffen et al., "Planetary Boundaries: Guiding Human Development on a Changing Planet," *Science* 347, no. 6223 (February 13, 2015): 1259855. I will discuss this further later in the chapter.

7. Antoine de Saint-Exupéry, *Wind, Sand and Stars* (Reynal & Hitchcock, 1939).

8. This observation remains true today: the entire human population stand-

ing motionlessly could fit in a small US state. However, the amount of land required to sustain this population is very high. One might not see a lot of people in a desert, but the resource shadow of humans is everywhere. See Mathis Wackernagel and William Rees, *Our Ecological Footprint: Reducing Human Impact on the Earth* (New Society Publishers, 1998).

9. Peter Kareiva, Sean Watts, Robert McDonald, and Tim Boucher, "Domesticated Nature: Shaping Landscapes and Ecosystems for Human Welfare," *Science* 316, no. 5833 (June 29, 2007): 1866–69.

10. See Peter M. Vitousek, Harold A. Mooney, Jane Lubchenco, and Jerry M. Melillo, "Human Domination of Earth's Ecosystems," *Science* 277, no. 5325 (July 25, 1997): 494–99.

11. René Dubos, *The Wooing of Earth* (Charles Scribner's Sons, 1980).

12. Rabindranath Tagore, "Towards Universal Man," in *Towards Universal Man* (Asia Publishing House, 1961).

CHAPTER TWENTY-SIX

1. Dr. Seuss, *The Lorax* (Random House, 1971).

2. Mildred D. Taylor, *Song of the Trees*, illus. Jerry Pinkney (1975; Puffin, 2003).

3. Carl Hiaasen, *Hoot* (Knopf, 2002).

CHAPTER TWENTY-SEVEN

1. David W. Orr, *Ecological Literacy: Education and the Transition to a Postmodern World* (State University of New York Press, 1992), 3.

2. US Census Bureau, "U.S. and World Population Clock," https://www.census .gov/popclock/ (accessed August, 6, 2017).

3. Jim Trelease, *The Read-Aloud Handbook*, 7th ed. (Penguin, 2013).

4. For an excellent review of the concept of environmental literacy (and adjacent literacies), see B. Brewer McBride, C. A. Brewer, A. R. Berkowitz, and W. T. Borrie, "Environmental Literacy, Ecological Literacy, Ecoliteracy: What Do We Mean and How Did We Get Here?," *Ecosphere* 4, no. 5 (2013): 1–20.

5. Xenia Hadjioannou and Eleni Loizou, "Talking about Books with Young Children: Analyzing the Discursive Nature of One-to-One Booktalks," *Early Education & Development* 22, no. 1 (2011): 53–76.

Index

Abram, David: *The Spell of the Sensuous*, 32, 300n10

Achebe, Chinua: *How the Leopard Got His Claws*, 46, 302n10

acid rain, 5

Adam (biblical), 73, 241, 304n3

Adams, Richard: *Watership Down*, 67, 303n3

advocacy, environmental, 4, 272, 276

aesthetics, 142, 304n5

Africa, 115, 150, 246, 259, 300n19

Albrecht, Glenn 56–57, 303n7 (chap. 4)

alchemy, 8, 78

Aleuts, 214

Allen, George, 296, 301n2

Allingham, William: "The Fairies," 86, 305n3

American wilderness tradition, 26, 102

Andersdatter, Anne Marie, 78

Andersen, Hans Christian, 14, 77–80, 305n12

angels, 85, 229, 304n3

animals, 3–7, 10, 22–24, 33, 44, 46, 60, 66–68, 108–13, 117, 153–54, 182–84, 216, 231–32, 246–48, 309n2, 313n13; anthropomorphic, 24, 44, 60, 66–67; domesticated, 84; pet, 61, 68; wild, 48, 112, 120, 130, 214

animal tales, 66

Antarctica, 52

antelopes, 77, 172

Anthropocene, 312n14

anthropology, 185, 311n1

antiquity, 113, 117, 134, 310n20

anti-urban bias, 92

ants, 1–2, 128, 183

anxiety, 115, 146

apocalyptic narratives, 216

Appleton, Jay: *The Symbolism of Habitat: An Interpretation of Landscape in the Arts*, 56, 114–16, 302n6, 306n6

apprivoiser, 267–68

Aran Islands, 58, 88

Arcadia, 42

Arcadian shepherds, 45–46

archipelago, 169, 172, 187, 189, 270

Aristotle, 309n3 (chap. 15)

arithmetic, 28, 247

art, 61, 73–74, 79, 105–6, 108–11, 113, 182, 302n2, 304n6, 304n8, 306nn1–2 (chap. 9), 311n8

Arthur, King, 181–83

artists, 61, 101, 105–6, 108–10, 143, 198, 315n3; shamanistic, 112

Ashdown Forest, 51–54

Asia Minor, 120

asteroids, 259, 262–63, 271

atmosphere, 5, 81, 282, 284

atolls, coral, 169–70

Attenborough, Sir David, 274; impersonation of, 58

attention-deficit/hyperactivity disorder, 26, 305n18

attunement, 9, 286, 288

Auden, W. H., 35–36

Australia, 171, 300n19, 316n4 (chap. 25)

automobile, 248, 251–52

Azores, 168, 175–77, 310n3

Babar, 244–53, 315n1 (chap. 22), 316n4 (chap. 24); Babar's excrement, 249

Bachelard, Gaston, 56

backcountry, 102, 157

badger, 43, 65, 183

Baggins, Bilbo, 40, 145

Baggins, Frodo, 145–47

bagpipes, 71, 130, 307n7

balance, 28, 33, 45–46, 56, 121, 186–89, 214

Ballantyne, Robert M., 170; *Coral Island*, 170, 217–18, 309n8, 314n4

baobabs, 259–61

Bar-ba-loots, 272–75

Barr, Noel, 17, 296n3

Barrie, J. M.: *Peter and Wendy*, 166, 170, 309n2

Baum, Frank, 152–53, 309n1 (chap. 13); *The Wonderful Wizard of Oz*, 152, 155, 309n1 (chap. 13)

beasts, 3, 6–8, 17, 108, 116, 120, 128, 130–31, 137, 143, 153, 172, 175, 184, 223

beauty, 60, 76–77, 80, 118, 124, 136, 161, 216, 266, 274, 276, 289, 298n1

Beckett, Samuel, 20, 22, 296n7; *The Unnamable*, 21–22, 296n7

Bedouin, 256

bedtime, 3, 6–8, 17, 25, 117, 293

Beerbohm, Max: *Zuleika Dobson*, 21–22, 297n10

bees, 31, 154–55, 182

Beethoven, Ludwig van, 100

beetles, 31, 49, 87, 152

Berenberg, Ben Ross: *The Churkendoose: Part Chicken, Turkey, Duck and Goose*, 17, 296n2

berries, 119, 160–61

Betjeman, John 35–36, 301n1; "Christmas," 301n1; "A Subaltern's Love Song," 35

Bias in Children's Literature and Learning Materials (Klein), 299n11

big fierce animals, 171, 310n14

biodiversity, 8, 91, 266

biography, 140, 185, 214, 301n22, 303n1 (chap. 5), 305n13, 308n1, 311n11, 312n3

biophilia hypothesis, 56, 115, 302n5, 306n7

birch, 99, 143

Birch, Thomas H.: "The Incarceration of Wildness," 131, 307n8

birds, 1–2, 71, 76–77, 84, 109, 111, 119, 172, 182–84, 207, 209, 216, 225, 228–29, 248–50

bison, 108–9

bison sorceress, 111

blackbirds, 64, 251

Black Forest, 270

Blake, William: "The Tyger," 5, 295n5

Bligh, William (captain), 169

Bloomsbury Good Word Guide, 29, 299n13

Blyton, Enid, 192, 196, 291, 309n5 (chap. 15), 312n2; Famous Five series, 174, 312n2; *Five on a Treasure Island*, 168, 174, 191–94, 196, 309n5 (chap. 15)

boar, 123, 128, 130, 172

bodach an chóta lachtna, 119–20, 307n1 (chap. 10)

bogs, 119, 136, 138, 144

Bond, Michael: *A Bear Called Paddington*, 245, 316n3 (chap. 24)

booktalks, 288

Bosch, Hieronymus, 77, 303n1 (chap. 6); *The Garden of Earthly Delights*, 71–72, 303n1 (chap. 6)

Bottiglieri, Jan, 3

Bouncer, Benjamin, 68

bourgeois, 248, 252

boys, 48, 50, 53, 55, 59–60, 87, 89, 116, 176, 180–83, 193, 195, 217–23, 272, 275, 279, 282

Brazil, 29, 185, 193, 201

Brazil, Angela, 193

Britain, 12, 59, 91, 119–20, 135, 144, 174, 176, 189, 191, 199, 217, 304n9

British admiralty maps, 170

British countryside, 141–42

British National Trust, 59

Brendan, Saint, 175

brothers, 35, 40, 48, 61–62, 126, 140, 177, 198, 216, 293

Brown, Marc: *Arthur's Nose*, 67, 303n5

Brown, Margaret Wise: *The Runaway Bunny*, 22, 40, 297n16, 301n1

Brunhoff, Jean de, 244–46, 248–49, 252–53, 315n1 (chap. 24); *Story of Babar*, 244, 246–48, 250–53, 315n1 (chap. 24)

bullock, equanimous, 305n8

bullying, 219, 241

bunnies, 23, 63–66

Burnett, Frances Hodgson: *The Secret Garden*, 7, 82, 305n17

Burren National Park, 91, 133–34, 138, 307n1 (chap. 11)

Burton, Virginia Lee: *The Little House*, 236–37, 315n4 (chap. 22)

business, 117, 204, 208, 273, 292

cabalistic signs, 182

Caldecott Medal, 12, 105, 237

Calder, John, 21

Calvin and Hobbes (Watterson), 239–43, 252, 315n3; *The Authoritative Calvin and Hobbes*, 239–40, 315n3; *The Days Are Just Packed*, 315n5 (chap. 23)

Canadian wilderness, 103

Canary Islands, 175

cannibalism, 125, 128, 158, 169, 200

cannibals, 183, 200, 202, 209, 211, 213

Captain Underpants series, 7

Carboniferous limestone, 133

career, 106, 299n9

Caribbean Sea, 23

Carle, Eric: *Very Hungry Caterpillar*, 22, 297n13

carnage, 152–53, 219

Carpenter, Hugh, 136, 139–40, 308n1

cars, fast, 121

Carter, Annie, 62

Casey, Edward S., 148–49, 308n9

castaway, 213, 216

castaway anxiety, 167

Catching Fire (Collins), 159, 209n5

cats, 2, 5, 19, 64, 68, 77, 111, 122, 153, 195–96, 202, 231, 235–36; domestic, 196; ferocious, 16; wild, 195–96

cattle, 59, 109, 134, 175

cattle rustling, 84, 149

Catton, William, 316n6

cave, 31, 107, 110–12, 117, 126, 131, 133, 306n2 (chap. 9)

cave artists, 111–13

cays, 23, 170, 297n17, 310n9

Celtic, 84, 135–36, 183

Celtic mythology, 135, 181, 311n4

Celtic Twilight, The (Yeats), 87, 305n5

CFCs (chlorofluorocarbons), 283

change, 28, 56–57, 66, 73, 112, 184, 186–87, 202–3, 207, 210, 247; climate (and greenhouse effect), 56–57, 241, 266, 284; revolutionary, 285, 316n6

Channel Islands, 214

charms, 43, 179, 246–47

Chauvet Cave, 109–10

Chawla, Louise, 298n7

Chellam, Ravi, 4, 295nn3–4

Chicago, 52, 194, 225–26, 291

chickens, 17, 61, 251

child, 2–3, 5, 7–8, 15, 23–24, 26–28, 36–37, 40–41, 53–54, 118, 200–201, 214, 228–29, 256–58, 285–88; asthmatic, 275; bookish, 28; inner, 106; naughty, 103

child-at-heart, 265

child-rearing practices, 282

children's literature, 5, 7–8, 10–12, 20, 22–23, 25, 44, 46, 59, 171–73, 179, 273, 276, 284, 286, 296n10, 299n11, 313n13; best-selling, 196; contemporary, 24; rare, 116; urban, 239

chironomid midges, 255

Christ, 71

Christianity, 120, 218

city, 37, 82–83, 150, 191, 228–30, 233, 236–40, 243–45, 247–53, 287, 315n1 (chap. 23)

civilization, 99, 107, 156, 161, 185, 196, 202, 204, 216–17, 219, 221–22, 263, 311n10, 315n2 (chap. 23)

Clare Heritage Centre, 133

classical mythology, 308n10

Classic Cinema, 59

Clements, Rhonda, 298n6

cliff, 88–89, 136, 220

climate change (and greenhouse effect), 56–57, 241, 266, 284

climate instability, 285

Clottes, Jean: *Cave Art*, 108, 306n2 (chap. 9)

Colinvaux, Paul A.: *Why Big Fierce Animals Are Rare: An Ecologist's Perspective*, 310n14

Collins, Suzanne, 12, 156, 197, 309n1 (chap. 14); *Catching Fire*, 159, 209n5; *The Hunger Games*, 13, 156–61, 309n1 (chap. 14)

colonies, 189, 246–47, 251, 276

colonizers, 85, 119, 202

Columbus, 176, 310n22

community, 8, 81, 109–10, 112–13, 307n6; biological, 109, 249; human, 107, 120; natural, 173

companions, 28, 51, 57–58, 61, 68, 96, 99, 124, 221–22, 293, 311n25

concept, 9–10, 101, 141, 188, 296, 299n10, 317n4; keystone species, 310n18; western park, 91

Connemara, 58, 90–91, 167, 303n8 (chap. 4), 309n4 (chap. 15)

conservation, 4, 5, 5, 8, 51, 59, 274, 295n4, 299n8

constellations, 117, 250

continents, 169, 171, 269, 300n19; lost, 176

Cooper, David E.: *A Philosophy of Gardens*, 304n7

Corey, Joshua: *The Arcadia Project: North American Postmodern Pastoral*, 301n7

Corfu, 177

cormorants, 192, 216

Corofin, county Clare, 133, 307n1 (chap. 11)

corpse, 89, 131

cosmic hunt, 306n9 (chap. 9)

Cowardly Lion, 152–53

Coyle, Kevin: *Environmental Literacy in America*, 279n23

coyotes, 239, 244, 315n1 (chap. 23)

crabs, 19, 193

creation, 4, 91, 134, 141, 143, 303n2 (chap. 6)

creatures, 5–6, 18, 25, 27, 67, 86, 121, 127, 130, 145, 152, 158, 187–89, 195, 205, 275; first terrestrial, 203; goblinesque, 143; monstrous, 152; mythological, 113; wild, 128

critics, 8, 42, 79, 103, 118, 199–200, 235, 302n9

crone, 126

Crumb, Robert D.: *A Short History of America*, 235–37, 314n3 (chap. 22)

Cub Scout manual, 240

Cú Chulainn, 18

cultural anthropology, 311n1

culture, 27, 42, 56, 101, 117, 159, 180, 185, 270, 299n11, 311n10, 315n2 (chap. 23); oral, 32, 233

Cuvier, Georges, 31–32

Cyclades, 169

Dahl, Roald: *Charlie and the Chocolate Factory*, 302n9

Daily Telegraph, 139, 142

Dalorto, Angelinus: *L'Isola Brazil*, 170, 310n11

dark satanic mills, 253

Darwin, Charles, 27, 30–32, 172, 189–90, 299n9

death, 20–21, 44–48, 61, 67, 70, 123, 125, 127, 129, 140, 158–59, 161, 228–29, 258, 261, 287

death-by-lion attacks, 4

decay, 81; excremental, 98; urban, 93, 235

deer, 18, 109, 117, 128, 152, 175

Defoe, Daniel 193, 196, 199, 201–2, 205, 211, 213, 312n8, 313n1; *Robinson Crusoe*, 195–96, 198–202, 205, 208–9, 211, 215, 312n8, 314n16 deforestation, 285

DeLoache, Judy S., 297n19

developmental psychology, 297n19

devil, 37–38, 89

d'Huy, Julien, 117, 306n9 (chap. 9)

Dickens, Charles, 78

Dillon, Eilís: *Lost Island*, 170, 310n12

Disney, 24, 49–51, 53, 183

diversity, 109, 112, 270, 306n3 (chap. 9); biological, 239

Doctor Dolittle (Lofting): *Story of Doctor Dolittle*, 28; *Voyages of Doctor Dolittle*, 29–31

dogs, 2, 117, 216, 231, 248; wild, 215–16

Dollo, Louis, 203

domestication, 196, 206, 267

domesticity, 145

donkeys, 47, 130

Dorfman, Ariel: *The Empire's Old Clothes: What the Lone Ranger, Babar, and Other Innocent Heroes Do to Our Minds* 246, 316n5 (chap. 24)

dragons, 41, 59, 128, 143, 180, 186–87, 189; little, 186

dreams, 43, 73, 79–80, 93, 99, 107, 113, 149, 237, 271; enchanted, 147

Dublin, 5, 18, 37, 83–84, 87, 169, 191

Dubos, Rene: *The Wooing of Earth*, 269, 305n7

Dunn, Christopher, 51, 292

Durrell, Gerald: *My Family and Other Animals*, 177, 311n24

Durrell, Lawrence, 177, 311n25; *Reflections on a Marine Venus*, 177

dwarfs, 41, 123–25, 241

dwelling, 10, 148–50; hermetic, 149; hestial, 149–50

eagles, 128

Earth, 52, 56, 58, 72, 74–77, 136, 138, 171, 262–64, 266–71, 282–84, 287, 300n19, 303n6 (chap. 4), 307n6

ecocriticism, 10, 314n2 (chap. 22)

ecoliteracy, 299n12, 317n1 (chap. 27)

ecological, 70, 126, 171, 173, 249–51, 258, 261–62, 271

ecological footprint, 317n8

ecological literacy, 299n12, 317n1 (chap. 27)

ecological restoration, 51

ecological system, 248; social, 262–63

ecologists, 93, 109, 173, 229, 287

ecology, 3, 8, 10–11, 30, 33, 69, 81, 99, 129, 166, 186, 250, 262, 310n14, 311n13, 316n4 (chap. 25); ecosystem, 250, 274; urban, 92, 244, 315n2 (chap. 24)

ecopsychology, 303n6 (chap. 4)

ecosystems, 249–53, 266, 273–74, 272, 276, 317n9

ecosystems services, 305n16

Eden, 73, 303n2 (chap. 6)

edible plants, 69

education, 3, 8, 181, 183, 312n5, 313n9, 317n1 (chap. 27); environmental, 28, 285–86

Eells, Elsie Spicer: *The Islands of Magic: Legends, Folk and Fairytales from the Azores*, 176, 310n23

Egypt, 114, 228

elephants, 130, 172, 242, 244–46, 248–51, 258; anthropomorphized, 250

elephant turd, weight of, 249

elf, 76, 148, 150

Ellis, Frank H.: *Twentieth Century Interpretations of Robinson Crusoe*, 199

Elton, Charles S.: *Animal Ecology*, 311n13

empathy, 10, 53, 229, 281, 285

Empson, William: *Some Versions of Pastoral*, 42, 44, 301n8

Enchanted Places, The (C. Milne), 48, 50, 147

endemophilia, 56

enemies, 48, 131, 139, 142

energy flows, 9, 249

England, 27, 49–51, 62, 138, 140, 183, 200, 211–12, 269

environment, 9–10, 20, 25–26, 43–44, 48, 113, 121, 125, 160, 185, 188, 203, 220, 223, 249, 269, 279, 283–84, 298n7

environmental attitudes, 295n6

environmental change, 3, 56

environmental ethics, 24, 295n6, 304n10, 307n8

environmental issues, 8

environmentalists, 56, 93, 272

environmental literacy, 7, 25, 28–30, 258, 287, 296n11, 299n12, 300n16, 317n4

environmental science, 5, 10, 92, 220

equilibrium, 186–87

Et in Arcadia ego, 45–46

Evanston Public Library, 292

Eve, 71, 73, 304n3

evil, 60, 73, 136–38, 186–88, 217

evolution, 183, 203, 313n11

excesses, 71, 242, 247, 249; capitalist, 273

exile, 50–51, 106, 201

fairies (faery), 15, 75, 80, 84–88, 125, 128, 131, 172

fairy tales, 29, 47, 75, 78–79, 81, 88, 121, 124, 126–28, 131–32, 176, 307n3 (chap. 10), 310n23

Falkenburg, Reindert Leonard: *The Land of Unlikeness: Hieronymus Bosch, The Garden of Earthly Delights*, 303n1 (chap. 6)

Famous Five series (Blyton), 174, 312n2; *Five on a Treasure Island*, 168, 174, 191–94, 196, 309n5 (chap. 15)

Fantastic Beasts and Where to Find Them, 184

farmers, 37, 54, 89, 199, 211

Fianna, 84, 119–20

Fine, Aubrey H.: *Handbook on Animal-Assisted Therapy: Theoretical Foundations and Guidelines for Practice*, 297n22

Fionn mac Cumhaill, 17, 84–85, 175

fir trees, 62, 68

fish, 23–24, 89, 128, 198, 215, 251, 309n3 (chap. 15)

Five on a Treasure Island (Blyton), 168, 174, 191–94, 196, 309n5 (chap. 15)

Fleischman, Paul: *Weslandia*, 239, 315n2 (chap. 23)

flesh, 195, 216; dried goat, 204; human, 121; marbled child, 123

flock, 41, 46, 130, 187, 206, 262

flowers, 41, 55, 76, 80, 160–61, 180, 260–

61, 271, 304n4; cultivation of, 73,
    304n4; loveliest, 75; wilted, 76
food, 64, 69, 73, 111, 121, 123, 127, 157, 159–
    60, 197, 202, 206, 215, 218, 249
food energy requirements, 309n3
    (chap. 14)
food webs, 9, 273
fool, 17, 184
forest, 46, 48, 50–51, 104–6, 120–24,
    126, 128–32, 143–44, 146–47, 152, 220,
    222–23, 245–48, 251–52, 273–76
forest creatures, 122
Fortnum, Peggy, 316n3 (chap. 24)
fox, 65, 128, 264–68
Frahm, Randy: *Islands*, 172, 310n17
friendships, 127, 200, 268, 276, 281, 292;
    botched, 44
fruit, 73, 122, 160, 232, 250, 274–75,
    304n4
fungi, 68, 81, 184

Gaines, Steven D., 310n19
Galápagos Islands, 172, 310n17
Galway (county), 88, 90–91
Gandalf, 145–46, 183–84, 311n7
Garden Cities, 248, 316n6
gardening, 64, 304n9
Garden of Earthly Delights, The (Bosch),
    71–72, 303n1 (chap. 6)
garden properties, 73
gardens, 9, 18–19, 37, 44–45, 54, 64, 67–
    70, 72–77, 80–82, 102–3, 121, 140, 264,
    303n2 (chap. 6), 304n5, 314n2 (chap.
    22); botanic, 304n5; healing, 82; par-
    adisiacal, 303n2 (chap. 6); power of,

81–82; productive food, 69; sublime,
    103; terrifying, 72; walled, 75
geology, 30, 96, 299n9
George, Jean Craighead: *My Side of the
    Mountain*, 151, 187, 308n16
Geraghty, Paul: *Great Green Forest*, 5–7,
    296n8
girl, 78, 89, 123–25, 129, 153, 156, 192–93,
    218, 231, 279, 312n6; little, 76, 279;
    starving, 129
Gleick, Peter H., 309n2
Glenveagh Valley, 87
goats, 38, 40, 112, 183, 205–6, 251
God, 73, 123, 208, 229, 240, 299n10, 303n2
    (chap. 6), 314n17
goddess, 149
Golding, William, 217–20, 222–23,
    309n7, 314n2 (chap. 19); *Lord of the
    Flies*, 169–70, 197, 217–20
Golley, Frank B.: *Primer for Environmental
    Literacy*, 30, 296n11, 300n17
Gollum, 133–34, 138
Good Life, 45
goose, 17, 183, 296n2
Grahame, Kenneth: *Wind in the Willows*,
    24, 42, 297n21, 301n6
grasses, 50, 55, 96, 153, 163, 197
Great Indoors, 20, 28, 33
Great Outdoors, 7, 26–27
Greece, 41–42, 169
Greek mythology, 113
Greene, Graham, 65, 70, 303n4
Greenland, 171, 175
Greeves, Arthur, 137
Gregory, Lady Augusta: *Visions and Be-*

liefs in the West of Ireland, 300n21

Greif, Martin J., 314n16

Grimm fairy tales, 47, 119, 127–28, 130–32; "The Children of Famine," 129; "Hansel and Gretel," 121–23, 125, 127–29, 131; "Hans My Hedgehog," 130; "Little Brother and Little Sister," 129; "Little Magic Table, the Golden Donkey, and the Club in the Sack," 131; "Little Red Cap," 131; "Little Snow White" 123, 127, 131; "The Old Woman in the Forest," 129; "The Summer and the Winter Garden," 131; "The Sweet Porridge," 129; "The Twelve Brothers," 126

Griswold, Jerry: *Feeling Like a Kid: Childhood and Children's Literature*, 310n13

ground beetles, 30, 252

Gubar, Marah: *Artful Dodgers*, 296n10

gun, 195, 204, 211

habitats, 56, 68, 88, 113–15, 120, 134, 144, 171

Hadjioannou, Xenia, 288, 317n5

Hamilton, Virginia: *The People Could Fly: American Black Folktales*, 67, 303n7 (chap. 5)

happiness, 47–48, 58, 77, 242, 302n13

"Happy Prince, The" (Wilde), 228–29, 314n1 (chap. 20)

Hardin, Garrett, 311n12

harmony, 39, 42, 44–48, 93, 215

Harry Potter and the Philosopher's Stone (Rowling), 7, 11, 13, 111, 178, 181, 184, 189, 193, 296, 306n4, 311n9

Hawaiian Islands, 169

health, 26–27, 43, 48, 110, 118, 292; mental, 27, 53; physical, 298n5

heart, 5, 19, 73, 152, 218, 229, 237, 265–66, 268–69; broken, 229

hearth, 28, 48, 116, 118, 121, 149, 308n11

Hedderwick, Mairi: *Katie Morag and the Two Grandmothers*, 168, 309n5 (chap. 15)

hedgehogs, 49, 62, 128, 130

Hegel, Georg Wilhelm Friedrich, 304n7

Hellfire Club, 37

Heneghan, Fiacha, 1, 6–7, 293

Heneghan, Oisín, 7, 239–40, 281, 288, 310n15

Heneghan, Paul, 35, 294

Heneghan, Vassia, 7, 125, 281

Hermes, 149–50, 308n10

hero, 22, 39, 42, 64, 67–68, 125, 128, 145, 149, 189, 201, 213, 276, 287

Hestia, 149–50

Heyerdahl, Thor: *Fatu-Hiva*, 169, 309n6

Hiaasen, Carl: *Hoot*, 276, 317n3 (chap. 26)

HMS *Bounty*, 169

Hobbit, The (Tolkien), 7, 18, 23, 41, 134, 144–46, 183, 296n5

hobbits, 7, 18, 23, 40–41, 134, 138–40, 144–50, 183, 296; demented, 133

Holy Family, 114

home, 5–6, 10, 40, 42–45, 50–51, 54–56, 59–64, 68, 121–22, 124–25, 137–38, 149–50, 178, 197, 243

Homer, 149

honeybees, 128, 270

horrors, 152, 213, 236, 253

hospitality, 293

house, 1–2, 18, 53, 55, 122, 124, 129, 142, 148, 196, 206, 236–37, 243, 253, 266–67

Howard, Ebenezer: *Garden Cities of Tomorrow*, 316n6

Hudgens, Ric, 308n6 (chap. 11)

"Human Domination of Earth's Ecosystems," 317n10

Humming-Fish, 273–75

Hundred Acre Wood, 51–52, 54

hunger, 89, 122, 129, 156, 158–60, 202

Hunger Games, The (Collins), 13, 156–61, 309n1 (chap. 14)

hunters, 117, 160–61, 166, 214, 219, 221–22, 245, 247, 250

Huorns, 143, 147

Hy-Brasil, 170, 175

hydrogen cyanide, 261

ice, 225, 227

Illinois, 51, 136, 293, 301n7

imaginary islands, 170, 175

imagination, 18, 33, 53, 87, 90, 106–7, 110, 113, 165, 194, 235, 303n2 (chap. 6)

immortality, 187–88

immrama, 175–76

Indians, 4, 31, 204

indigenous people, 102, 214

Inis Mór, 88

Ireland, 49, 52, 58, 83–85, 87–88, 90–92, 119–20, 133–38, 142, 167–68, 174–76, 217, 225, 300n21, 304n9; mythological tradition of, 174

Irish literature, 17, 83–84

Island of the Blue Dolphin (O'Dell), 197, 213–14, 216, 314n1 (chap. 19)

islands, 11, 49, 98–100, 163–80, 189, 191–98, 200–223, 251, 257, 287, 309n1 (chap. 15), 310n10, 310n12, 312n1, 314n1 (chap. 19); barrier, 169; continental, 168, 171

Jesus, 103

John Newbery Medal, 12

Joyce, James, 37, 79, 199

Judgment Day, 130

Kareiva, Peter, 266, 317n9

Katniss Everdeen, 157–61, 197

Katz, Eric, 304n10

Kellert, Stephen R., 115, 302n5, 306n7

keystone species concept, 310n18

Kilby, Clyde S., 136

Kincaid, Eric: *Nursery Rhymes*, 231, 314n1 (chap. 21)

king, 46, 104, 126, 130, 178, 181, 183, 246, 262

King Arthur, 181–83

Kirkman, Robert: *The Walking Dead*, 216

Klein, Gillian: *Reading into Racism: Bias in Children's Literature and Learning Materials*, 299n11

knife, 64, 199, 204

Kohl, Herbert R.: *Should We Burn Babar?: Essays on Children's Literature and the Power of Stories*, 246, 316n4 (chap. 24)

Koran, 73

Kroeber, Alfred, 185, 311n10

Kroeber, Theodora, 185, 311n11

Kuo, Frances 292, 305n18

lake, 71, 86, 97–100, 226–27, 275
Lake District, 62
Land of Oz, 152
landscapes, 9, 11, 36, 50, 52–54, 56–57,
72, 90–91, 113–15, 127–28, 133–35, 137–
38, 160, 235–36, 251–52; bleak, 272;
fantasy, 179; humanized, 45; natural,
114, 300n19
Lane, Margaret: *The Tale of Beatrix Pot-
ter: A Biography*, 303n1 (chap. 5)
Lanes, Selma G.: *The Art of Maurice Sen-
dak*, 105, 306n1 (chap. 9)
Lascaux cave, 110
Lear, Linda: *Beatrix Potter: A Life in
Nature*, 303n9
Lee, Bruce, 59–60
Lefcourt, Herbert M., 296n9
Le Guin, Ursula K., 178, 311n3, 311n8,
312n15; Earthsea cycle, 178–79, 186–
87, 189–90, 198, 311n3
Leopold, Aldo, 103, 161
Leprechaun, 86
Lerer, Seth: *Children's Literature: A
Reader's History from Aesop to Harry
Potter*, 296n10
Lettergesh beach, 167
Lewis, C. S.: *The Lion, the Witch and the
Wardrobe*, 136–37, 141, 143, 150, 308n12
Linnean Society, 68
lions, 3–5, 77, 109, 112, 120, 128, 150, 152–
54, 172; lion-human conflict, 295n4
Lion, the Witch and the Wardrobe, The
(Lewis), 136–37, 141, 143, 150, 308n12

literacy, 29, 32; formal, 28–33
Little House, The (Burton), 236–37, 315n4
(chap. 22)
Little Prince, The (Saint-Exupéry),
256–69, 287
LoBue, Vanessa, 24, 297n19
Lofting, Hugh, 28; *Story of Doctor
Dolittle*, 28; *Voyages of Doctor Dolittle*,
29–31
Loizou, Eleni, 288, 317n5
London, Jack, 22, 297n11; *The Call of the
Wild*, 22
loneliness, 21, 202, 208, 213, 215–16, 264;
existential, 240
Long Arrow, 29, 31–32
Lopez, Barry, 222, 302n4, 314n5
Lorax, The (Dr. Seuss), 272–76, 317n1
(chap. 26)
Lord of the Flies (Golding), 169–70, 197,
217–20
Lord of the Rings trilogy (Tolkien), 133–
35, 143–44, 146, 183
Lost Boys, 166, 172
Louv, Richard, 26, 33, 296n6, 298n3,
302n4; *Last Child in the Woods*, 33, 53,
296n6, 298n3, 302n4
love, 5, 8, 10, 18, 21, 25, 27, 56–58, 143,
157–58, 268, 271, 285, 287–88, 294
Lug, 120
Luke's Gospel, 39

macabre, 72, 125
Macfarlane, Robert, 170, 310n10
MacKillop, James: *Dictionary of Celtic
Mythology*, 181, 311n4

Madame Mim, 183

magic, 128, 176, 178, 180, 186–87, 189–90, 214, 310n23, 311n1; shamanistic, 116; sleight-of-hand, 181

magicians, 178, 311n27

Mallard Island, 98, 100–101, 293

Malthus, T. R.: *An Essay on the Principle of Population*, 259, 316n3 (chap. 25)

Manhattan, 225

maps, 57, 95–97, 111, 220

Mare, Walter de la: *The Three Mulla-Mulgars*, 150, 308n13

market, 128, 232, 304n4

Marris, Emma: *Rambunctious Garden*, 74, 304n11

marshes, 139, 144, 166

Martin, Bill: *Brown Bear, Brown Bear, What Do You See?*, 22, 297n14

Martyn, Florence, 134

Marx, Karl, 204, 259

Marx, Leo: *Machine in the Garden*, 235, 314n2 (chap. 22)

Marxist critic scribbling vitriol, 246

mass, 88, 163, 194

Matthiessen, Peter: *The Tree Where Man Was Born*, 259, 316n2

Maupassant, Guy de, 88

McGonagall, Minerva, 111

McGrew, Mike: *Saint Brendan and the Voyage Before Columbus*, 310n22

Meade, L. T. (Libby), 191–94, 196, 291, 312n7; *Four on an Island*, 191–92, 194, 196; *A Very Naughty Girl*, 193, 312n7; *World of Girls*, 192, 312n6

meadow, 235–36

Medawar, Sir Peter: *Advice to a Young Scientist*, 300n18

medicine, 29, 157

melancholia, 129, 141, 211, 236, 281

memory, 19, 32, 36, 54, 57, 60, 106, 121, 194, 245, 296; earliest, 17; photographic, 193

Merlin (Merlyn), 178, 181–84, 189, 311n5

meteorology, 30

mice, 49, 128

Michelangelo, *David*, 249

Middle-earth, 137–38, 141, 144–46, 150, 184, 308n6 (chap. 12)

migration, 83, 150, 229, 262

Mill, John Stuart: *Autobiography*, 200, 313n8

Miller, Mara: *The Garden as an Art*, 73, 304n6

Milne, A. A.: *Winnie-the-Pooh*, 7, 44, 48–49, 50, 53, 55, 57, 302n1

Milne, Christopher, 53–58, 302n3; *The Enchanted Places*, 53, 55, 57, 302n3

minimal biological requirements, 160

minimal hydration requirements, 158

Mirkwood, 145–46

Modern Library, 21, 22 297n9, 305n4, 313n14

mole, 42–43

mollusks, 18–19

money, 206–7, 314n17; pots of, 206, 208

monkeys, 2, 23, 130, 150, 172, 245, 297n17; flying, 154

monsters, 166, 183, 189

Montreal Protocol, 283

moon, 85, 105, 122, 167, 231, 243

Moore, Tony, 216

moral relativism, 200

mortality, 47, 70, 143, 256

Morton, Timothy: *The Ecological Thought*, 312n14

Morton Arboretum, 51

mother, 17, 19, 22, 60, 64, 67, 89, 107, 123, 129–30, 139, 180, 245–47, 250, 298n6; beloved, 143; dead, 245; dumbfounded, 241

mountains, 31, 37, 82, 85, 111, 150–51, 180, 197, 220, 223, 308n10

mouse, 49, 64–65, 69, 183, 197

movement, 20, 26–27; bowel, 158; "co-mix" magazine, 235

Mozart, Wolfgang, 100

Muir, John, 26, 103

Murray, Declan, 255

Myers, Gene: *The Significance of Children and Animals: Social Development and Our Connections to Other Species*, 297n18

mystic, 223

Napoli, Donna Jo: *The Magic Circle*, 307n4

narcissism, 79, 263

Nash, Roderick, 101, 306n3 (chap. 8)

natural history, 6, 29–31, 88, 143, 172, 178–79, 181–82, 184, 192, 229, 307n2 (chap. 11)

naturalists, 20, 28–32, 60, 123, 295n1, 298n1; great, 27, 29, 33, 259; greatest, 31–32

natural world, 5, 8, 10, 21, 25, 27–28, 32, 68, 81, 140, 183, 190, 220, 284–86, 300n21

nature, 20–24, 26–28, 30–33, 44–45, 52–55, 81–83, 90–92, 102–3, 139–42, 179–80, 187–89, 221, 269–70, 283–88, 298n7, 299n10, 300n16; forces of, 75, 157, 214; inanimate, 232; pristine, 315n3; reading the book of, 299n10; revolutionary, 79; savage, 102; urban, 286; wild, 88, 142, 174

nature ascetic, 274

nature-deficit disorder, 26, 53, 296, 298n4, 302n2

necromancer, 133, 146, 183

Negev desert, 270

nest, 90; ant, 295n1; solitary wasps, 182

Neverland, 166, 170, 172

Newbery, John, 297n20

New Testament, 208

New York City, 170, 225, 238

nightmares, 227, 232

Nikolajeva, Maria, 296n10

Noah, 196, 275

Nobel Prize, 283

Nodelman, Perry: *The Pleasures of Children's Literature*, 296n10

North Africa, 120

North America, 50, 111, 144, 175, 185, 270, 300n19, 311n11

nostalgia, 45, 52, 56–57, 84, 108, 141, 156, 194, 235, 258

nursery rhymes, 12, 230–31, 233, 314n1 (chap. 21)

Oberholtzer, Ernest, 100–101, 306n1 (chap. 8)

Oberholtzer Foundation, 98

ocean, 115, 169, 171, 189–90, 198

octopus, 3, 23

O'Dell, Scott: *Island of the Blue Dolphin*, 197, 213–14, 216, 314n1 (chap. 19)

Odum, Eugene, 252, 316n7 (chap. 24)

O'Flaherty, Liam, 88–89, 305n7

Oisín (mythological), 17, 175

Ojibwe people, 99

Old Forest, 146–48

Old Irish, 136

Old Testament, 303n2 (chap. 6)

Ollivander's wand shop, 185

O'Meara, John Joseph: *The Voyage of Saint Brendan: Journey to the Promised Land*, 310n21

Opie, Iona Archibald: *Oxford Dictionary of Nursery Rhymes*, 233, 314n2 (chap. 21)

Opie, Peter: *Oxford Dictionary of Nursery Rhymes*, 233, 314n2 (chap. 21)

optimism, 101, 170; unbridled technological, 263

ordeal, 123, 198, 219

organisms, 30, 188, 203

Orians, Gordon H.: *Snakes, Sunrises, and Shakespeare: How Evolution Shapes Our Loves and Fears*, 115, 306n8

Orr, David W., 317n1 (chap. 27)

Orwell, George: *Animal Farm*, 22, 297n12

out-of-doors, 26–27, 242–43, 295n6

owl, 21, 54, 109, 182–84, 197–98, 242, 276

Oxford English Dictionary, 29, 148, 166, 304n4

Oz, 152

ozone loss, 283

Paddock, Joe, 99, 306n

Paine, Robert, 172, 310n18

painting, 10, 45–46, 71, 108, 114, 143

Paleolithic, 109, 117, 232

Palaeolithic mythology, 306n18

Pan, the great god, 38, 42, 45, 303n9

paradise, 71–73, 77, 84, 215, 303n2 (chap. 6)

parents, 2–3, 7–8, 20, 24–25, 27, 39, 41, 44, 86, 122, 191–92, 243, 281–82, 284–86, 288

park, 91, 138, 226–27, 238, 307n1 (chap. 11); local, 225; national, 20, 83, 91, 133

parrot, 207, 209–10; offensive, 31

pastoral, 11, 38, 40–43, 45, 47, 61, 69, 84, 91–93, 201, 214, 286–87, 301n1, 302n9; environmental, 48

pastoralism, 41

pastoral poems, 41

pastoral promise, 39

Paterson, Katherine: *Bridge to Terabithia*, 46, 302n11

Paulsen, Gary: *Hatchet*, 150, 308n15

pencil, 49, 101

Pennypacker, Sara: *Pax*, 150, 308n14

Peter Rabbit. *See* Potter, Beatrix

pets, 19–20, 285

Pfister, Marcus: *The Rainbow Fish*, 22, 297n15

Phaedrus, 300n20

philosophers, 36, 74, 148–49, 199–201

philosophy, 2, 8, 10 74, 220, 304n7; fox's, 266, 268–69

phoenix feather, 185

pigeons, 122, 251

Piggy (*Lord of the Flies*), 217–19, 221–22

Piglet, 49–50, 54

pigs, 39, 130, 222, 231, 242

pike, 183; quasi-Nietzschean, 183

Pishon, 73

Pixar, 24

place, 1, 27, 35–36, 55–59, 87, 100–101, 103–4, 106–7, 118, 135–37, 140, 144–46, 148–50, 156–57, 236–37; beautiful, 161; bucolic, 235; desolate, 144; natural, 141, 150; pristine, 266; unhappy, 216

planet, 10, 111–12, 241, 259–60, 262–63, 266–67, 286, 306n5; small blue-green, 15; tamed, 266

plants, 72, 75, 77, 80–81, 105, 111, 134, 139, 172, 180–81, 184, 232–33, 249, 261, 267

Plato, 300n20

playground, 279

Pleistocene, 107–9, 111, 113; art, 108

poetry, 42, 78, 144

pond, 189, 225, 273

Popo Agie Wilderness, 95–96

populations, 4, 189, 215, 233, 259, 263, 274, 283–84, 316n3 (chap. 25), 317n2 (chap. 27)

porcupines, 2, 172

porridge, 119, 129

Potter, Beatrix, 7, 59–61, 297n21, 303n2 (chap. 5); *The Tale of Benjamin Bunny*, 64–65; *The Tale of Mr. Tod*, 63–65; *The Tale of Peter Rabbit*, 44, 48, 71; *The Tale of the Flopsy Bunnies*, 63–65

Poussin, Nicolas: *Et in Arcadia Ego* (*The Arcadian Shepherds*), 45

predators, 69, 261

prince, 28, 39, 47–48, 75, 77, 119, 124–25, 129–30, 172, 210, 228–29, 257–65, 267–68, 271; foreign, 119, 132

Queen, 123–25, 220, 246

rabbits, 19, 22, 49–50, 62–65, 67, 69, 71, 128, 192

Rackham, Arthur, 296n4

Radagast, 184

Rainy Lake, 98, 100

rat race, the, 42

Rawls, Wilson: *Summer of the Monkeys*, 23, 297n17

rebellion, 156–57

reef, 170, 198

Reenadina Woods, 87

religion, 136, 138; shamanistic, 111

Rembrandt, *Landscape with the Rest on the Flight into Egypt*, 114

reveries, 44, 107, 173

revolution, 79–80

revolutionary politics, 156

Rivendell, 150

Robinson, Tim, 58, 167, 303n8 (chap. 4), 309n4 (chap. 15)

robinsonades, 196–97, 213–15

Robinson Crusoe (Defoe), 195–96, 198–202, 205, 208–9, 211, 215, 312n8, 314n16

rocks, 99, 107–8, 110–11, 178, 186, 192–93, 197, 205, 215, 220, 250, 264

Roman Empire, 119–20

romantic, 81, 281

Ross, Stephanie: "Aesthetics of Gardens," 304n5

Rousseau, Jean-Jacques, 201

Rowling, J. K., 7, 13, 184, 296n12, 306n4, 311n9; *Harry Potter and the Philosopher's Stone*, 7, 11, 13, 111, 178, 181, 184, 189, 193, 296, 306n4, 311n9

Royal Ballet, 60

royalty, 78, 158, 246

Rudd, David, 312n3

Ruelle, Karen Gray: *The Tree*, 238, 315n5 (chap. 22)

Saint-Exupéry, Antoine, 256–58, 260, 262–63, 266–67, 269, 287, 316n1, 316n7 (chap. 25); *The Little Prince*, 256–269, 287; *Wind, Sand and Stars* (*Terre des hommes*), 263, 316n7 (chap. 25)

Sauvage (forest), 182

savages, 207, 211–12

savanna hypothesis, 115

Sayer, George, 136

scarecrow, 64, 152, 154

Scotland, 11, 52

sea, 84, 88–89, 102, 114, 163, 167–68, 172, 175, 179, 181, 192–93, 203–4, 223, 251, 299n9

sea elephant, 215

Second World War, 54–55, 141, 217

Sendak, Maurice: *Where the Wild Things Are*, 103–6, 107–8, 113, 116, 306n1 (chap. 9)

Seuss, Dr., 272, 274, 317n1 (chap. 26); *The Lorax*, 272–76, 317n1 (chap. 26)

sex, 159; excessive, 71

sexism, 312n5

Shakespeare, William, 115, 178, 306n8, 311n2; *Macbeth*, 179, 311n2

shamans, 110–11, 113, 117

shame, 33, 97, 262–63

Shannon diversity, 109, 112, 306n3 (chap. 9)

She-Goat, 205

shellfish, 198, 215

Shepard, Ernest H., 49–50, 297n21

shepherds, 41, 45–46

ship, 104, 204–5, 231

shipwreck, 33, 193, 195, 204–7

shit, 10, 19, 249, 251

Short History of America, A (Crumb), 235–37, 314n3 (chap. 22)

Sidhe, 84–86

Silverstein, Shel: *The Giving Tree*, 305n16

simpleton, 130, 247

sisters, 17, 48, 63, 89, 122, 126, 198

skin, 9, 130, 195, 228; cormorant, 215; hedgehog, 130; wearing animal, 207

snails, 61, 76, 128, 180, 252; pet, 61

snakes, 2, 24, 115, 128, 185, 271, 306n8; poisonous, 48

Snape, Professor, 185

snow, 178, 225–27

snugness, 171, 173

soil, 8, 81, 99, 118, 135, 261

solastalgia, 56–57, 141, 303n7 (chap. 4)

solitude, 96, 100, 197, 202, 208, 211

son, 6, 29, 39–40, 43, 78, 126, 130, 175, 186, 201, 282

souls, 149, 202, 266, 298n1, 301n6

South Africa, 140

South African, 5

sparrows, 58, 251

species, 4, 52, 56, 109, 111, 117, 128, 143, 189, 203, 205, 214, 216, 244, 251

species extinction, 173

species loss, 284

spell, 32, 180, 300n19

spiders, 24, 115, 231; grey, 47

Spyri, Johanna: *Heidi*, 82, 305n17

stars, 46, 48, 111, 117, 198, 240, 242–43, 263, 266, 271, 316n7 (chap. 25)

starvation, 127, 159

Steig, William, 197, 313n3; *Abel's Island*, 197–98, 313n3

Stephen, Leslie, 199

Stephens, James, 84–85, 296n4, 305n1

Stevenson, Robert Louis, 169, 202, 309n7, 313n10; *Treasure Island*, 168, 174, 191–94, 196, 309n7, 312n10

stings, 154, 295n1

stone, 61, 80, 182–83, 186

Stoney, Barbara: *Enid Blyton: The Biography*, 312n3

stories, 11–13, 39–41, 44–45, 47–48, 60–67, 75–78, 88–90, 101–5, 115–21, 125–27, 173–76, 199–203, 213–16, 228–30, 286–88; animal, 59; children's picture, 108, 110; cosmic hunt, 117; environmental, 127, 239, 287; nature-based, 284

storm, 11, 18, 112, 120, 142, 192–93, 197–98, 225

storytelling, 6, 112, 118

suburban, 37, 141, 239–40, 243, 287, 252

sun, 6, 43, 75, 85, 96, 120, 142, 147, 182, 249, 264

supernatural, 110, 178

survival, 23, 112, 115, 127, 158, 170, 189, 192, 197, 200, 208, 229

sustainability, environmental, 56, 92, 274

swallow, 228–29, 251

Swift, Jonathan, 199

sword, 119, 182–83, 311n6

Tagliaferro, Linda: *Galápagos Islands: Nature's Delicate Balance at Risk*, 172, 310n17

Tagore, Rabindrinath, 269, 317n12

Táin Bó Cúailnge, 84

tales, 12, 23–24, 56, 66, 79, 87, 92, 124–27, 176, 179, 311n3, 314n1 (chap. 20); environmental, 13, 127; tall, 176; traditional survival, 156

Tao of Le Guin, 186

Tatar, Maria: *Enchanted Hunters: The Power of Stories in Childhood*, 296n10

Tattersall, Ian: *Masters of the Planet: The Search for Our Human Origins*, 111–12

Taylor, Mildred: *Song of the Trees*, 276, 317n2 (chap. 26)

Taylor, Theodore: *The Cay*, 23, 297n17, 310n9

teachers, 2, 18, 98, 180, 191, 217, 281, 286

technology, 10, 210, 235, 273

teenagers, 22, 52

Templeogue Village, 37, 163, 166

Terenure Village, 37

terra incognito, 118

terror, 9, 65, 118, 176, 243

Teutonic wizard, 183

Theocritus, 301n4

thief, 75, 149

thirst, 129, 156, 158–60, 286

Thoreau, Henry D., 27, 207, 298n2, 313n14, 314n1 (chap. 22); *Walden*, 207–8, 313n14

tigers, 2, 5, 77, 152, 172, 240, 242

Tigris, 73

tin whistle, 100, 125

Tolkien, Arthur, 140

Tolkien, Christopher, 307n3 (chap. 11)

Tolkien, J. R. R., 7, 18, 41, 133–46, 150, 183, 296nn2–3, 301n3, 307n3 (chap. 11), 308nn1–7; *Farmer Giles of Ham*, 144; *The Hobbit*, 7, 18, 23, 41, 134, 144–46, 183, 296n5; "Leaf by Niggle," 143–44, 308n5 (chap. 12); Lord of the Rings trilogy, 133–35, 143–44, 146, 183; *The Silmarillion*, 136, 144, 308n4 (chap. 11); *Unfinished Tales of Númenor and Middle-earth*, 144, 308n6 (chap. 12)

Tolstoy, Leo, 79

Tolstoy, Nikolai: *The Quest for Merlin*, 181, 311n5

tools, 29, 53, 57, 113, 204–6, 247, 282, 285; revolutionary, 58

toponesia, 57

topophilia, 35–37, 56, 302n5

topsoil, 282

towns, 120, 127–28, 133, 180, 226, 230, 232–33, 235, 247

toxic waste, 241

toys, 55, 57, 279

trail, 95–97, 122, 222

tramps, 89, 119

traumas, 60, 219, 228, 245–46, 266

Treasure Island (Stevenson), 168, 174, 191–94, 196, 309n7, 312n10

trees, 50–51, 54, 84–85, 114–15, 139–40, 142–44, 146–48, 153–54, 235–36, 238, 242, 249–51, 259, 273–74

Trelease, Jim: *The Read-Aloud Handbook*, 284, 317n3 (chap. 27)

tribulations, 44, 126, 209, 233, 240; small, 18

Ulrich, Roger, 305n18

uncanny landscape hypothesis, 53

United States, 1, 12, 49–50, 102, 184

universe, 9, 144, 172, 232

urban adapter, 244

urban life, 229, 232, 235, 244, 302n9

urinous stench, 225

valleys, 41, 48, 54, 62, 95–97, 205

value, 5, 20, 76–77, 81, 102–3, 173, 207, 262, 288; civilized, 216, 219, 222–23, 247; materialistic, 257

vanity, 77, 257, 271

vegetables, 64–65, 69, 73, 304n4

vesper time, 100

Virgil, 47; *Eclogues*, 42, 46, 301n5

Vitousek, Peter M., 317n10

Vivaldi, Antonio Lucio, 100

Voldemort, Lord, 185

voyages, 27, 32–33, 175–76

Walden (Thoreau), 207–8, 313n14

Wallace, Alfred Russel, 301n22

walls, 49, 73, 75, 81, 104–5, 163, 182

wanderer, 114, 183

warm-blooded mammals, 158

Warne, Frederick, 62

Wart, 182–83

wasps, 37, 252

waste, 10, 249

water, 68, 72, 76, 98, 100–101, 114, 148, 157–61, 166–67, 176–77, 181, 201–2, 220, 226–27; fresh, 198; refreshing lake, 245

Watterson, Bill, 240, 315n3; *The Authoritative Calvin and Hobbes*, 239–40, 315n3; *Calvin and Hobbes*, 239–43, 252, 315n3; *The Days Are Just Packed*, 315n5 (chap. 23)

waves, 36, 88–89, 96, 168, 194, 202, 227, 276; rogue, 198

wealth, 47, 126, 128, 187–88, 211, 246; rejecting, 207

weather, 112, 229, 231; inclement, 226, 229

Webster, Deborah, 141, 308n3

wedding, 125, 130

Wells, H. G.: *The Island of Dr. Moreau*, 165, 309n1 (chap. 15)

western park concept, 91

Where the Wild Things Are (Sendak), 103–6, 107–8, 113, 116, 306n1 (chap. 9)

White, E. B.: *Charlotte's Web*, 46, 302n12

White, T. H.: *The Sword in the Stone*, 182, 184, 311n6

Wicked Witch of the West, 153–54

wild beasts, 122, 127, 131, 196, 200, 202–3, 244

Wilde, Oscar: "The Happy Prince," 228–29, 314n1 (chap. 20)

Wilder, Laura Ingalls: *The Little House on the Prairie*, 7, 151

wilderness, 11, 91–93, 97–98, 100–103, 107, 118, 120–21, 128, 144–46, 150, 156–57, 161, 233, 287, 306n3 (chap. 8), 307n6; biblical, 102; child's, 103; forested, 121, 124, 130, 146; idea of, 92, 101–3, 107, 116–18; paradisiacal, 249; post-apocalyptic, 272; sublime, 161

Wilderness Act, 307n6

wilderness adventure, 105, 156, 214

wildlife, 1, 195, 239, 251

wildness, 74, 90, 101, 131, 165, 170, 269, 286, 307n8

wild places, 26, 92, 150, 165, 197

Wilson, E. O., 56, 115, 302n5, 306n7

Wilson, Ruth: *Nature and Young Children: Encouraging Creative Play and Learning in Natural Environments*, 300n16

wings, 1–2, 54, 149, 255

Winnie-the-Pooh (Milne), 7, 44, 48–49, 50, 53, 55, 57, 302n1

winter, 97, 163, 176, 181, 197–98, 225; harsh, 197

witchcraft, 11, 184

witches, 122–23, 128, 150, 154, 178–81

Wittgenstein, Ludwig, 90–91

wizards, 41, 146, 148, 178–79, 181, 183–84, 186, 189, 198

wolves, 39, 48, 104, 107, 113, 128, 153–55,

172, 197; famished, 200; Pyrenees, 200, 211; starving, 211

woman, 27, 68, 78, 80, 109, 129, 169, 176, 198, 213–14, 226, 231

Wonderful Wizard of Oz, The (Baum), 152, 155, 309n1 (chap. 13)

woodcutter, 16, 121–22, 128

woodlands, 20, 26–27, 33, 46, 18, 51–54, 63–64, 68, 128, 137, 144, 146, 235–36, 240–41, 291; great yew, 87

Wordsworth, William, 62

Wyss, Johann David, 172, 310n16; *Swiss Family Robinson*, 172, 310n16

Yeats, William Butler 86–87, 305n4; *Fairy and Folk Tales of the Irish Peasantry*, 186

Yi-Fu Tuan, 56, 302n5

young adults, 23, 46

youths, 7, 26–27, 37, 52, 59, 104, 107, 114, 218–19, 234, 248; impressionable, 59; plutomanical, 275; power-hungry, 181

Zeno, 17, 296n

Zipes, Jack, 79, 305n15

Zneimer, John: *The Literary Vision of Liam O'Flaherty*, 305n6